Unplugging Popular Culture

Unplugging Popular Culture showcases youth and young adult characters from film and television who defy the stereotype of the "digital native" who acts as an unquestioning devotee to screened technologies like the smartphone. In this study, unplugged tools, or non-digital tools, do not necessitate a ban on technology or a refusal to acknowledge its affordances but work instead to highlight the ability of fictional characters to move from high tech settings to low tech ones. By repurposing everyday materials, characters model the process of reusing and upcycling existing materials in innovative ways. In studying examples such as *Pitch Perfect*, *Supernatural*, *Stranger Things*, and *Get Out*, the book aims to make theories surrounding materiality apparent within popular culture and to help today's readers reconsider stereotypes of the young people they encounter on a daily basis.

K. Shannon Howard *is Assistant Professor in the Department of English and Philosophy at Auburn University Montgomery, USA.*

Routledge Research in Cultural and Media Studies

115 Cultural and Political Nostalgia in the Age of Terror
The Melancholic Sublime
Matthew Leggatt

116 New Feminisms in South Asian Social Media, Film, and Literature
Disrupting the Discourse
Edited by Sonora Jha and Alka Kurian

117 Women Do Genre in Film and Television
Edited by Mary Harrod and Katarzyna Paszkiewicz

118 Reclaiming Critical Remix Video
The Role of Sampling in Transformative Works
Owen Gallagher

119 Ecologies of Internet Video
Beyond YouTube
John Hondros

120 Panic, Transnational Cultural Studies, and the Affective Contours of Power
Edited by Micol Seigel

121 Ethnic Media in the Digital Age
Edited by Sherry S. Yu and Matthew D. Matsaganis

122 Narratives of Place in Literature and Film
Edited by Steven Allen and Kirsten Møllegaard

123 Unplugging Popular Culture
Reconsidering Materiality, Analog Technology, and the Digital Native
K. Shannon Howard

For a full list of titles in this series, please visit www.routledge.com

Unplugging Popular Culture
Reconsidering Materiality, Analog Technology, and the Digital Native

K. Shannon Howard

Routledge
Taylor & Francis Group

LONDON AND NEW YORK

First published 2018 by Routledge

2 Park Square, Milton Park, Abingdon, Oxfordshire OX14 4RN
52 Vanderbilt Avenue, New York, NY 10017

Routledge is an imprint of the Taylor & Francis Group, an informa business

First issued in paperback 2020

Copyright © 2019 Taylor & Francis

The right of K. Shannon Howard to be identified as author of this work has been asserted by him in accordance with sections 77 and 78 of the Copyright, Designs and Patents Act 1988.

All rights reserved. No part of this book may be reprinted or reproduced or utilised in any form or by any electronic, mechanical, or other means, now known or hereafter invented, including photocopying and recording, or in any information storage or retrieval system, without permission in writing from the publishers.

Notice:
Product or corporate names may be trademarks or registered trademarks, and are used only for identification and explanation without intent to infringe.

Library of Congress Cataloging-in-Publication Data
A catalog record for this book has been requested

ISBN: 978-1-138-58839-4 (hbk)
ISBN: 978-0-367-66371-1 (pbk)

Typeset in Sabon
by Apex CoVantage, LLC

Contents

	Introduction: "It Forces You to Play Differently"	1
1	"My Charade Is the Event of the Season:" Celebrating *Supernatural* With Materiality, Music, and Generations X to Z	21
2	Beca as Bricoleur: How *Pitch Perfect* Characters Embrace Materiality and Music	43
3	Analog Dinosaurs and Abandoned Kids in *Jurassic World*	63
4	"Don't Adjust Whatever Device You're Hearing This On:" (Dis)Embodiment and Analog Technology in *13 Reasons Why*	85
5	Complicating Materiality and Generational Labels: *Get Out* and the Role of the Collector	105
6	Solving Z for X: Extending Generational Paradigms in *Stranger Things*	126
	Conclusion: Blooming (and Burning) Where You Are Planted: The Optimism of Generation Z	147
	Index	162

Introduction
"It Forces You to Play Differently"

This project is primarily about reconsidering the abilities of today's young people and framing them within the cultural language of popular film and television narratives. Too often we associate today's children and young adults, those born in the 1990s, with an addiction to screened technologies like smartphones and handheld computers. This book interrogates this portrayal and extends the definition of what it means to be one of these "digital natives."

I question the supremacy of the digital in the world because material items like cassette tapes, walkie talkies, antique cars, and analog television still affect characters from these narratives in key ways. These are things that, as Timothy Morton says, "are not exhausted by our use, but rather persist beyond it" (190). In other words, the things featured in these shows and movies do not exist as mere props but as co-participants in constructing reality. For instance, the below photo illustrates how today's

Figure 0.1 A Fan Dressed in Cosplay at Sakura Con in Seattle Pays Tribute to the VCR/TV Combo

Source: Author photo

young people create beyond their screens. The VCR/TV combo on the girl's head is not only a relic of an age past but a testament to this young woman's knowledge of such technology *and* her talent for making objects part of her costume and persona. The creative powers of today's young people continue to surprise those of us who believe they cannot and will not look up from their smartphone screens. For example, if we simply browse the social network Pinterest for the words "graduation cap," we discover how graduating college and high school seniors, ones holding their smartphones and snapping selfies, also adorn their caps with glitter, ribbons, and quotations from their favorite stories or authors. These self-fashioned hats often represent their love for popular culture narratives like the ones featured in this book. Another example to consider is the trend of bullet journaling, where individuals painstakingly design notebooks with colored pens in order to keep personal lists or words and art that encourage them. Numerous Facebook groups exist inside which "bujo," or bullet journal, practitioners post photos of their art, poetry, calendars, and mental or physical health inventories. These examples merely scratch the surface of what it means to be a young person who unplugs in a digital age.

I use the word unplugged in the book's title partly because of the role music and soundscapes play in shaping some of the character's journeys. Beca Mitchell in *Pitch Perfect* learns to create music both with and without traditional instruments and technology. Maeve and Marie in *Supernatural* stage a haunting a cappella rendition of "Carry On, Wayward Son" in the concluding scene of the show's celebratory 200th episode. Jonathan Byers in *Stranger Things* introduces his younger brother to the Clash just as he offers some life-saving advice. In *13 Reasons Why*, Clay remembers his most romantic moment with the deceased Hannah when his best friend gives him a cassette, not a series of mp3 files. This is all to say that part of reconsidering analog technology, materiality, and today's digital natives involves thinking about the tools, formats, and spaces characters use to navigate their worlds, and most of the time these tools and formats transfer some kind of noise or music. Music, as Jonathan Sterne argues, is a part of the material world and the study of materiality (186).

The word unplugged refers specifically to a cable television experiment in the late 1980s and early 90s where simple, acoustic performances aired on Music Television, a channel where all the most recent rock videos—complete with elaborate settings, effects, and sounds—played continually on a loop. *MTV Unplugged* was successful because it showcased the versatility of its performers, those capable of navigating the recording studios and music video stage sets and the intimacy of smaller venues where acoustic instruments were common. Guitarist Mike McReady of

Pearl Jam once explained to *Rolling Stone* that "It forces you to play differently. You can't rely on feedback. It forces you to use dynamics, and to look at each song in a different way. Some songs turned out good acoustically, and some just didn't quite happen" (Greene). Musicians like McReady, while speaking about their craft, often reveal the very characteristics that today's Generation Z characters on film and television require. They must play or create in different ways, some analog and some digital, in order to meet their personal needs as well as the needs of their communities. They sometimes fail and sometimes succeed in these endeavors; however, in both cases these characters act as what Claude Levi-Strauss would refer to as bricoleurs, people forced, like *MTW Unplugged* musicians, "to play differently" under a wide variety of circumstances.

Levi-Strauss in *The Savage Mind* discusses the role of bricoleur as someone who takes the available resources of a given situation and is able to create something new from the limited supply. Put another way, the bricoleur does not anticipate or request tools that are absent but fulfills the objective of a given time and place with the objects and concepts already present. Levi-Strauss explains, "It might be said that the engineer questions the universe, while the 'bricoleur' addresses himself [or herself] to a collection of oddments left over from human endeavors" (19). She is able to "'make do' with 'whatever is at hand,' that is to say with a set of tools and materials which is always finite and is also heterogeneous because what it contains bears no relation to the current project" (17). Musicians like Pearl Jam's McReady and others have all used unlikely materials to create something new.

Being a bricoleur, however, requires new circumstances and tools with which to experiment. It often involves taking someone out of their usual surroundings and challenging them to adapt to new places. Peter Sax in *The Revenge of Analog* shares a story of Camp Walden, where digital devices are confiscated so that summer campers may nurture face to face relationships. Although Sax is more heavy-handed in his critique of an increasingly digital world, his points about analog's resurgence in different communities are hard to dismiss. In his epilogue, "The Revenge of Summer," Sax reports on how the director believes a technology-free campus facilitates growth and interpersonal relationships. By leaving Instagram behind, campers are more likely to go outdoors, form lasting relationships, and "endure a little hardship." He says, "[P]eople push you and help you to succeed, and you end up with friendships, confidence, and an inner fortitude that ends in a sense of belonging to a greater independent community" (Sax Epilogue). Sax agrees that this part of the human condition is often eclipsed by digital immersion in screens.

The example of summer camp brings to mind the natural world, one of the largest representations of unplugged life. Although nature remains unpredictable, youth in these narratives will find ways to make such untamed and unique settings work for them. Moonee, a six-year-old character from the film *The Florida Project*, makes the observation that her favorite tree is the one that is "tipped over" but "still growing." This acceptance of nature's imperfections is key to developing humility, particularly for adults who still subscribe to the Scientific Revolution's view of humankind as superior to nature, a philosophy in which the "earth exists for humans" (Dobrin and Weisser 71–72). However, the good news is that part of what young people have in common with nature is nature's ability to "acclimate," or to "change and change again" when needed (Dobrin and Weisser 76). Since adults often become set in their ways, it is up to youth to interrogate and improve upon the anthropocentric views of nature as inferior to humans. Knowing how to shuttle effectively between analog and digital platforms also entails accepting nature as part of the analog sensibility.

However, beyond Nirvana's soulful performance and the idyllic settings of the natural world, the word unplugged suggests a lack of power. If we pull the plug on something, we imagine dark screens or silent rooms, perhaps caused by storm fronts that cause citywide blackouts. The idea of an unplugged world makes us think of the Luddite who blames cell phones and texting for the pollution of the English language (Warnock 301–07). It may call to mind older generations who never adjusted or adapted to email or social networks. In *Cobra Kai*, a contemporary spinoff of the original *Karate Kid* films, Johnny, a fifty-year-old man down on his luck, has to ask his high school classmate, "What's a Facebook?" He uses a flip phone and refers to most screen technologies as iComputers. His apartment shows a collection of CDs and tapes from the 1980s not because he is a bricoleur or a collector of vintage items, but because he is out of touch with contemporary society. Therefore, a teenager must show him how to set up a website for his business and adapt to marketing to a new generation.

This is not to say that the word never invokes positive connotations. People have often referred to going unplugged as taking a break from various stressors found on screens. This habit has become more frequently discussed with the advent of the Trump administration in the 2010s and the polarization between the right and left sides of the political spectrum. News often creates division in communities, and this way of life prompts people to ignore it in order to protect their mental stability. In this age self-help gurus also encourage people to take breaks from social media in order to allow their brains time to recharge and to allow themselves to experience boredom as a way to generate new ideas. Additionally, more prolonged periods of unplugged life are typical on hiking trails or on vacations where part of the appeal is to leave screen-mediated life behind. Many agree it can be salutary to balance the plugged and unplugged parts of daily living.

Materiality

I define the term unplugged by connecting it to materiality, which acts as a positive force for consideration in popular culture, multimodal composing, pedagogy, and media studies. Materiality as a term may initially remind some of us of the classic 80s song "Material Girl" by Madonna. In this song Madonna mentions her desire for a mate who "saves his pennies" and has "cold hard cash." "Mr. Right" is the man who not only provides for his partner but lavishes expensive gifts on her. This message echoed the materialistic themes of that particular decade, where only the rich would have the opportunities to succeed in business and in life (the yuppie being a central example of this). The 80s, therefore, provides a rather pejorative image of what materiality means.

In scholarly work researchers have reclaimed this word to mean something quite different: an attitude of respect toward our surroundings and the objects found in them. In this approach to the term, the human immersed in the physical world does not attempt to conquer or purchase the spaces and tools in her midst. The physical world instead becomes an agent in its own right, able to effect changes that humans cannot fully understand. In an ideal world, a focus on materiality keeps us humble rather than greedy, just as it does when we adapt to nature's imperfections. Most chapters in this book will showcase materials and humans as co-participants and positive allies in creating reality, but Chapter 5 (and some of Chapter 3) will hearken back to Madonna's message and the gift shop mentality of possessing things to amass wealth and status. It is important to show both sides of materiality in order to maintain a realistic view of how people may choose to colonize and control the physical world as much as some attempt to respect it.

When speaking of materiality in this text, the term means the physical environs and properties of a given space as well as the objects and/or tools located inside those same spaces. This definition aligns with Christina Haas's definition, where material consists of "having mass or matter and occupying physical space" (4). While this definition appeals to common sense, it will be used more specifically in this book to invoke the world of analog furniture and tools: cumbersome televisions, twisted cords on landline rotary phones, and clocks that still require winding either on our wrists or mounted on a wall. However, materiality as a concept moves beyond the idea of analog and digital. As Samantha Coole and Diana Frost describe,

> At every turn we encounter physical objects fashioned by human design and endure natural forces whose imperatives structure our daily routes for survival. Our existence depends from one moment to the next on myriad micro-organisms and diverse higher species,

on our own hazily understood bodily and cellular reactions. . . . In light of this massive materiality, how could we be anything other than materialist?

(1)

Coole and Frost provide a necessary call here, but there may be one key way that we should not be materialist, and it involves the frequency of difficult terminology and dense prose to describe the mysteries of the world around us. Topics like materiality and the scholarship associated with it must be ideally made translatable to the public as well as the members of the academy. Some scholarship, especially the kind associated with materiality and its various theoretical framings, like new materialism, object oriented ontology, and even agential realism, becomes almost impossible to wade through, particularly for laypeople. An easy excuse is that topics like agential realism are not supposed to be portable or applicable outside a circle of scholars because they deal in philosophical concerns that only high theorists can appreciate. I respectfully disagree. Terms like agential realism and the like are fruitful for those involved in philosophical discussions about the nature of being in the world, but they do not necessarily facilitate a meaningful, daily relationship with the physical matter surrounding people.

For example, the term glitch is central to the analysis of *13 Reasons Why* in Chapter 4. Research, therefore, led me to a particular scholarly piece that addresses the phenomenon of glitch artwork and its relationship to rhetoric. The abstract explains glitch art with terms like "bi-stable oscillation," "metastable orientation," and "metastability." While the author of this piece has an impressive record of scholarship on and about the topic(s) of new materialism and materiality, his terminology may alienate an audience composed of adults who choose not to specialize in the critical philosophy surrounding concepts like the glitch. Undoubtedly, these individuals are not his target audience here, and such scholarship does help advance knowledge so that we may better understand the intersections of humans and nonhumans (materials and creatures alike) to act persuasively. Still, I have seen glitch art as well as accidental glitches in pictures and on television, and terms like metastable orientation fail to do it justice. It is beautiful and confusing and bold, featuring splashes of color dripping across error messages or distorted pixels from a computer screen. The terminology above reinforces that the study of glitch art is off limits to a layperson, and this particular academic approach to studying the world around us creates limitations and boundaries rather than dwelling in possibilities.

A more direct and clear explanation is that the glitch, like the one featured in the example above, becomes a nonhuman agent suggestive of instability. It captures where stops and starts, or errors, happen frequently and cause inconvenience. Therefore, parts of glitch art as a genre cannot be easily dissected because they *embrace* error and mystery rather than shy away from it.

Figure 0.2 A High Definition Television Experiences a Glitch during a Storm
Source: Author photo

To be fair, a scholar like Timothy Morton, one who dwells in vernacular, pop cultural, *and* more esoteric discussions of philosophy, might remind today's audiences that the job of philosophies like object oriented ontology (OOO) *is* to "reconfuse us" about the status of language "we take for granted" (154). Vocabulary used to explain the glitch, however clear or obtuse, reminds all audiences that so much of the world defies categorization or easy dissection in prose. As the image above illustrates, the glitch happens when technology remains plugged but frozen, stuck in a limbo between the efficient and sleek world of the digital and the heavier, less malleable world of the analog appliance. Because the glitch occurs somewhere between the world of plugged and unplugged machines, it both fascinates and frustrates laypeople and scholars alike.

Analog and the Use of Parachronisms

Most people use the word analog to refer to non-digital technology. Indeed, Sax applies this very concept to his own text *The Revenge of Analog*: he says that "analog, in the broadest sense of the term . . . is the opposite of digital." His definition of digital guides most of this work: "[i]f something is connected to the Internet, runs with the help of software, or is accessed by a computer, it is digital" (Introduction). The *Oxford English Dictionary* confirms this distinction between analog and digital as one that is popular today. However, there is more involved. To think a bit more technically, we might add that analog technologies, as the *OED* also explains, "operate by the manipulation of continuously variable physical qualities," which include "voltage, space, and time." Nicholas Negroponte reminds us that analog processes use atoms while digital ones use bits; for example, "when you go through customs, you declare your atoms, not your bits" (4). Analog is embodied. To use middle school science in a reductive analogy here, analog is to a solid or a liquid what digital is to the invisible gas.

If most people imagine that the digital exists somewhat abstractly in the nebulous clouds, cyberspaces, or online environments of the world, they also associate analog with more pejorative concepts like unwieldy boxes, slowness in delivery, or regular glitches in performance. Trevor Pinch and Frank Trocco explain the current analog revival in the music industry as a return to "knobs and wires" (317). They also say in their study of the musical synthesizer that those who use analog instruments "appreciate the subtle complexities that arise from things not quite working as they should" and embrace the mystery of how such instruments work (223, 294). Likewise, analog is often associated with older technologies, while digital, or newer, technologies often allow for "greater ease, efficiency, or beauty" as well as "increased speed" (Ronda 79).

Analog technology also provides multiple opportunities to demonstrate how nonhuman agents and human agents work together in unpredictable ways. For example, Aden Evens describes musicians as having particularly complex relationships with their instruments, ones that must include a "friction" that humbles rather than empowers the musician when honing her craft. He explains,

> Defined by its resistance, the instrument does not just yield passively to the desire of the musician. It is not a blank slate waiting for an inscription. Likewise, the musician does not just turn the instrument to his own ends, bending it to his will against whatever resistance it offers. Rather musician and instrument meet, each drawing the other out of its native territory. The instrument itself has a potential, a matter-to-be-determined, and its use is always in relation to its own character as well as the desire of the musician.
>
> (160.1)

This relationship to the instrument holds special significance to those who champion the analog over the digital in music. Evens uses the following adjectives to characterize how some musicians view the digital—as "sterile, dry, or cold" and "lacking detail" or "spirit" (10.1). Those who prefer albums over CDs feel that "though the right notes are all there in the right places, the music does not move and so does not gather up the listener into its motion." Evens calls such fears of CD music "misapprehensions" rather than valid critiques: it is not that the digital is inferior in quality but that it is coded and arranged differently (10.1). If taken too far, such romantic notions of analog technology can be obstacles to this argument, which is that the characters in these narratives are able to shuttle *between* the analog and digital in some ways that previous generations did not. Part of analog's beauty in the narratives discussed here is that objects become actors, just like the cast members in these stories do.

Analog descriptions remain a fixture in our culture, if only in the form of dead metaphors, where the present and the past fuse in linguistic expression. For example, I still tell people to "dial" my number even though the smartphone has no physical dial. I still answer the smartphone with "Hello?" as if I have not yet been informed who the caller is (and I have). These habits recall wall mounted phones or even rotary devices before them where the finger moved in circles to enter numbers. I might also tell people to "flip" the channel on my television even though large knobs that used to do this trick rarely present themselves today. Rather than simply dismiss them as dead metaphors, people may find this lingering analog terminology may function in a different way—through parachronism. Originally defined as an "error in chronology," the parachronism is similar to the anachronism but works retroactively instead of forwardly. If an anachronism is a clock of standardized time in a Shakespeare play, a thing too futuristic to belong in a narrative set in medieval Scotland (see *Macbeth*), the parachronism works in the opposite direction, by using a dated reference to amplify the present situation (Howard). The winding and flipping suggest that parachronism is most effective when stressing its use of material objects, some of which seem displaced in the present. In other words, a parachronism often occurs as a *thing* or as a reference to a *thing* rather than as an abstract phenomenon.

In the discussion of *13 Reasons Why*, parachronism works as a descriptor for Hannah Baker's choice of recording a suicide note on cassette tapes. Her choice is one not born out of nostalgia for an earlier time; indeed, her reasoning for making the decorated tapes (she paints them with blue nail polish), wrapping them in a box, and including a paper map with marker has present day implications. Hannah Baker explains on the first tape (Tape 1, Side A) that cassette tapes are more valuable as a tool for recording her suicide note because "it's not supposed to be easy, or I would have emailed you an mp3." For Hannah the tapes carry a physical (but also emotional) weight that digital media does not possess. In the absence of her own body, destroyed by suicide, the tapes are embodied. The thirteen tapes, all messages to those whom she blames for her death, are meant to be handled and weighed, physically and emotionally, as they pass from student to student. While Hannah's tapes are the dividing marks between episodes, the Netflix streaming service launches each episode without a single command from us, the viewers. While streaming the show, Hannah in the fictional realm is urging her peers to slow down, confront the possibility of glitches, and do more work.

What the parachronism also does is subvert expectations: rather than reflect the exact "cultural moment in which the films [and television narratives] were made," according to Bronwyn Williams and Amy Zenger (6), a narrative may exist beyond the confines of periodization and the trap of becoming "dated." All narratives are still in some way a product of the "ideological truths and values" (6) of a given time, but the parachronism works to dissolve any lines existing between one era and the next by changing the shape and context of the materials. Margaret Ronda cites Walter Benjamin's focus on "wish images," or images in which the "new is permeated with the old," as one frame through which to study the act of obsolescing technologies (86). She further stresses that certain physical objects meant for retirement (e.g. phone booths) exist in a place that straddles past and present partly because they linger with us in "undead" form, unable to decompose (Ronda 76–77, 81). It could be suggested that the authors or directors indulge in "wish images" as well, allowing their readers and viewers to move beyond epochal specificity and into the realm of the universal.

With the juxtaposition of ancient life forms and contemporary ones, the *Jurassic Park* franchise engages in parachronism regularly. In most cases, the action displays an irreverence for time's past and present constraints since the goal of the scientists is often to make the past seem "present" in more ways than one. While doing so, these same scientists and entrepreneurs are regularly betting on new technology and its effect on their children's futures. This matters because constant manipulation of time remains central to understanding how generations adapt different world views. In the case of *Jurassic World*, the younger generations show more respect for nature's unpredictability, but such respect does not make them immune to the joy associated with scientific discovery and the entertainment it might bring.

The definitions of analog and digital will often be used colloquially in this text rather than scientifically. In other words, the book is dealing with the public, mass perceptions of such terms rather than the jargon-specific way of looking at analog and digital. If the glitch as an event is accompanied by an "awareness" of the medium in which something is composed (Betancourt), I would then say that analog technology, too, involves an awareness of medium, but it also involves an awareness of the physicality of things. Florian Cramer, who attempts to unravel the implications of a term like "post-digital," reminds her audience that terms like analog and digital are frequently slippery rather than understood universally. She reminds us from a purist's perspective that "[s]omething can very well be 'digital' without being electronic, and without involving binary zeroes and ones. It does not even have to be related in any way to electronic computers or any other kind of computational device." She goes on further to explain that analog "does not necessarily mean non-computational or precomputational. There are also analog computers. Using water and two measuring cups to compute additions and subtractions—of quantities that can't be counted exactly—is a simple example of analog computing." While this book deals primarily with public perceptions rather than purist definitions, Cramer's notes will be important when dissecting the use of technology in a narrative like *Stranger Things*, where Morse code, an arguably non-digital practice, actually involves what Cramer refers to as the "discrete, countable units" of something. It will also come in handy when analyzing the use of genetic engineering in *Jurassic World*, an act that involves both discrete splicing and insertions of matter while also making room for unpredictable outcomes. Cramer might argue that these acts are, in fact, digital, perhaps even more so if we consider that digits, even fingers called digits, are making the communication or creation of something possible to begin with. In sum, I take Cramer and others into account but put forth a more colloquial perception of analog and digital since the narratives in this project appeal to a wide range of viewers who are often more interested in the fictional characters than the nuanced treatment of any one vocabulary term. This interest leads naturally, then, to an explanation of how today's digital natives, or Generation Z characters, become significant.

The World of Generation Z

If we slow down and observe the young people around us, we might find it surprising how often they rely on analog as well as digital tools, even as we insist on labeling them digital natives. While students today may text and take notes on a smartphone, they also write in Moleskine notebooks and read hard copies of magazines. Although students love capturing moments on their smartphone camera, the Polaroid camera has made a comeback in recent years, perhaps due to the immediate physicality of a printed image (I remember how surprised I was to see my own niece photographing a sunset on the water with her Polaroid camera a few years ago). Also, record shops frequently sell LPs to this generation's mp3 collectors, and live music still reigns supreme on college campuses (see Sax Introduction, ch1, ch3, ch6).

Adults refer to today's youth not only as digital natives but by other titles: "Generation Z," "the Homeland Generation," and occasionally, but poignantly, "the Post 9/11 Generation" (see Horovitz; Strauss and Howe). Also, the term millennial (and occasionally post-millennial) often acts as a parachronistic description of this cohort since we have used the term for two decades—millennial may refer to a 30-year-old adult and also describe a high school teen in 2017. However, this teen group is especially associated with a time of great financial unease, terrorist threats, and "iCulture." Generation Z in this book consists mainly of those characters born in the mid-1990s (some flexibility exists since Beca in *Pitch Perfect* and Chris in *Get Out* might straddle the cultural divide of millennials and Generation Z). Generation Z is also more clearly defined by the attack on the World Trade Center on September 11, 2001 and subsequent mental and emotional processing of that traumatic event. While representations of children in the twentieth century (and earlier) also include traumatic moments, years since the terrorist attack of 2001 have seen a proliferation of narratives reacting to and reflecting on an unstable world. The past two decades have also seen an increase in domestic terror threats with mass shootings in schools and at public events, the most recent being the massacre at Marjory Stoneman Douglas High School in Florida.

In the midst of this instability, characters from Generation Z distinguish themselves by embracing both analog and digital tools. To be forthright, their habit of doing so has certainly raised some eyebrows and provoked memes of young people "using their typewriters in the park" only to promote their own uniqueness or "hipster" image (Cramer). Additionally, older generations often call such habits, common to people of various ages, an attempt at engaging in retro or nostalgic behaviors rather than genuine ones. In fiction, however, Generation Z students frequently use analog and digital materials in order to prepare for all possible outcomes in their future, particularly outcomes that are negative. Therefore, knowing how to use a bow and arrow to find food in a dystopian landscape, like Katniss Everdeen in *The Hunger Games* trilogy, becomes just as important as knowing how to avoid cyberbullying on social networks. Knowing how to make earplugs out of cotton like the character Chris in *Get Out* is just as important as knowing ways to use earbuds or headphones in a crowded space where one seeks privacy.

Due partly to the pressures and dangers unique to this generation, suicide rates for young people have increased in recent years, as seen in *13 Reasons*. Yet materiality not only exposes human mortality but the entropy surrounding us. Popular culture and even casual observations of the cities in which we live often point toward a new preoccupation with decay and ruin. This focus has led photographers, explorers, and scholars across various disciplines to document the physical changes in our world: structures like former indoor malls, vacant downtown shops, and foreclosed homes form a new landscape that reveals the nature of a precarious time. Appreciation for materiality cannot help but address what Matthew Christopher calls "an age of consequences." By "age of consequences," Christopher explains what his work as a photographer of abandoned places has revealed to him: that such places are not "anomalies" but ubiquitous reminders of "our current culture and the losses and failures that we are now sustaining" (4). These examples often point toward some anxiety about entropy and destruction on a more global scale. Environmental philosopher Timothy Morton, in his description of what he terms "ecological thought," explains that changing perspective through attention to the physical world is vital to understanding how to live responsibly: "It isn't *like* thinking about where your toilet waste goes. It *is* thinking about where your toilet waste goes" (127). Scholars like Morton and others see the things of our world and the humans in it as participants in a large network of forces, as both are caught up in what Morton describes throughout his work as a "mesh" of existence. Jane Bennett views the "starting point of ethics" to be "recognition of human participation in a shared, vital materiality" (14), and she uses the word "linger" to characterize what we should be doing when encountering the material world (17). She further observes how the habits of consumerism veil the wondrous surprises of our material surroundings: "It hit me then in a visceral way how American materialism, which requires buying ever-increasing numbers of products purchased in ever-shorter cycles, is *anti*materiality. The sheer volume of commodities, and the hyperconsumptive necessity of junking them to make room for new ones, conceals the vitality of matter" (5). As people consider where and how they throw things away and replace them with new ones, their relationship with the physical world changes considerably.

While some young people today favor LPs and cassette tapes over new technology because "before was always better," as Tony says using his tape player in his car in *13 Reasons Why*, their reasons for operating such devices go deeper than a desire to show off vintage collections of things. Experience with college students in my own classrooms has led me to question whether the digital natives actually enjoyed the virtual lives we assume they lead. On my campus, students carry and use their smartphones, but most do not enjoy the oversaturation of technology that has some teachers excited. One group of freshmen I taught even explicitly commented on my evaluations that they were tired of "remembering passwords" and "making social media accounts" for class activities; what they wanted was simplicity in course requirements and a positive relationship with the teacher.

The generation after millennials has been born with screens and Internet use as a fact of life, but if this is so, then we might ask how much they regularly embrace the meaning such an existence. Phill Alexander describes the problems inherent in assuming that students today are "natives" of such a terrain:

> We have to work against the fatalistic generalization that the young understand technology and the old do not. Digital is not a place. You are not native to it, nor do you need to apply for residence on its shores. You're not too old, nor are you so young that you'll

have magic powers that cause you to innately understand everything digital.

(328)

Inhabiting the digital world requires understanding of rhetorical choices that users make, but rarely do people slow down to examine why analog or digital constraints exist in any given situation. For example, in most college classrooms a hybrid of analog and digital tools exists. A whiteboard or dry erase board accompanies the digital display of an overhead projector. Rarely does a teacher wish to use one without the other as an option. Instructors find themselves displaying text on both, and it is important to tease out the reasons we love colored markers and handwritten notes just as it is important to teach the nuances of digital platforms and their limitations. When the whiteboard leaves traces of a class discussion behind, ghosts of ideas linger on the walls rather than disappear with the stroke of a delete button. This act of ghosting, which is, in fact, the technical term for stained whiteboards whose age prevents complete erasure of markings, suggests a physical reminder of communication in ways that a delete button cannot. A joke left on the board in faint blue ink, or a definition underlined in black, remains behind to prompt curiosity of what happened in the room just prior to the next group's arrival.

Why Film and Television? Why Pop Culture?

If school classrooms offer artifacts that could easily articulate this argument, and neighborhoods remain peppered with abandoned buildings that serve as evidence of materiality's encroachment upon a digital world, why look to fiction to reveal iterations of the analog alongside the digital? First, the primary data in popular culture is accessible to the reader of this text who need only rent or stream the examples discussed here. Such data is meant to appeal to a wide audience rather than a particular community that only my neighbors and me can access and describe. Data in popular culture is also plentiful. In terms of analog tools like a whiteboard, we do not have to look far for examples of what is commonly known as the "big board trope" in popular culture. One poignant example occurs in the series *Battlestar Galactica* in the 2000s. In the pilot episode, set in outer space, the main cast seeks refuge from their enemies, the Cylons. Camera shots often feature ticking clocks on the walls because the enemy launches an attack every "33 Minutes" (name of episode) and tests the combat flight crew's ability to forsake sleep for days on end. Indeed, many pilots are given stimulants as a way to survive the ongoing attacks. During the repeated losses of their men and women, the humans keep track of how many survivors remain. Because the human race has almost been wiped out, the number dwindles, and each time the Cylons come, their leader must change the ongoing tally of survivors on a whiteboard with her markers. The characters, surrounded by all the accoutrements of sci-fi technology, use one small board to document the shrinking number of surviving humans. Meredith Woerner remarks specifically on this one object as being "the exact moment when *Battlestar Galactica* won our hearts": she says, "I'm not sure if any post apocalyptic or survivor series (since BSG) has been able to recapture the simple weightiness of the whiteboard. We've seen spaceships blast Earth to bits, but I've yet to witness a series where the stakes were this clear and this important. It shows that sometimes the simplest devices hold the most power. . . ."

Likewise, this project will focus primarily on pop culture examples of fictional characters as its main data source because characters offer different perspectives for us to explore, and these characters have the potential to act as models for different ways of living within certain contexts and conjunctures. Storytellers and filmmakers also believe these points to be true, or they would not traffic in ideas and the dissemination of them with such joy and possibility. If, as Jonathan Sterne says, "the work of cultural studies is to redescribe context, to analyze conjunctures, [and] to attend to the relations of people, power, and practices built into any phenomenon or problem" (29), then storytelling allows for ample contexts and conjunctures of what could be. It poses what Jerome Bruner calls a number of "possible worlds." In Stephen King's memoir *On Writing*, he recalls the moment when someone first told him to "make up his own story." He says,

> I remember an immense feeling of possibility at the idea, as if I had been ushered into a vast building filled with closed doors and had been given leave to open any I liked. There were more doors than one person could ever open in a lifetime, I thought (and still think).
> (King 28)

In other words, storytellers do not offer a fictional view of the world just for transitory entertainment purposes. They also offer countless possible ways of experiencing and reimagining life, and this approach is central to how we create with the materials available to us.

In doing so, narratives like the ones studied in this book, Laura Briggs and Jodi Kelber-Kaye argue "less optimistically," ones "that become consumable by a large popular audience" like *Jurassic World* and *Pitch Perfect*, do "offer rather familiar re-workings of stories that the culture can assent to, consume, and enjoy" (93). Yet this project is not a literary one but a rhetorical one, which means that the narratives involved in this study are studied in connection with audience responses and audience habits in a twenty-first century world. The concern over the schism between high art and popular blockbusters need not halt the forward trajectory of the argument. In rhetoric, "familiar re-workings" help the author or director behind each franchise create characters that reflect the existing public just as the public, in turn, identifies with them. Easy identification and consumption are necessary for a message to resonate with others.

As mentioned before, environmental crises, terrorism abroad and at home, and collapse of the economy provide ample evidence of why Generation Z might not just imagine but *expect* the end of the world to occur within their lifetime. However, analog devices may be used to suggest innocence and joy. The protagonist of *Guardians of the Galaxy* listens to a song on his Walkman in the opening scene of the film franchise's sequel. Star-Lord (Chris Pratt) uses this tool to remind him of his childhood before his mother was killed. As Rebecca Tuhus-Dubrow describes, we see the character "dancing spunkily through a cavernous extraterrestrial landscape. The Walkman is his prized possession. When a prison guard confiscates it and Peter sees him wearing the headphones, he cries, 'That song belongs to me!'" As Tuhus-Dubrow further explains, the analog tool "is thus portrayed alternately as a source of comfort, thrills, and enchantment," and she reports that this scene inspired purchases of Walkmans on eBay, where "[they] sold for up to $820" (see Chapter 3). This example, while rooted in nostalgia for the character's past, has material implications for today's consumers who also wish to capture the thrills and enchantment of analog music—not just to be a part of a retro trend, but to feel as elated as Star-Lord does as he dances in outer space. Perhaps, they may even escape, via their bulky sound-canceling headphones, the negative news they hear every day on television and the Internet. Tuhus-Dubrow would remind us that the Walkman both increases auditory pleasure *and* insulates the listener from the outside world. This very fact serves as a reminder that even analog materials separate humans from their communities; smartphones alone are not to blame.

Moving forward, this book includes many examples of creativity made in unplugged circumstances. Such circumstances often result in the character's ability to create something new; and, like the original *MTV Unplugged*, the use of simpler instruments showcases the adaptability of creators rather than a disdain for technology. Romanticizing unplugged composing or creating is not productive even if Chris Pratt's character Star-Lord finds it so: every tool has its affordances and limitations, including the ballpoint pen. Nor should we privilege low tech activity over high tech activity. The goal here is something less stratifying: to celebrate the creative ways characters use tools that exist beside, behind, between, above, below, and among the screens we use. Therefore, this book is a celebration of and an investigation into material spaces and objects that have not been previously explored as parts of Generation Z culture. The range of examples supplied in this text will vary from positive to negative as some characters confront obstacles related to the overuse of digital devices. While Beca in Chapter 2 becomes a respected bricoleur capable of navigating various spaces and tools, Chris in Chapter 5 finds that materials are used to trap him into servitude. This set of examples is meant to offer a range of perspectives on how living an unplugged life affects the quality of young people's lives.

In Chapter 1, "Fan Fiction," the television show *Supernatural*'s 200th episode and self-proclaimed tribute to its most steadfast fans, explores the excitement and creativity of high school students as they transform (via a very "meta" narrative) *Supernatural* into a musical for their community. Unlike later chapters of this book, where trauma often accompanies the unplugged world, this section celebrates the joy two teenagers experience when they bring one of their favorite stories to life through a combination of digital tools and material props. Additionally, the episode "Fan Fiction" reflects on the main characters' own preoccupation with material items like the 1967 Chevy Impala the two brothers Sam and Dean drive, and it reminds the audience that the characters of this particular narrative continually struggle with the lack of agency or free will that accompanies a rich material world that operates on macro and micro scales of being.

Chapter 2 will demonstrate that tech-savvy characters, like those in *Pitch Perfect*, are the people who are most likely to surprise us by manipulating tools and spaces that require no electric power. Beca Mitchell, female protagonist of the film, performs in unlikely settings (and with unlikely props) and inspires others to do the same. In this narrative characters are just as likely to stack CDs as they are to digitally mix tracks on a laptop. The low fidelity world of a capella music in both the first film and its sequel *Pitch Perfect 2* features empty swimming pools, shower stalls, plastic cups, campfires, and candles as co-participants in musical performances. Beca becomes a leader of the Barden Bellas, an a capella group, because she effectively navigates both worlds with attention to audience needs. She works with both material and digital artifacts to show her talent: one key scene is her manipulation of a plastic cup to create rhythm on the stage floor. In the film's sequel, Beca and her teammates confront high tech performances by European performers. Going unplugged helps these young female artists "find their sound" even as they compete against the most sophisticated singing group in the world.

Chapter 3 addresses the characterization of youth in the *Jurassic Park* franchise, starting with the original film based on Michael Crichton's novel and ending with the recent summer blockbuster *Fallen Kingdom*, a sequel to the 2010s reboot *Jurassic World*. From its inception the mythos surrounding this story of genetically engineered dinosaurs has featured children abandoned or neglected by their parents during times when survival is uncertain. Likewise, the films unveil a problematic desire for hybridizing analog and digital tools for financial gain, and such hybridizing is accompanied by every glitch imaginable. These movies find creative ways to link the problems of abandoned children to the de-extinct animals whose welfare remains secondary to humankind's need for entertainment.

The use of time manipulation to muddy the lines among the past, present, and future also heightens the challenges faced by characters of all ages.

In Chapter 4, about *13 Reasons Why*, protagonist Hannah Baker uses cassette tapes to compose a lengthy suicide note to her peers. While the cassettes are the most tangible example of unplugged, or analog, technology, other examples serve as catalysts in the plot, such as a classmate's 1990s style zine magazine, Moleskine notebooks for poetry, and the graffiti written on bathroom walls. Hannah composes on old technology to make statements about the limitations and dangers of screen technologies, especially as they are used in cyberbullying and transmission of photographs via smartphones. Most importantly, however, Hannah's use of analog technology acts as a form of embodiment that speaks directly to the horrors of suicide and the disembodiment caused by violence to the self.

In Chapter 5's analysis of *Get Out*, a film whose reviews were unanimously full of praise, the central conflict exists between a white upper middle class family and a young African American man named Chris, whose first visit to his white girlfriend's childhood home becomes a fight for survival. Throughout Chris's visit, the audience views the house itself as a place where the father collects souvenirs in order to "experience another person's culture." In a more sinister moment, the audience realizes that the Armitages are also in the business of collecting African American bodies to fulfill dreams of athletic and artistic genius. Chris's encounters with the material world remain dangerous ones; indeed, this narrative showcases the repeated unplugging of a smartphone so that Chris may not call for help. *Get Out* serves as a counterpoint to earlier chapters because the Armitage family as a unit has made a life out of dominating the material world and rendering it helpless. The triumph occurs only when Chris is able to repurpose the Armitage family's heirlooms and escape the house.

Chapter 6, which addresses *Stranger Things*, reveals that analog *sensibilities*, not just its tools, define childhood in the 1980s. In this series a boy named Will Byer's disappearance triggers a series of supernatural events in a small town, and the boy's best friends find creative ways to locate him, using existing technologies like short-wave radio. However, once Will returns, the trouble continues because holes now exist between different realities that threaten to annihilate all life. Will's own artistic talents demonstrate how children, even at their most powerless, find ways to save their families and friends from destruction. This chapter finally demonstrates how children born in every generation, not just Generation Z, have used older forms of technology to outsmart the more contemporary tools of their adult counterparts.

The conclusion then reminds readers that this generation's use of both digital and analog technologies makes for rich storytelling because characters become stewards of the physical world while also developing complex relationships with humans. In sum characters from these narratives look to the physical world for both inspiration and survival in desperate circumstances, and such lessons may be applicable to our own encounters with Generation Z. I offer two final examples that have implications for future study: the web-based television series *Cobra Kai* and the independent movie *The Florida Project*. The characters from both of these narratives have little financial stability on which to lean, and this scarcity of resources prompts them to engage in "rasquache," a technique that involves not only bricolage but a form of resistance to typical capitalist structures and conventions. Such a technique may signal the way forward for Generation Z and the generations than follow them.

These encounters with characters will be made richer by a refusal to accept digital native as the main descriptor of their lifestyle. While young people continue to use screens, adult readers here will benefit from taking careful note of their interest in the physical world as well. We then recognize, through engagement with popular culture, how the use of materiality in narrative might inspire viewers to engage in their own acts of bricolage and their own efforts to conserve and sustain resources in the world around them.

References

Betancourt, Michael. "Critical Glitches and Glitch Art." *Hz-Journal*, no. 19, July 2014, www.hz-journal.org/n19/betancourt.html.

Briggs, Laura, and Jodi I. Kelber-Kaye. "'There Is No Unauthorized Breeding in *Jurassic Park*': Gender and the Use of Genetics." *NWSA Journal*, vol. 12, no. 3, Autumn 2000, pp. 92–113.

Bruner, Jerome. *Actual Minds, Possible Worlds*. Harvard University Press, 1987.

Coole, Samantha, and Diana Frost. "Introducing the New Materialisms." *New Materialisms: Ontology, Agency, and Politics*, edited by Samantha Coole and Diana Frost. Duke University Press, 2010, pp. 1–46.

Cramer, Florian. "What Is 'Post-Digital?'" *APRJA*, vol. 3, no. 1, 2014, www.aprja.net/what-is-post-digital/.

Evens, Aden. *Sound Ideas: Music, Machines, and Experience*. University of Minnesota Press, 2005.

Greene, Andy. "Flashback: Pearl Jam Play Intense 'Black' on 'MTV Unplugged'." *Rolling Stone*, 5 Mar. 2015, www.rollingstone.com/music/music-news/flashback-pearl-jam-play-intense-black-on-mtv-unplugged-47702/.

Guardians of the Galaxy 2. Directed by James Gunn, performers Chris Pratt, Zoe Saldana, and Vin Diesel, Marvel Studios, 2014.

Haas, Christina. *Writing Technology: Studies on the Materiality of Literacy*. Routledge, 1996.

Horovitz, Bruce. "After Gen X, Millennials, What Should Next Generation Be?" *USA Today*, 4 May 2012, usatoday30.usatoday.com/money/advertising/story/2012-05-03/naming-the-next-generation/54737518/1.

Howard, K. Shannon. "Why Are We Here? Parachronism as Multimodal Strategy in *Grey's Anatomy*." *Journal of Multimodal Rhetorics*, vol. 1, no. 1, Spring 2017, http://multimodalrhetorics.com/1-1-howard-html.

King, Stephen. *On Writing*. Pocket Books, 2000.

Levi-Strauss, Claude. *The Savage Mind*. University of Chicago Press, 1966.
Madonna. "Material Girl." *Like a Virgin*. Sire Records, 1984.
Morton, Timothy. "Attune." *Veer Ecology: A Companion for Environmental Thinking*. University of Minnesota Press, 2017, pp. 151–67.
———. *Hyperobjects: Philosophy and Ecology After the End of the World*. University of Minnesota Press, 2013.
Negroponte, Nicholas. *Being Digital*. Knopf, 1995.
Pinch, Trevor, and Frank Trocco. *Analog Days: The Invention and Impact of the Moog Synthesizer*. Harvard University Press, 2002.
Ronda, Margaret. "Obsolesce." *Veer Ecology: A Companion for Environmental Thinking*. University of Minnesota Press, 2017, pp. 76–89.
Rose, Frank. *Embracing Analog: Why Physical Is Hot*. J. Walter Thompson Company, March 2013, www.jwtintelligence.com/2013/03/qa-on-embracing-analog-why-physical-is-hot/.
Sax, Peter. *The Revenge of Analog: Real Things and Why They Matter*. Public Affairs, 2016. iBook.
Sterne, Jonathan. *MP3: The Meaning of a Format*. Duke University Press, 2012.
Strauss, William, and Neil Howe. *Generations: The History of America's Future From 1584 to 2069*. HarperCollins, 1992.
"Tape 1, Side A," *13 Reasons Why*, season 1, episode 1, July Moon Productions, 31 Mar. 2017, *Netflix*, www.netflix.com/watch/80117471.
Tuhus-Dubrow, Rebecca. *Personal Stereo*. Bloomsbury, 2017. Kindle.
Warnock, Scott. "Texting Ruins Students' Grammar Skills." *Bad Ideas About Writing*, edited by Cheryl E. Ball and Drew M. Loewe. Digital Publishing Institute, 2017, pp. 301–8.
Woerner, Meredith. "The Exact Moment When *Battlestar Galactica* Won Our Hearts." *io9 Television*, 14 Dec. 2014, io9.gizmodo.com/the-exact-moment-when-battlestar-galactica-won-our-hear-1670313315.

1 "My Charade Is the Event of the Season"

Celebrating *Supernatural* With Materiality, Music, and Generations X to Z

The Winchester Mystery House sits on a corner in San Jose, California, offering tours of its twisting turrets and narrow staircases every day except Christmas. As the brochure describes, features of this "mystery house" include "a window built into the floor, staircases leading to ceilings, a chimney that rises four floors to stop just 1 ½ feet from the mansion's ceiling, and doors that open onto blank walls." It includes a Winchester Firearms Museum so that visitors may learn about the rifle that was known as "The Gun that Won the West," and its rooms total 160 in all. The world's "most unusual and sprawling mansion" is also considered one of the most haunted locations in America. As Colin Dickey explains, lore surrounds and infects it; stories tell of ghosts, séances, fear of death, and symbols always in numbers of thirteen.

I begin with a description of the Winchester home because it acts as an appropriate analogy[1] for studying materiality in the sprawling mythology of *Supernatural*, a show that has been running for fourteen consecutive seasons on the CW (formerly WB) channel. The house itself, according to fans, also inspired the showrunner Eric Kripke to use the last name Winchester for his two male protagonists. Like the Mystery House, *Supernatural* (2005–present) contains countless metaphorical corridors and rooms in its mythos, some of which lead to architectural insight and some of which simply end in unfinished staircases and doors to nowhere. If we even begin to talk about how the material world of objects, places, and powers influence this narrative, we certainly will, figuratively speaking, travel farther than just 160 rooms. The show extends into multiple dimensions of Heaven, Hell, and Purgatory as Judeo-Christian descriptions of the cosmos and its devils and angels permeate the narrative's trajectory (see Brown).

Supernatural has dealt specifically in images of materiality since its pilot. A story of two brothers who hunt supernatural creatures, it features a material horror in the mysterious death of their mother Mary and, twenty years later, one brother's girlfriend at Stanford University ("Pilot"). In this material death, the body, stabbed and bleeding, becomes stuck to the ceiling, with flames shooting out around her and burning

Figure 1.1 Winchester Boulevard near the Winchester Mystery House in San Jose, CA
Source: Author photo

her corpse. The search for the thing or man responsible for this act (later identified as a demon named Azazel) drives both brothers out into the towns and forests of rural America, where similar supernatural events occur and jeopardize the lives of innocent civilians. Dean Winchester, the older brother at twenty-six years old, has already devoted years of his early adult life to "hunting" evil, and he comes to recruit younger brother Sam to join him, mainly because his father, a fellow hunter and mentor to Dean, has gone missing. While Dean's purpose is linked to a family crisis, the reunion seems grounded in something else: the desire for Dean to find a hunting partner in Sam despite Sam acting as a foil to him with an academic career and plans for law school.

Although Sam's future stands in contrast to Dean's rootless existence, the sudden tragedy of Sam's girlfriend's demise (and its similarity to his mother's fiery death) drives Sam out on the road to locate the murderer, whom the brothers find and kill at the end of the second season ("All Hell Breaks Loose, Part 2"). However, the death comes with a price: Dean must be willing to sell his soul to a demon so that Sam may live. When an angel finally rescues Dean from Hell in Season Four ("Lazarus Rising"), the mythos expands to include both angels from Heaven and demons from Hell, all warring for Sam and Dean's attention. After years sleeping in the car and using fake credit for food and gas, the two brothers realize that, despite their tireless work and frequent encounters with death, they make a rather dysfunctional but effective hunting team. However, the angels and demons in their midst use them repeatedly to serve a different agenda as a final apocalypse approaches in Season Five.

This chapter's main focus is an analysis of a tenth season episode titled "Fan Fiction" (2014), which also happens to be the show's 200th episode and what showrunner Jeremy Carver has called "a love letter to fans" (Herbig and Herrmann 754). Written by Eric Kripke and Robbie Thompson, "Fan Fiction" contains frequent references to earlier seasons, some of which are only recognized by loyal viewers. Although more than 200 episodes exist currently, "Fan Fiction" does constrain its references to the first five seasons of the show since those are viewed as being part of Chuck Shurley's fictional book series *Supernatural*. Chuck, known by the pen name Carver Edlund, is a character in the show itself, and his encounters with Dean and Sam allow for a level of meta-commentary on fan behavior, convention culture, and fan fiction.[2]

Most of the examples that follow, therefore, come from the first five seasons, although references to Season Six and beyond will occasionally be pertinent to the analysis of "Fan Fiction." However, before using the 200th episode as a case study for *Supernatural*'s emphasis on materiality as it relates to Generation Z—since "Fan Fiction" centers on the creative efforts of high school girls as they launch their own musical—I review some moments in the show when materials act as co-participants to the brothers who hunt monsters. This chapter will first examine materiality as it works at large in this particular television narrative, and then it will narrow its focus to one particular object's agency in the *Supernatural* mythos: the 1967 Chevrolet Impala. Finally, it will conclude with a close analysis of "Fan Fiction," the episode featuring high school students whose efforts prove that Generation Z is capable of moving between high and low tech environments in order to create a musical version of two brothers' lives on the road.

Supernatural and Materiality

One simple but representative example in *Supernatural* of how nonhuman materials come to possess power equal to that of humans occurs in Season Four's "After School Special," where the two brothers, Dean and Sam, must solve a case of murder at an Indiana high school. After interviewing the different citizens of the town, they discover that several children have died and that one of the parents, a school bus driver, is keeping a lock of his deceased son's hair in his Bible. Sam and Dean burn the cursed lock of hair and, therefore, set the school community free from the homicidal evil spirit that is possessing both students and adults alike. This focus on a material good, the hair, as the key through which spirits may gain their energy is just one moment during which the brothers must acknowledge that larger forces and even smaller ones often thwart the efforts of well-intentioned human beings. References to cursed objects abound, and such curses often render something inanimate animate. Still, the lock of hair acts as more than a cursed object from a horror story. It becomes the source of comfort and security that the grieving boy's father needs after losing his son. The lock also empowers other humans to murder others in grotesque ways, so its power extends beyond the father's grief and into the world at large.

One need only consult the *Supernatural* wiki (supernaturalwiki.com) to review the number of references that pertain to weapons, talismans, and more mundane objects in the show's mythology. For example, a particular gun, the Colt, receives as much background information as the characters do on this encyclopedic website. In *Supernatural* the Colt is a special weapon that John Winchester uses to bargain with the demon Azazel for Dean's life ("In My Time of Dying"). The gun continues to change hands throughout the entirety of the series, with characters desperate to use it because it has the power to kill some of the worst monsters in the series. On the wiki page, information about this one weapon includes 6,133 words (the length of an average academic article in a scholarly journal). Additionally, the section on weapons and mystical artifacts includes eighty separate pages of encyclopedic notes on objects as diverse as salt, a rabbit's foot, a hyperbolic pulse generator, cat's eyes, horcruxes, and the Staff of Moses. Even Dean and Sam's last name, Winchester, brings attention to their armory since relatives of the historical Winchester family (the same family responsible for the Winchester Mystery House) are responsible for inventing one of the nation's most famous rifles (Dickey).

Likewise, the otherworldly creatures in this show are neither fully embodied nor completely ephemeral, which makes for a fascinating study of how the material world intersects and influences humans. The title of the *Supernatural*-themed volume of the *Journal of Transformative Works* in 2010 may have been titled "Saving People, Hunting Things" (which also serves as a line from a song in "Fan Fiction"), but the two actions listed there are rarely that neatly divided. For example, the Season Four episode "Family Remains" proves just how frustrating a case becomes when two children haunting a home are actually live human beings who have been sealed off from the world. On the other hand, another Season Three *Supernatural* episode named "Ghostfacers" showcases the characters entering a haunted location called the Morton House where they search for the Leap Year Ghost, an entity who surfaces once every four years. Sam and Dean's search for such entities includes measuring the air quality for traces of electromagnetic energy and, in other episodes (such as the aforementioned story about possession), collecting traces of ectoplasm that, as in Season Two's "No Exit," serve as material manifestations that guide the hunters to their prey. In "Ghostfacers," some ghosts are caught in a loop via a "Death Echo," which places them directly between the spirit and material realms.

World building in any narrative may often contain an astonishing catalog of detail from those willing to author it, but *Supernatural*'s own databases seem particularly rife with things that possess screen time and agency in ways that other stories fail to accomplish. This will become especially important in "Fan Fiction" because the girls attend to these details carefully, bringing their narrative to life through carefully selected props that the actors use to tell *Supernatural*'s story. All in all, the analog world of weapons and artifacts in *Supernatural* far outnumbers the digital resources the boys use to solve their cases. In most episodes the best way to defeat evil is to retrieve a certain object and use it sparingly and respectfully (e.g., the Colt can hold only thirteen rounds to kill demons). Objects may sometimes stand directly between the protagonist and his or her security and/or safety from harm, and humans are not exempt from becoming such objects: Sam is told in Season Five that he is the bodily vessel for Lucifer ("Free to Be You and Me"), and Dean is informed that he is the vessel for the archangel Michael's sword ("Sympathy for the Devil").

This malleable border among humans, objects, and spirits may be why the characters often refer to human bodies as merely "vessels" or "meat suits." Human forms are often subject to manipulation by larger forces.[3] Likewise, objects play a significant role in honoring the dead in episodes like "Children Shouldn't Play with Dead Things:" Sam buries his father's military dog tags at his mother's grave after John Winchester dies. Such actions foreshadow the eventual return of the parents in different spiritual and bodily forms. John the father returns as a ghost to help the boys defeat Azazel in Season Two, and Mary, the mother, is brought back to life at the end of Season Eleven when Dean pleases an unstoppable force called the Darkness.

An emphasis on materiality in *Supernatural* cannot be divorced from the characters' own heroic actions and persistence as they locate, use, protect, and even become artifacts; yet the message, one articulated by Castiel, an angel who rescues Dean from Hell, is always that "there is a bigger picture here" ("Are You There God? It's Me, Dean Winchester"). Indeed, angels both good and corrupt must consistently remind Dean and Sam that their human vision is "limited" ("Dark Side of the Moon"). Although such an idea seems pessimistic, part of celebrating the materiality of the physical world includes acknowledging macro and micro matter that influences events on a global scale. A primary example that Timothy Morton uses to describe this phenomenon is climate change, which he refers to as a hyperobject. In layperson's terms, a hyperobject is an agent/object of such size that humans are unable to control, contain, or even fully grasp it: the result of its impact is to "humiliate the human, decisively decentering us from a place of pampered privilege in the scheme of things" (47). It may then be fair to say that hyperobjects, or macrostructures in *Supernatural*, include God, the Darkness, angels, demons, Leviathan, Hell, and Heaven. (We might go even farther and argue that the fandom itself is a hyperobject, rarely contained and controlled.)[4] Likewise, on a micro-level the viewer sees that something as mundane as a magical coin ("Wishful Thinking") has the ability to change reality for the humans in the narrative, and its use may also affect the macrostructures that continue to dwarf and reduce human power. In his research Sidney Nagel shares his fascination with the macro and micro orderings of the material world when he says, "I am struck by the observation of Victor Hugo: 'Where the telescope ends, the microscope begins, and which has the wider vision? You may choose.' I am seduced by the shape of objects on a small scale. The forces that govern their forms are the same as those that are responsible for structures at ever increasing sizes. . ." (29).This reality in which small and large forces have equal footing with human efforts is one that is best described as a supernatural realm, making the show's title quite fitting. Still, not all objects that help defeat evil spirits are made of ghost ectoplasm or a cursed lock of human hair. Some initially appear to blend in with the background rather than stand out as agents capable of saving the world. One of these objects is the 1967 Chevy Impala.

The Impala as Material Agent

As both Winchesters attempt to destroy the supernatural creatures they encounter on the road, multiple camera shots zoom in on the material contents of Dean's Impala, where knives, guns, crossbows, salt, fake FBI badges, and pistols are stored beneath and above the floor of his trunk. These weapons and objects sometimes catch the eye more quickly than the vehicle that holds them. It is harder to understand the car as a weapon or a tool because it exists as a container for the Winchesters' belongings. However, the Impala becomes agential in the fight against evil and often gets just as immersed in ghostlike and supernatural activity as the brothers do. In the very first episode, Dean's Impala actually chases and attempts to run down both him and Sam because it is haunted by a woman in white who lures unfaithful men to their deaths ("Pilot").

This does not mean that life on the road is always dangerous; sometimes it is mundane and tedious. In Season Four Dean admits, under the spell of a fever, that spending "eight hours a day" in the Impala, which he nicknames Baby, "listening to the same five tapes" with Sam is a fate he abhors ("Are You There God? It's Me, Dean Winchester"). However, fans of the show feel differently. Academic articles feature the Impala as a central "shibboleth" or object that links fans together across time and space. Media scholar Mark Stewart explains,

> There have been times, while teaching, that I've raised the TV series *Supernatural* in discussion. Inevitably, if I am providing a brief context of the series to students, I describe the two brothers, the Winchesters, who travel across the country fighting demons in their black 1967 Chevy Impala. It is when I mention the colour, make, and model of the car that I see eyes begin to light up within the room.

Stewart goes on to show pictures of fans who cosplay as the car itself, which provides rather startling proof of how agential objects in this universe have become for devoted viewers. Even the writers affirm the car's importance, for in Season Five's finale "Swan Song" the narration, from Chuck Shurley, begins with a description of the vehicle's birth and life:

> On April 21, 1967, the 100th million GM vehicle rolled off the line at the plant in Janesville—a blue two-door Caprice. There was a big ceremony, speeches. The lieutenant governor even showed up. Three days later, another car rolled off that same line. No one gave two craps about her.
>
> But they should have. Because this 1967 Chevrolet Impala would turn out to be the most important car—no, the most important *object*—in pretty much the whole universe.

Chuck's narration above refers specifically to how the Impala and the objects inside it save Sam from possession by the devil and the completion of the Judeo-Christian apocalypse. As Lucifer takes control of Sam's physical form, he assaults Dean with the intent of killing him and then bringing the world to an end.

However, just as Sam/Lucifer is about to deliver the final punch, his eyes catch the way the light reflects off the vehicle's window, and his gaze redirects to a plastic toy soldier caught in an ashtray ("Swan Song"). This gaze triggers a host of memories that enables Sam to recover control of his body and force Lucifer back into his subterranean cage. Earlier Chuck explains to the audience, "The army man that Sam crammed into the ashtray. He's still stuck there. The Legos that Dean shoved into the vents—to this day, heat comes on, and they can hear them rattle. These are the things that make the car theirs—really theirs. Even when Dean rebuilt her from the ground up, he made sure all these little things stayed, 'cause it's the blemishes that make her beautiful" ("Swan Song"). What Chuck suggests throughout this episode is that Dean's ability to recognize the value in these small objects creates a chain of events that prevents the deaths of millions. On macro and micro scales, the car acts as an agent that changes the history of this fictional world, although few knew its value when it rolled off the Janesville lot.

The description of the car above leads to one of the most important points about materiality: appreciation for it helps us protect the world around us, even if its day to day usage renders it initially unremarkable. On the surface level Jane Bennett stresses this appreciation is key to "looking for a road that leads to more sustainable consumption practices" (269). On a deeper plane the Impala and other objects like it help humans, as Eileen Joy beautifully puts it, to pause or slow down, "paying better attention to what is close at hand and is already always intimate with us—which is everything—welcoming the Other, not taking ourselves too seriously, and working together to add beauty to the world" (172). This point, while perhaps naively sentimental, describes the lingering effect of "Swan Song," the episode that some fans believe should have concluded the series for good.

Despite Sam's emotional connection to the vehicle in the Season Five finale, the car is most often associated with older brother Dean. Like the car in Stephen King's *Christine*, although not as temperamental or deadly, the Impala, originally belonging to John, the boys' father, functions as a partner to Dean, one that stays with him even as family disappears (e.g., John's disappearance and later death). At the beginning of Season Two, where Sam suspects Dean has only a few days to live, Sam begs his friend Bobby to restore the vehicle, even though it is totaled beyond repair ("In My Time of Dying"). In his mind, the car and Dean are inseparable as entities. As Melissa Bruce observes, Dean as a character "touches the Impala and emotes beside it more than we see him do with any other object, or even person. To separate the two is to leave Dean remarkably unstable." Peter Schwenger analyzes how King tackles this same concept in *Christine*. As his character Arnie devotes all of his time to restoring Christine, the titular character in the form of a 1958 Plymouth Fury, "the work he invests in the car consolidates his identification with her" (79–80). It is in this sense that Schwenger illustrates how "ownership, which seems to be a relation of control over objects, has a reverse side in which the owner becomes no more than a sum of his objects, indeed may feel himself to be an object among objects" (75). While Dean's situation may not seem as dramatic since his efforts to work on the car do not result in homicidal tendencies, one episode reinforces the idea that a stranger need only to compliment Dean's precious car in order to earn his friendship and trust ("Sex and Violence"). This compliment is the beginning of Dean's manipulation by a male Siren, who later convinces Dean to kill his brother so that the Siren may take his place. In this case, the viewer may recognize that Dean's seduction via material compliments emasculates or robs him of agency rather than enforcing it.

Dean further asserts his belief in cars as active, thinking agents when he stumbles upon an old model of what appears to be Little Bastard,

James Dean's car, in an episode rife with material imagery called "Fallen Idols." This episode features a wax museum where charmed objects bring the wax celebrity dolls to life and render them lethal. However, Dean suspects the first culprit is James's cursed Porsche, which has been missing since 1970. Although the car turns out to be somewhat of a red herring, the viewer sees Dean carefully moving beneath the vehicle, afraid that any sudden move will offend the spirit whom many believe to be deadly. As Dean explains to Sam, "Death follows this car around like exhaust. Nobody touches it and comes away in one piece." He first approaches the vehicle by saying, "Okay, baby, I'm not going to hurt you so . . . don't hurt me."[5] Dean refers to the Impala as Baby, too, throughout the narrative ("Fallen Idols").

Co-participation means that the Impala neither works solely as a masculine symbol or a prop but functions as a nonhuman actor that propels the narrative in specific directions. The girls in "Fan Fiction" will later capture this interpretation with their own musical, where the Impala features prominently at the center of the stage and becomes the topic of several songs (e.g., "On the Road So Far" and "Carry On, Wayward Son"). And while spending eight hours a day in the vehicle sometimes wears Dean and Sam out, the excitement of materiality still remains intact with high school student Marie's vision of the quests that the brothers undertake: one lyric boasts excitedly that "We are in Dad's car!" The final lines of the play also intone, "Out on the road, just the two of us" as the actors smile fondly at each other before the last musical number. The consistent backdrop throughout the play is a painting of a highway, one that diminishes as it runs straight toward the horizon.

Examining "Fan Fiction": Generational Differences in *Supernatural*

Because *Supernatural* has been on the air for fourteen years, characters featured in its various episodes come to represent more than one generation. Even Sam and Dean, in their twenties when the story begins, are approaching forty when the most current season airs, and their lack of identification with younger generations becomes pronounced. Describing an encounter with a ghost in Season Ten, a college student meant to represent a more tech-savvy generation than the brothers' own informs Dean and Sam that her boyfriend's truck "had a mind of its own" because the "Trini" (i.e., Siri) application on her phone kept giving false directions that led to an accident. When Dean looks puzzled at the notion of a map that talks to its users, Sam explains with some embarrassment,

> You have to excuse my partner. When it comes to technology, he's a little behind. He just learned how to poke on Facebook.

> Janet: Um, Trini is the nav app we were using. It's—it's like a talking map. [Dean looks at her, confused.] You're Gen X. Right.
> Dean: Ok, so Trini and everything else in the truck went all "Christine."
> Janet: Who's Christine?
> Dean: It's a Gen X thing.
>
> ("Halt and Catch Fire")

This explicit distinction drawn between Dean and the college student reveals a stereotypical view of how Generations X and Y view one another. In this episode, appropriately titled "Halt & Catch Fire," the characters in college take selfies in their dorm rooms, use wireless speakers, and engage in instant messaging on social networks. In some ways, the above exchange may be naïve, since individuals Dean's age do use such technologies to navigate, and people Janet's age, at least a few, *have* heard of Stephen King's novels. Still, the dialogue sets up the manner in which the writers of *Supernatural* bring generational differences to light. Sam, the younger brother closer to the student's age, often acts as the translator for Dean and the young characters he meets while solving cases.

Dean and Sam, having been born in the late 1970s and early 80s, belong to Generation X not only because they fail to recognize contemporary technology but because their own backgrounds reflect the cultural zeitgeist of that time. Still, some generations have more in common than one might initially suspect. For example, Dean and Sam must grow up without guardians due to their father's hunting activities, and the new Generation Z girls of "Fan Fiction" also find themselves devoid of mentorship when they need it. The motivations behind these adult absences in a narrative, however, differ. While Marie, the author/director of the musical version of *Supernatural*, is abandoned by her drama teacher, one might consider that Generation Z students *must* escape adult supervision to exercise true creativity. Generation Z youth especially welcome these chances to create away from the parents' watchful eyes because, as danah boyd explains in her study of contemporary social networks and today's teens, "Even in suburban enclaves where crimes are rare, teens are warned of the riskiness of wandering outside" (86). Lack of unstructured playtime drives teens deeper inside technological rabbit holes out of desperation, not addiction, boyd argues. In this sense, the narratives featuring unchaperoned teenagers and young adults serve as opportunities to fantasize an alternate reality, one where freedom really exists on the road, especially for youth who are surrounded by privilege (e.g., a private high school in the case of "Fan Fiction").

This stands in contrast with Sam and Dean's situation, where an important feature of materiality for them is the emphasis on what Julia Wright says is the latchkey kid trope, a popular representation of life without parents during the 1970s and 80s. The key became the co-participant that twentieth-century children—members of Generation X—used to let themselves into a domestic space without the help of parents to greet or protect them. Raised by a mechanic in the 70s and 80s and, therefore, members of Generation X themselves,[6] the Winchester brothers also understood the limits of their financial situation early on. Wright says, "Although they have access to money through credit card fraud, the money is directed entirely at basic living expenses and the work; they stay at cheap motels, eat take-out food, and only buy new clothes when needed for hunting. . . ."

Two common associations with Generation X include analog technology and the conspicuous absence of guardians or parents (Strauss and Howe). Indeed, John Winchester and his friend Bobby work as mechanics in their day to day lives but often disappear for stretches of time to fulfill their roles as hunters, leaving Dean to watch over Sam during their childhoods. Dean and Sam certainly fit the latchkey kid trope mentioned earlier. Viewers also note the references to analog culture in the brothers' journeys. Dean in particular listens to classic rock by Kansas, Led Zeppelin, and Bob Seger on cassette tapes, makes references to Memorex ("Dark Side of the Moon") and the 80s comedy *Perfect Strangers* ("The Man Who Would Be King"), and fears that his parents never loved him. He imagines instead that he was a "burden" his parents were "shackled to" ("Dark Side of the Moon"). His mother's ghost goes on to say that "the one silver lining" to her violent, fiery death was that at least she "was away from [Dean]."

Marc Prensky, the educator and speaker who coined the term "digital natives" in 2001, would also consider the brothers "immigrants" who learn to use the laptop computer and mobile phone technologies for their own benefit but do not understand fully how online communities work. In other words, Sam and Dean are horrified to discover that not only do *Supernatural* fans exist (as in Edlund's books, not the television program) but that they often write speculative fiction about the two brothers in a romantic relationship (a trope called Wincest). Their horror is evident in their encounter with a millennial fan of Carver Edlund's books named Becky ("Sympathy for the Devil"). Becky, a fanfiction writer and avid fan of *Supernatural*, remains obsessed with Sam's character and is thrilled to meet him in person. However, Becky, as portrayed in the series, is often demanding and self-centered, a stereotype that Generation Y, or millennials, must consistently struggle against (Stein). Season Seven would even feature Becky drugging and manipulating Sam into marriage ("Season Seven, Time for a Wedding!").

However, Sam, Dean, and Becky are important not just as representatives of their respective generations. They are important as precursors to the Generation Z portrayal of Marie and Maeve, who are neither Generation X latchkey kids nor millennial sycophants but something entirely different. By Season Ten, the year in which *Supernatural* aired "Fan Fiction," Dean and Sam are now the mentors or guardians, while the Generation Z teens at St. Alphonso's Academy are the youth that initially appear to require protection. Both brothers arrive in Flint, Michigan to discover that the drama teacher, Mrs. Chandler, has disappeared from a private school for girls, only to discover later she is being held prisoner by Calliope, an otherworldly muse of the arts.

While Dean and Sam's arrival to a new hunt usually features a con job of impersonating FBI agents in handsome suits and ties and charming information out of locals, a careful viewing of "Fan Fiction" reveals that the Winchester brothers fail to impress the school community in a similar manner: they are both too disturbed by the creation of a musical script about their lives and seem to bumble around like older men uncertain of their purpose. Furthermore, as soon as Sam and Dean whip out their fake FBI badges, the actors in front of them hold the same kind of fake badge as a prop for the play, and this mirroring exposes, with some humor, the very playacting that the Winchesters do as they travel. Although Sam discovers the identity of the antagonist Calliope, the muse who harms members of the former cast and crew, that revelatory moment is perhaps eclipsed, albeit humorously, by the many times Marie and Maeve must warn him and Dean not to "touch anything." Unlike Becky, Marie and Maeve find the two men unimpressive, even after they discover who they really are.

Although some studies of Generation Z teenagers claim students no longer read critically (Seemiller and Grace), Marie demonstrates quite the opposite. She hones her vision of Carver Edlund's books to such a specific point that she is able to justify all of her creative choices: her refusal to insert Chuck in his own narrative, her inclusion of material through Season Five, and her desire to have all details rendered as faithfully as she can. For example, she scolds an actor for not wearing what she calls the "Samulet," a necklace that symbolizes the brothers' love and appears throughout most of the seasons. She justifies this complaint by explaining to the cast member that her script includes events *before* the work "Dark Side of the Moon," Edlund's brilliant but unpublished story of Dean and Sam's journey through Heaven.

While all of this behavior sounds fanatical, and it is partly meant to seem so, Marie's main goal is different from the average fan's priorities. She focuses primarily on finding a publisher for her writing instead of obsessing about the characters and creating fantasies about them, as Becky does. Her desire centers on the creation of something new, a need to finish an abandoned series of books that failed to provide closure for its readers. Marie is also quick to identify the parts of *Supernatural* she dislikes, particularly the insertion of the author inside his own text and the metanarrative references. And while she enjoys the scenes with Dean and Sam bonding as brothers, she is able to poke fun at them by labeling them "melodrama." Becky's priority is to imagine herself coupled with Sam, even as she writes Wincest fan fiction. On the other hand, Marie stresses her belief that while it may be possible that some monsters exist in the world, the characters in *Supernatural* are fictional. Even Carver Edlund/Chuck Shurley views Becky as a flighty and annoying young woman, especially after he dates her for a short time. Years later, however, this same character as the writer/publisher will look upon Marie and Maeve with some admiration and tell them that their adaptation was "not bad."

The choice of antagonist for this episode reinforces the image of Marie's authorship and productivity. Calliope, one of the muses from Greek mythology often pictured with a writing tablet in hand, offers an interesting juxtaposition to the usual demons and monsters who oppose Sam and Dean. However, Calliope makes it her goal to punish any author who fails to make her vision come to fruition, and she enchants certain props to attack any person who stands between the artist and her purpose. This ability leads to another person's disappearance from the theater: the actress playing Sam in the musical. Because she finds Marie's leadership cloying and the lack of attention to canon disturbing, she threatens to see the principal and have the musical shut down before opening night, yet Calliope captures her before she achieves that goal.

Marie, in her view of character relationships, represents a more open-minded take on sexuality since she acknowledges the implicit homoeroticism in her musical without finding such an undercurrent problematic. While the Generation X brothers often seem horrified at the notion of "Destiel" and "Wincest," two tropes that support a sexual interest with the angel Castiel and Dean or with Dean and Sam, Marie is more nonchalant about the fact that the actors who play Castiel and Dean in her musical version are female partners in real life. While Dean looks concerned, Marie sees no issues in same-sex relationships both on and off stage. Nor does she call special attention to the bonds of fictional or nonfictional people at all until Dean directly questions her about it. Her attitude is one of acceptance but not in such a way that she must call special attention to it the way Becky does when she writes her own fan fiction about Sam and Dean. The Gen Z student has been raised in the most diverse population yet, and as such she does not find gender or sexual orientation something to fetishize.

Not only is Marie revising the stereotype of Generation Z through her critical artist's eye, she also stands in direct contrast with the mostly absent drama instructor, who, as it turns out, cannot wait to use her smartphone either to text or surf the Internet when the girls are rehearsing or to place a call the moment she steps out of the auditorium. Her parting words to the students include the following: "I have had three weeks of this crap show, and I am done. There is too much drama in the drama department." We see Mrs. Chandler then pull out a flask and take a sip as she continues to disparage the drama students to her friend. Marie and

Maeve, upon being questioned about their teacher's whereabouts after she disappears, iterate that Mrs. Chandler is an alcoholic divorcee whose main activities beyond school include drinking and sobbing. The place to find her is, therefore, the neighborhood bar, a place Dean also frequents in many prior episodes to deal with the stressors of hunting.

Put simply, one might say that while Generation X members are getting drunk and/or using smartphones, Marie and Maeve are hard at work past nightfall, trying to perfect their creative work. The viewer never sees Marie or Maeve take a call or place a text; indeed, their personal screens do not appear at all. The viewer, however, might still witness some changes in generational caretaking: Mrs. Salazar, the principal of the girls' school, is clearly hands on and present for her charges after the teacher vanishes, and the cast and crew parents fill almost all audience seats on opening night of the play (despite their unfamiliarity with the script or its source material). Dean and Sam also play the roles of guardians to the girls when they attempt to solve the case of Mrs. Chandler's disappearance. When both brothers reveal their true identities, the girls merely laugh and say that both of them look "too old" to be Sam and Dean. Maeve suggests instead that they might make an effective "Rufus/Bobby combo," two older hunters who act as father figures to the Winchesters after they lose their parents. This line reminds viewers just how long the road through thirteen seasons has been, since Dean and Sam are no longer young adults by Season Ten but tired hunters approaching middle age. In a sense, "Fan Fiction" includes a transfer of power from the old guard to the new: Sam and Dean certainly play their part and defeat Calliope, but otherwise their tactics and tricks seem worn and cliché next to the teens' painstaking efforts to capture the magic of the brothers' narrative. This narrative is one that Dean and Sam find tedious now; we hear them complain that "it's time to go back to staring at motel room walls." The girls, however, are the inventive characters now, ready to follow in the hunters' footsteps by standing up to the evil that threatens their classmates. They remind the original characters why their mission matters and why their journey is still relevant to a new generation of students.

Nevertheless, "Fan Fiction" deserves attention for other reasons. Maeve proves herself to be a bricoleur (Levi-Strauss), one who is able to work with the materials available to her under time constraints. She also shuttles effectively between high and low tech equipment. After the brothers arrive at St. Alphonso's, Maeve takes Sam up to the lighting booth, and she mocks his question of "hearing anything strange lately" by operating the different sound cues that reveal "supernatural" sounds from Marie's narrative. When Sam reminisces about his own technical theater experience by describing CD players in his old booth, Maeve, on headset, receives a message that she must "sign for something" in front of the theater, and she exits before Sam finishes his journey down analog memory lane. Additionally, Maeve uses the same headset to call all the cues in the live performance. Sound design and musical direction for the entire production remain under the girls' purview since even their piano accompanist is a high school student.

The student crew, led by Marie, also designs the entire production's set, costumes, and props. They fashion their objects and costumes to imitate the kind of materials described in earlier parts of this chapter. When Dean sees the assortment of plastic and wooden weapons, fake FBI badges, and talismans on the prop table backstage and asks Marie where she found everything, Marie replies with a phrase that remains integral to perceiving her generation with new eyes: "Some parts homemade, some parts repurposed. All of it . . . awesome."

Marie also solves the problem of special effects in her version of the narrative. In *Supernatural* demons must be defeated by driving out a material product: black smoke. While demons inhabit human bodies, their essence is more ephemeral, which means that forcing the black smoke out of the possessed body's mouth usually destroys the demon's essence, or keeps it at bay. In Marie's design, the musical shows Dean defeating demons by pulling a black sheet out from behind the actor and raising it to the ceiling, an effect that impresses the audience both in the episode and behind the screen. This craftsmanship renders the experience of the spiritual world as a tactile one, one that engages the senses. In this sense, Marie's choice to have rain ponchos cover the front row of the audience also echoes this same need to have her viewers physically engaged. She even quips that the result will be "full on Gallagher," a reference to a comedian, which, oddly enough, only Generation X might immediately recognize.

"Hey, Man, I've Got Another Song": Unplugging With Kansas and Generation Z

It takes a play created by high school women to encapsulate the power of a material cosmos in *Supernatural*, which is part of why "Fan Fiction" is important as a 200th episode. In this narrative the Generation Z characters, who take time to ensure the accuracy of the artifacts' appearance, prove themselves capable of championing analog materials while also using technology when appropriate (through light and sound effects in particular). Although the writers focus their episode primarily on the new students, their narrative allows for space to practice a "recursive" form of "polymediated" storytelling, where past, present, and future events overlay and inform one another. Herbig and Herrmann explain that polymediated narrative allows us to "examine the building of worlds in which storytellers and fans interact, change, shift, and contribute" to the culture of the narrative (749). In this sense, viewers may exist inside and outside the fictional world simultaneously and, therefore, associate other media beyond the small screen with the story of Sam and Dean.

Just as focusing on the Impala gave materiality a specific focal point for Generation X members Sam and Dean in the first half of this chapter, the use of the song "Carry On, Wayward Son" in Marie's musical gives us a similar point of view for Generation Z, even though it was first released in 1976. The song's influence is felt across seasons of *Supernatural* when used as a musical interlude for flashbacks at the start and end of certain seasons. It is played at yearly conventions for fans, and most fans, even casual viewers, find it hard now to listen to the classic song without thinking of this show. The cueing of the song at the outset of *Supernatural*'s "previously on" segments has become a tradition that fans believe establishes the Kansas track as the show's anthem. However, one might say its most moving incarnation is the unplugged, or stripped down, version Marie stages in her second act. Featuring only six female actors in the roles of the Winchester family and Bobby, the song receives mainly piano accompaniment rather than a full rock band of sound. As the students sing, Dean and Sam are left watching in the wings. This moment in the unplugged version of Kansas's ballad encapsulates the spirit of "love letter" to the fans perhaps more than any reference in the play before it.

Materiality, even in the form of a song, works to connect people across eras and geographical distances. In his work *Stone: An Ecology of the Inhuman*, Jeffrey Cohen emphasizes the role that Stonehenge as a historical site has had on the creation of his book while, at the same time, hinting at the myriad of ways the structure has had influence on people's imagination at large. The site continues to move people throughout history in different ways, coming to mean something new for each population who theorizes its purpose or parodies its importance with blogs like "Clonehenge" (168–169). No one would argue that "Carry On, Wayward Son" is as significant as a structure that has lasted this long or suggested such mystery, but Cohen's description of how the thing links disparate peoples and entities helps describe how "Carry On" functions, like the Impala over fourteen years of narrative, as a shibboleth or rallying point for *Supernatural* fans across the globe.

Indeed, the band Kansas experienced some of the same stress Marie the character feels before her musical goes live. As Marie faces the wrath of the antagonist Calliope and a missing actor in the lead role of Sam, she refuses to give in to fear and decides to "Barbra Streisand this bitch" by taking on an acting role in addition to her directing and writing roles. This decision, like the decisions of many bricoleurs in narrative, prompts Marie to problem solve and make do with the materials she possesses rather than the ones she must do without. Likewise, as the documentary *Miracles Out of Nowhere* reveals, songwriter Kerry Livgren's story of composing "Carry On, Wayward Son" includes multiple references to the pressure his band was under to create a billboard single. Since the other songwriter had been lagging behind in creating new tracks for their album, Kerry as guitarist and keyboardist also found himself with the lion's share of writing lyrics, much as Marie finds herself playing multiple roles in order to bring her vision to life. Kerry's creation of "Carry On" came at the "last minute," according to his band mates, when at the end of a long rehearsal he exclaimed, "Hey, man, I've got another song." In the same spirit of unplugging in the literal sense, Livgren also wrote "Dust in the Wind," which he insisted should only be accompanied by acoustic guitar (and later violin). Like other bricoleurs who use unlikely materials to create something new, Kansas's most famous and haunting song was born from Livgren's simple guitar exercise and a suggestion from his wife "to do something with that" (*Miracles*).

The song's message speaks to the nature of Dean and Sam's journey. Its lyrics promise "peace" for those who have what seems to be never-ending responsibilities, just like Sam and Dean, whose lives on the road never seem to change or offer rest. David Wild of *Rolling Stone* puts it best in the documentary: "Is there a thirteen-year-old boy on earth who does not either think of themselves as the wayward son or want to be?" (*Miracles*). This universal message encapsulates what the protagonists of *Supernatural* experience: a rootless and rebellious experience in direct conflict with societal norms like family or economic security. Although "Wayward Son" could be an appropriate song for Generation X at large, given what we know about latchkey kids and their absent parents, its importance extends beyond the 1970s and 80s when Marie adapts it as a simple, heartfelt ballad for her musical. The song could reflect Marie's personal struggle to satisfy her artistic goals at the risk of killing herself at Calliope's hands; but, more importantly, it acts as a parachronism (a cultural reference or thing that blurs the borders between past and present) that speaks to Generation Z's conditions of existence. As Seemiller and Grace put it, these students are "growing up in a post-9/11 era in which the United States has been at war for years and terrorist acts occur regularly around the world. This has been the reality since these kids were no older than kindergarten age. . . ." (110–111). The authors go on to illustrate this fact with references to school shootings at all levels, including elementary schools, and events like the Boston Marathon bombing.

A series of violent events plague this generation in a manner similar to that experienced by Sam and Dean when they hunt fictional monsters. Or, speaking more realistically, one of Generation X's few defining traumas was to watch the Challenger explode on live television, but Generation Z experiences similar horrors on a yearly if not monthly basis, all within reach of a handheld screen or phone. Still, they are encouraged to "carry on," a phrase that has become a popular hashtag for *Supernatural* fans on Twitter when referencing Kansas's song.

As we return to the musical, the spotlight falls on the girls who represent the Winchester family, and the lyrics begin. Dean and Sam watch from the theater wings as the students bring their story to life. Instead of mocking, their expressions belie a tenderness for these actors. A list of trivia items associated with the filming of "Fan Fiction" includes a reference to how this portion of the show was filmed (imdb.com). Instead of practicing with Dean and Sam present during all of the musical rehearsals, actors Jensen Ackles and Jared Padalecki witnessed the girls sing the ballad for the first time when the camera zooms in on their faces. It may have been as emotional for them as it was for us after 200 episodes of working together to tell the brothers' story.

The hit single "Carry On, Wayward Son" acts as polymedia while also serving as an excellent example of materiality at work. The viewer cannot hold or touch the song in the same way we might hold an object like a coin. Rather than touch we, like the actors in the musical, must rely on sound to activate the senses. Still, a song brings a network of agents together in this case. The song itself, whether found on cassette, CD, or digital device, possesses agency as it intersects with the themes of the brothers' journey, Dean's love of classic rock on cassette tapes, the unplugged parts of Marie's musical, the love of the fans who use the hashtag during their viewing, the struggle of carrying on in an age of domestic and foreign terrorism, and the legend of Kansas's ability to create under high pressure circumstances. All of these associations help us understand how the song itself is a co-participant in the unfolding story. Materiality in *Supernatural* is no different than the surprising extensions inside the Winchester Mystery House: just as it seems to reach a mundane end, the thing or object that participates in the life of the scene uncovers a new purpose, perhaps an incomplete one, but one that inspires people and characters across generations. To paraphrase Kansas, Marie's musical is "the event of the season" not because it is merely a "charade," but because it involves a network of materials and humans that effectively communicates the love of one storyteller for another. And it carries on.

Notes

1. After completing my first draft of this chapter, I realized that Dickey in his work *Ghostland* had also used the house as a symbol of the city of San Jose itself. I am indebted to his descriptions and mythbusting detail of how this house grew in the public consciousness. The idea of this house as a metonymic device for *Supernatural* was also reinforced by my own tour in 2017.
2. For more information on this use of meta-commentary, see Wilson and Torrey.
3. A discussion of *Supernatural* and materiality in early seasons and in the 200th episode "Fan Fiction" might be viewed as a safe way to approach this show, whose writers and producers connect to their fan base in complicated ways. This is all to say that the human concerns and issues surrounding the cult television show have grown controversial over time, and a consideration of nonhuman agents has been ignored to allow space for fan studies work on the actors, the fans, the characters, and the creative team that profits from increased contact with its audience via social media, conventions, and elsewhere (Torrey and Cole). As Aja Romano argues, few women, people of color, or individuals with different sexual orientations are ever featured on *Supernatural*, and those

who are often meet premature deaths (see also Busse). Additionally, fans often demand more attention be paid to the LGBT community and felt betrayed when the one lesbian character they had grown to love was murdered. Because the narrative still refuses to incorporate queer storylines of any substance even as it develops memorable and increasingly homosocial male bonds, fan fiction remains the central outlet for fans to express their desires. This may be partly why the 200th episode was titled "Fan Fiction": since showrunners reported, as mentioned elsewhere, that they wanted to write what they call a "love letter" to loyal fans.
4. At a fan convention in Seattle, Washington, Jared Padalecki and Jensen Ackles state explicitly that the show and the fandom is "so much bigger" than just the actors.
5. This is not the only time Dean holds a dialogue with a vehicle: in the episode "Changing Channels," the car speaks to Dean as K.I.T.T. when forced to play the role of Knight Rider in order to entertain the trickster archangel Gabriel. However, in this case, the car is clearly being used as a prop for Gabriel rather than a co-participant. On the other hand, years later Season Eleven would feature an entire episode titled "Baby," which told the story of a hunting case from the Impala's perspective (all action takes place in or around the vehicle). However, this story did not feature an anthropomorphic take on the vehicle but mostly a change in camera angles. Still, writers hint at the car's sentience when a girl fails to locate her purse in Baby's backseat, and that purse with its pennies appears in time to save Dean from the monsters whose undead souls will only depart if a copper coin is placed inside their mouths.
6. Divisions among generations are never so neat as to allow any certainty about an individual's place in the world; indeed, Sam, born in 1983 (according to wikis and fan sources), would actually be considered by some to be one of the earliest members of Generation Y (see Strauss and Howe), just like Becky Rosen, who graduates high school in 2001. However, the emphasis here is on the cultural work and message that his character represents within the context of the show. Within the realm of popular culture, it is possible to acknowledge that the narrative paints most members of a cohort with the same brush, yet this brush may still provide valuable moments of identification. This is simply another layer to uncover in the study of how characters make meaning in their fictional universes and how this meaning influences our own views of young people.

References

"After School Special," season 4, episode 13, Warner Bros. Television, 29 Jan. 2009, *Netflix*, www.netflix.com/watch/70223102?trackId=200257859.

"All Hell Breaks Loose, Part 2," season 2, episode 22, Warner Bros. Television, 7 May 2007, *Netflix*, www.netflix.com/watch/70223073?trackId=200257858.

"Are You There God, It's Me, Dean Winchester," season 4, episode 2, Warner Bros. Television, 25 Sept. 2008, *Netflix*, www.netflix.com/watch/70223091?trackId=200257859.

"Baby," season 11, episode 4, Warner Bros. Television, 28 Oct. 2015, *Netflix*, www.netflix.com/watch/80120454?trackId=200257859.

Bennett, Jane. "Powers of the Hoard: Further Notes on Material Agency." *Animal, Vegetable, Mineral*, edited by Jeffrey Jerome Cohen. Oliphant Books, 2012, pp. 237–69.

boyd, danah. *It's Complicated: The Social Lives of Networked Teens*. Yale University Press, 2014.

Brown, Nathan Robert. *The Mythology of Supernatural: The Signs and Symbols Behind the Popular TV Show*. Penguin, 2011. Kindle.

Bruce, Melissa M. "The Impala as Negotiator of Melodrama and Masculinity in *Supernatural*." *Journal of Transformative Works and Cultures*, vol. 4, 2010, http://journal.transformativeworks.org/index.php/twc/article/view/154.

Busse, Kristina. "Fan Labor and Feminism: Capitalizing on the Fannish Labor of Love." *Cinema Journal*, vol. 54, no. 3, 2015, pp. 110–15.

"Changing Channels," season 5, episode 8, Warner Bros. Television, 5 Nov. 2009, *Netflix*, www.netflix.com/watch/70223119?trackId=20025785.

"Children Shouldn't Play with Dead Things," season 2, episode 4, Warner Bros. Television, 19 Oct. 2006, *Netflix*, www.netflix.com/watch/70223055?trackId=200257858.

Cohen, Jeffrey Jerome. *Stone: An Ecology of the Inhuman*. University of Minnesota Press, 2015.

"The Colt." *Supernatural Wiki*, http://supernatural.wikia.com/wiki/The_Colt. Accessed 13 Jul. 2018.

"Dark Side of the Moon," season 5, episode 16, Warner Bros. Television, 1 Apr. 2010, *Netflix*, www.netflix.com/watch/70223127?trackId=200257859.

Dickey, Colin. *Ghostland: An American History of Haunted Places*. Penguin, 2017. iBook.

"Fallen Idols," season 5, episode 5, Warner Bros. Television, 8 Oct. 2009, *Netflix*, www.netflix.com/watch/70223116?trackId=200257858.

"Family Remains," season 4, episode 11, Warner Bros. Television, 15 Jan. 2009, *Netflix*, www.netflix.com/watch/70223100?trackId=200257859.

"Fan Fiction," season 10, episode 5, Warner Bros. Television, 11 Nov. 2014, *Netflix*, www.netflix.com/watch/80061137?trackId=200257859.

"Fan Fiction." *Internet Movie Database*, www.imdb.com/title/tt3845910/?ref_=fn_al_tt_2.

"Free to Be You and Me," season 5, episode 3, Warner Bros. Television, 24 Nov. 2009, *Netflix*, www.netflix.com/watch/70223114?trackId=200257859.

"Ghostfacers," season 3, episode 13, Warner Bros. Television, 24 Apr. 2008, *Netflix*, www.netflix.com/watch/70223086?trackId=200257859.

"Halt and Catch Fire," season 10, episode 13, Warner Bros. Television, 10 Feb. 2015, *Netflix*, www.netflix.com/watch/80061145?trackId=200257859.

Herbig, Art, and Andrew F. Herrmann. "Polymediated Narrative: The Case of the *Supernatural* Episode 'Fan Fiction.'" *International Journal of Communication*, vol. 10, 2016, pp. 748–65.

"In My Time of Dying," season 2, episode 1, Warner Bros. Television, 28 Sept. 2006, *Netflix*, www.netflix.com/watch/70223052?trackId=200257859.

Joy, Eileen A. "You Are Here: A Manifesto." *Animal, Vegetable, Mineral*, edited by Jeffrey Jerome Cohen. Oliphaunt Books, 2012, pp. 153–72.

Kansas. "Carry on, Wayward Son." *Leftoverture*. Kirshner, 1976.

King, Stephen. *Christine*. Scribner, 2016. iBook.

"Lazarus Rising," season 4, episode 1, Warner Bros. Television, 18 Sept. 2008, *Netflix*, www.netflix.com/watch/70223090?trackId=200257859.

Levi-Strauss, Claude. *The Savage Mind*. University of Chicago Press, 1966.

"The Man Who Would Be King," season 6, episode 20, Warner Bros. Television, 6 May 2011, *Netflix*, www.netflix.com/watch/70223153?trackId=200257859.

Miracles Out of Nowhere, directed by Charley Randazzo, performers Kansas, Orchard Studio, 2015. *Amazon Prime*. Viewed 2 Dec. 2017.

Morton, Timothy. *Hyperobjects: Philosophy and Ecology After the End of the World*. University of Minnesota Press, 2013.

Nagel, Sidney R. "Shadows and Ephemera." *Things*, edited by Bill Brown. University of Chicago Press, 2004, pp. 23–30.

"No Exit," season 2, episode 6, Warner Bros. Television, 2 Nov. 2006, *Netflix*, www.netflix.com/watch/70223057?trackId=200257858.

"Pilot," season 1, episode 1, Warner Bros. Television, 13 Sept. 2005, *Netflix*, www.netflix.com/watch/70223016?trackId=200257859.

Prensky, Marc. *From Digital Natives to Digital Wisdom*. Sage, 2012.

Romano, Aja. "Why Fans Have High Hopes (but Low Expectations) for *Supernatural*." *The Daily Dot*, May 2014, www.dailydot.com/parsec/supernatural-season-9-predictions/.

"Season Seven, Time for a Wedding!" season 7, episode 8, Warner Bros. Television, 11 Nov. 2011, *Netflix*, www.netflix.com/watch/70245747?trackId=200257859.

Schuderer, Sherry. "2017 SPN Seattle Con J2 Afternoon Panel." *YouTube*, 10 Apr. 2017, www.youtube.com/watch?v=owNIvNb6C3Q.

Schwenger, Peter. *The Tears of Things: Melancholy and Physical Objects*. University of Minnesota Press, 2006.

Seemiller, Corey, and Meghan Grace. *Generation Z Goes to College*. Jossey-Bass, 2016. iBook.

"Sex and Violence," season 4, episode 14, Warner Bros. Television, 5 Feb. 2009, *Netflix*, www.netflix.com/watch/70223103?trackId=200257859.

Stein, Joel. "The New Greatest Generation." *Time Magazine*, vol. 181, 20 May 2013, http://time.com/247/millennials-the-me-me-me-generation/.

Stewart, Mark. "A Black 1967 Chevy Impala: Fan Shibboleths as Cultural Password." *Flow: A Critical Forum on Media and Culture*, 2014.

Strauss, William, and Neil Howe. *Generations: The History of America's Future, 1584–2069*. HarperCollins, 1992.

"Swan Song," season 5, episode 22, Warner Bros. Television, 13 May 2010, *Netflix*, www.netflix.com/watch/70223133?trackId=200257859.

"Sympathy for the Devil," season 5, episode 1, Warner Bros. Television, 10 Sept. 2009, *Netflix*, www.netflix.com/watch/70223112?trackId=200257859.

Torrey, K. T., and Shannon Cole. "I Used to Think Maybe You Loved Me (Now Baby, I'm Sure): The Reconstruction of the *Supernatural* Fangirl." Society for Cinema and Media Studies Conference, 29 Mar. 2015.

Tosenberger, Catherine, ed. "Saving People, Hunting Things: A Special *Supernatural* Themed Edition of *Transformative Works and Cultures*." *Transformative Works and Cultures*, vol. 4, 2010, http://journal.transformativeworks.org/index.php/twc/issue/view/5.

Wilson, Jules. "The Epic Love Story of *Supernatural* and Fanfic." *Fic: Why Fanfiction Is Taking Over the World*, edited by Anne Jamison. BenBella Books, 2013, pp. 309–15.

"Winchester Mystery House: Estate Guide." Winchester Mystery House, LLC. San Jose, CA. Tour on 23 Nov. 2017.

"Wishful Thinking," season 4, episode 8, Warner Bros. Television, 6 Nov. 2008, *Netflix*, www.netflix.com/watch/70223097?trackId=200257859.

Wright, Julia M. "Latch-Key Hero: Masculinity, Class and the Gothic in Eric Kripke's Supernatural." *Genders 1998–2013*. University of Colorado Boulder, 2008.

2 Beca as Bricoleur

How *Pitch Perfect* Characters Embrace Materiality and Music

The Screen Junkies, comedians behind the video series "Honest Trailers," mockingly provide the following voiceover about *Pitch Perfect* and its college freshman protagonist Beca Mitchell: "Meet Beca: a snarky, pretentious wanna-be DJ, who hates her dad for paying her tuition. Hates this cute guy for flirting with her. Hates these girls for wanting her to join their club. Hates her job for making her do any work. And hates movies. All of them." At the start Beca resembles any other young character that we might label as, well, entitled. The film does its part in making Beca unsympathetic, perhaps to show us more clearly why our perceptions of young people are incomplete by the end of the story. In watching her journey, the audience has the opportunity to move from a position of annoyance toward her to one of respect.

Beca's goal is to become a music producer in Los Angeles, and her father, a professor at Barden University, promises that if she makes the effort to join a club and immerse herself in the college community, he will not stand in the way of her dream. The Barden Bellas, an a cappella group still smarting from the failure to win a national singing championship, decide to loosen their audition standards enough to accept Beca's alternative music and style. As Beca grows close to these girls (played by actresses Rebel Wilson and Brittany Snow among others), she both antagonizes but later inspires their leader Aubrey (Anna Camp) to try new mashups of contemporary songs to replace the predictable singing the girls do at every competition. She also opens herself to the possibility of romance as she befriends fellow singer Jesse (Skyler Astin), who, like the Screen Junkies, initially views Beca as aloof and full of hatred for things she considers beneath her. By the end of the film, the Bellas reign supreme in both the national a cappella scene and back home at Barden University. With Aubrey graduating, Beca looks like the next leader of the Bellas.

In *Pitch Perfect 2*, the viewer witnesses Beca and her group's ascendancy to national renown, which culminates in an invitation to sing for the President of the United States at Lincoln Center. However, now that the Bellas have won the national a cappella championship three times (Beca and her peers are college seniors now), their style has morphed from

Figure 2.1 Set of Large, Noise-canceling Headphones
Source: Wikimedia Commons

a more endearing rendition of inspiring songs to a spectacle of song that includes props and special effects to wow the audience. Their performance even features a circus-like suspension as one young woman enters in aerial fashion to her solo of "Wrecking Ball" by Miley Cyrus. This elaborate showmanship backfires since the costume rips during her swings from the rafters, and the entire audience sees her nude bottom half hanging upside down from her harness. The negative press associated with this faux pas results in the Bellas being banned from competition at Barden University, and their only hope of restoring the group's reputation is to enter and win a world singing competition. The remainder of the narrative focuses on how the Bellas can recapture their original sound in order to succeed against rival German group Das Sound Machine. At first, the Bellas attempt to beat Das Sound Machine "at their own game" by using advanced pyrotechnics and digital screen designs to augment their presentation. However, the more effects and props the Bellas add, the more the audience finds their performance off putting. Rather than strive for simplicity, the Barden singers now believe that less is not more and that a bigger budget will solve the rather empty content their group has begun to stage.

Although a third film exists, I will explain in the second half of this essay why the summaries and analysis stop here. For now I will argue that *Pitch Perfect* and its sequel do valuable cultural work beyond offering a delightful romp through the dorm rooms of today's young adults and the politics of college a cappella groups. This chapter highlights examples of materiality with its use of unplugged music, its reliance on unique spaces to create meaning, and its use of handheld tools to reveal character motivation. In this particular film, the Barden freshmen (and later seniors in the sequel) are the oldest members of Generation Z in this book. Indeed, the cast may also be easily grouped with stereotypes of millennial entitlement since the Screen Junkies, among others, take pleasure in highlighting their narcissism. Still, Beca in this narrative reminds us that, at least in this fictional world of choral performance, not all of today's youth are married to their laptops and phones. They also know how to manipulate objects and spaces to make new meaning out of old customs and rituals. Beca is what Claude Levi-Strauss calls a bricoleur—one who is able to make things and create meaning from available materials. The idea of mashups and remixes—the stuff of bricolage—is not new, but *Pitch Perfect*'s characters demonstrate that authentic bricolage as practiced in digital culture does not always remain in digital culture but expands into the physical world to join material and human efforts.

As stated in the Introduction to this book, Levi-Strauss in *The Savage Mind* discusses the role of bricoleur as someone who takes the available resources of a given situation and is able to create something new from the limited supply. The bricoleur operates within "constraints imposed by a particular state" rather than going beyond them (19). She is able to "'make do' with 'whatever is at hand,' that is to say with a set of tools and materials which is always finite and is also heterogeneous because what it contains bears no relation to the current project" (17). Mark Deuze then describes digital culture as a place where people are "making do" every day as they "accept the fact that reality is constructed, assembled, and manipulated by media." He explains that "the only way to make sense of that mediated world is to intervene and thus adjust our worldview accordingly—which in turn shapes and renews the properties of media, more closely reflecting the identity of the remediating bricoleur instead of the proverbial couch potato" (66). Deuze stresses the bricoleur's role as different from the image of the lazy consumer because we intervene *as* we consume. In working through bricolage, users manipulate and design messages so that new meanings result from their efforts. In *Pitch Perfect* we initially see Beca mixing different musical tracks on her laptop, and this above quotation resonates with her efforts in the film. This marriage to digital media, however, is not the only avenue through which the work of bricolage is explored. Here the term bricoleur is, albeit somewhat paradoxically, rooted in a study of materiality, where places, things, and animals possess the same potential to make arguments as humans do. This material world hosts and creates new meaning with us rather than remaining subordinate to our human efforts. Gaining a new perspective of tools and places in our world reminds us, most importantly, that humans are not the only architects of our world; rather, we are co-participants in it.

The Plastic Cup

This analysis begins with a dissection of a key moment in the franchise: Beca's freshman audition for the Barden Bellas. Because Beca is typically seen with her laptop, working on sonic compositions and layering tracks, the audience expects to see her use some form of technology in her audition. As she describes her process to her friend Jesse, her musical talent consists of "find[ing] songs that have the same chord progression and creat[ing] a track that blends them together." Because she has little experience with a cappella singing, the audience may anticipate her departure from the standard audition of repeating Kelly Clarkson lyrics. Beca does depart from convention, but she uses a simple object to create rhythm while she sings rather than rely on digital tools or effects. Upon beginning her song, she leans over to the table where the two directors sit and retrieves a plastic yellow cup filled with their pens. Dumping the pens on the table, she uses the empty cup to mark a complex beat sequence on the floor of the stage as she sings without musical accompaniment.

The plastic cup serves as an example through which to study the creativity of humans while also honoring the nonhuman objects in their midst. Most philosophers who celebrate object oriented ontology, a vital part of material rhetoric that focuses on physical entities, stress that the world exists beyond what we can know and manipulate in terms of our thinking. This line of belief may seem to run counter to the celebration of a bricoleur, who manipulates objects to fit her needs. The very heart of most philosophies surrounding materiality reveals some desire to decenter the human, or at least acknowledge human limitations in the presence of other physical agents, many of which are non-sentient. At the moment of marking rhythm with the yellow cup, Beca proves her ability to work with her hands when no technology is present. She hits the plastic cup as it turns downward and then upward, manipulating the object in a manner almost too fast to imitate or track. Her work with the cup is admirable not just for the hand-eye coordination she displays but also for the ability to "make do" with available tools in her environment. While other auditions feature the same song over and over again, Beca's departure from the norm seems, at least initially, welcomed, since the judges' faces indicate curiosity at her efforts.

The protagonist's use of the plastic cup also unveils another aspect of Generation Z culture. The trait of being able to see beyond an object's original design so that it may be upcycled rather than trashed is one that Generation Z characters seem primed to do. As she thinks like a bricoleur, Beca finds a way to circumvent a problem that has global implications: the damage done by single use plastic items. In an era where more and more studies point to plastic's devastating effects on the ocean and its frightfully long decomposition process (see Trowsdale, Housden, and Meier), it may be folly to assume that one plastic cup repurposed by a college student would have any impact on the problem.

Nevertheless, the placard on the next page shows just how commonly the rhetoric of one person making a small but significant contribution permeates Generation Z's culture. Teens and children frequently see reminders like the one above when they enter public and commercial spaces and are

Figure 2.2 Hotel Room Placard Asking Guests to Save Water
Source: Author photo

reminded that "each person CAN make a difference." As Alex Blasdel's encomium to Timothy Morton describes, "We live in a world with a moral calculus that didn't exist before. Now, doing just about anything is an environmental question." Consequently, one plastic cup or one towel hung on a rack in a hotel does have an impact on the amount of environmental waste produced by humans.

The second and third films in the trilogy would hearken back to the cup scene in different ways. In the second movie the Bellas are sitting around a campfire on a retreat, where Aubrey has charged the girls to recapture their "Bella sound" so that they may win the world competition. Chloe then begins the "Cups" song that Beca first sang when they met her. In this version, the voices alone make harmony; the singers use no tools to accompany the performance. The song is also slower in this iteration. By the time they finish, the Bellas realize that they have rediscovered what traits make them special: traits of originality, simplicity, and bricolage on which Beca relied in her audition. In the final competition, the Bellas win the world prize partly because they learn that advanced pyrotechnics and multiple props are distracting. The two groups even offer different views of technology in their song titles. While Das Sound Machine sings

"Light em Up" and uses pyrotechnics, the Bellas sing an original song called "Flashlight," which hearkens back to the value of something small to create a powerful effect. Having gotten back to their original vision, the singers choose to rely only on small flashlights held in each woman's hand. This use of a handheld tool in contrast to Das Sound Machine's ostentatious display of light and sound effects works for their purposes as they reveal an entire sisterhood of Bella alumnae who sing along with the current cast.

On the other hand, the third film mocks the first film's use of the cup as a tool to make music. When the former Bellas are invited to a reunion, three years after their graduation, Chloe actually holds up a plastic cup and proclaims that they are ready to sing, only to have another girl knock it out of her hand in embarrassment. The narrative in this particular film capitalizes on the original "Cups" song and its titular prop as something that is outdated and unnecessary rather than innovative. The very tossing aside of the cup also shows why the third film deviates from its original premise of music shaped by specific spaces and tools. By the conclusion, the film subverts the original premise of the a cappella medium by showing how the girls, particularly Beca, must succumb to the presence of instrumental backgrounds and the ideas and compositions of people like commercial rap artist D J Khaled (who guest starts in the movie). The story also places greater emphasis on the power of the individual to achieve fame instead of the value of a community singing together. In *Pitch Perfect 3*, D J Khaled and his staff choose Beca to appear onstage by *herself* mainly because she possesses talent with digital mixing on expensive equipment.

The digital and analog tools present in these films connote opposing images in most examples. The analog work of singing without digital accompaniment, the use of things like cups and hands and sticks to make sound, and the creative manipulation of space is often associated with community. The use of digital screens and tools often results in isolation. It first seems that Beca works best alone, creating mashups on her laptop (this is what we see her doing in the very first shot of the first film), but she later learns how to work in an ensemble and use her ability as bricoleur to change her community. The third film features how she regresses, albeit reluctantly, to her role as a soloist and music producer, unable to take her friends with her in the next phase of her career.

Beyond the Cup

In the first film Beca's character arc includes a journey from apathy toward material culture to a position of celebrating its uses. In particular, hand held objects like the cup receive significant attention rather than acting as background props. Beca's internship with the local radio station provides frequent evidence of this. Inside the studio the viewer sees an overabundance of things used to play and make music. Upon arriving at the studio for the first time, Beca realizes her first duty as lowly freshman is not to actually mix music or use a mixing board but rather to "stack CDs." Once the camera pans and scans the space, viewers note the design as one that might be referred to as vintage studio design. Beca's father characterizes the station as a "dark and dirty" place; the rooms are covered in old rock posters, and the architecture, complete with peeling paint on window trimmings that separate the DJ's seat from the larger library, suggests that the building was a private residence at some point in the past. WBUJ's staff, rather than mixing tracks initially, appears to work primarily with a collections of LPs and compact discs archived on two floors.

In other words, all of this material culture seems to suggest that the world of musical production, especially in a small college town like the one in this film, still depends largely on items that can be physically touched rather than just simply remixed digitally. Indeed, musicians often have paid tribute to the material world in which they have been immersed, and recent scholarship highlights ways they have done so. Mandy Suzanne-Wong explains in an opening editorial of *Evental Aesthetics*, a journal recently featuring the importance of materiality in art, that one musician Morton Feldman "spoke of [sound] composition as a collective act of human and nonhuman agents" (4); his material process is one in which a musician "worked by letting materials work on him" (5). Here the materials work on Beca in a similar fashion, but only when she allows them to enter her frame of reference. That is, Beca's disappointment over her CD stacking duties may be first read as a reaction to being given a menial task, but we may also consider that the reaction is grounded in her previous experiences of storing and mixing music in digital forms. She has often, in musical design, "worked on the materials" in ways they could not possibly "work on her," to borrow Suzanne-Wong's words. A song on CD or album remains, in one view, a frozen structure incapable of fluid combinations with other tracks. Beca's experience with music has always allowed her to change a song's DNA through editing of various sounds. As she is thrust into a studio that uses dated technology and tools from the past, her view of music changes from one that is primarily focused on digital culture to one that is aware of material culture, too. Unlike digital culture, material culture, at first glance, seems to offer no easy way to produce new compilations of tracks. This realization sets the mood for the a cappella culture to come: where singers may use only their minds and mouths to harmonize.

Beca repeatedly tries to get her music showcased at the local radio station but becomes humbled by the process. Each time she completes a new mashup, she saves the work and brings it to her supervisor, who then tosses the small thumb drive into a large, indistinguishable pile of similar objects with her name on them. Tools associated with digital compilation of tracks appear discarded rather than honored, forgotten rather than utilized. The remixing or engineer work submitted individually by an artist seems to exist in a vacuum (Beca's musical mix is played at the station, finally, but only when most of the campus departs for spring vacation). The focus shifts from a world of digital remix to a world where music is made primarily through human voices in unique locations.

This material culture does more than offer a glimpse into past styles of musical consumption and production. Through stacking materials with another intern, Beca begins her first friendship with a boy named Jesse who also enjoys singing a cappella. This is important because through engaging in the menial job of organizing compact discs, relationships form more readily than when Beca uses her digital tools in isolation. Just after the expositional scene in the studio, the camera cuts to Beca as she is mixing two tracks on her computer. Although she works outside on the Quad, where her father says students come together to socialize, she remains isolated and glances around her at the other groups of students talking and laughing together. Beca sits alone, holding the laptop and wearing large headphones that block out any sound but the one she mixes. Upon seeing her isolation, Beca's father urges her to join a group on campus; he is so sure that extracurricular involvement will foster a sense of community that he promises to help her move to Los Angeles to pursue music if she remains unhappy at the end of the year.

This example echoes another moment in which material items are used in place of technology to establish human connection: Jesse's makeshift movie picnic. Upon spotting Beca outdoors, Jesse brings a blanket, juice packs, and a set of classic DVD films to share. When hearing Beca disparage movies, he mocks her for not enjoying them and reveals his desire to educate her through "movication." She explains that her lack of enthusiasm is due to the predictability of the endings; she often gets "bored" in the first half because she figures out the plot in advance. Again, Beca's preference for a more digital platform where predictable or traditional media may be remixed rather than accepted as static forms again holds sway here. A movie, packaged on a DVD, much like the CDs she must stack in the radio station, must be endured rather than enjoyed because of its traditional, ossified plot formations and execution. In material culture, Beca sees only limitations, at least at first. Later she learns that these items possess the same capacity for remix when she adapts the concluding song from *The Breakfast Club* to sing at a national competition.

The presence of *The Breakfast Club* as a key text also supports a focus on materiality. In this 1980s narrative, the movie's plot features a group of motley characters whose relations to one another are random and ill fitting. Sentenced to a Saturday detention, they spend the day in conflict but end in some degree of harmony as they learn to appreciate one another's differences and backgrounds. Like Ian Bogost, who praises the power of the "list" as testament to a flat ontology (where all items are equal but not necessarily connected), the *Breakfast Club* script concludes with a list of characters, presented like a set of ingredients. The voiceover of the narrator(s) insists that each character is both alone and together:

a brain,
an athlete,
a basket case,
a princess,
and a criminal

even if the characters fit one stereotype more than the rest. This list emphasizes the "thing-ness" of life in high school where stereotypes tend to crystallize personalities into contained identities with specific properties. In material rhetoric Bogost refers to this process of listing disparate elements as calling attention to the "jarring staccato of real being" (40) and best illustrates the "rhetoric of lists" when he shares a commercial from Trader Joe's grocery store:

It's a box of soup
It's a bell from a boat
It's yogurt made
From the milk of a goat
A handle that rips
On a paper sack
That checker you like
Who'll never be back
    (45)

This making of lists, or habit of "cataloguing" reality (Bogost 38–45), also echoes the strange juxtaposition of parts that characterizes the bricoleur's work when she cannot choose but "make do" with those things available to her. By the time the Bellas compete at Lincoln Center, Beca has amassed a list of songs to feature in her performance, including "Party in the U.S.A.," "Don't You Forget (About Me)," "Just the Way You Are," "Titanium," and "Turn the Beat Around," among others. In a sense, the Bellas are like the characters in *The Breakfast Club*: they all singularly and together represent the fun of 80s pop music, the brashness of Miley Cyrus, the soulfulness of Bruno Mars, and the empowerment of female singers like Sia. Mixed together, the parts still remain intact, but all songs become a part of the material rhetoric that makes up the Barden Bellas, just as the list above helps characterize the shopping experience of Trader Joe's. It is also worth noting that Timothy Morton's work on object oriented ontology also opens with an example of sonic mashup similar to what Beca and her teammates use to win the competition. His discussion of the 1990s track "Set Adrift on Memory Bliss" by P.M. Dawn as a way to understand the material world and the memory of his schizophrenic brother shows how useful objects and musical compositions are as examples of persuasion in themselves:

> And of course, that's what the song does: it attends to an affective state, memory bliss, over and over, as a way to say goodbye to someone—or to hold them in mind, not letting go. We just can't be sure. It's why the song works. It's a hip-hop song, made of pieces of other songs, samples. The song is almost like something you'd sing over one of your favorite records, a cherished object you play over and over again.
>
> (15)

Likewise, Beca's triumph is her ability to use all the previous experiences and "affective state[s]" of the girls—conservative and radical alike—to help compile a winning mashup that earns them the title of national champions. Finally, we see where viewing bricolage as "overcome[ing] the usual dichotomy between consumption and production" (Farmer 34) takes full force: Beca both consumes *The Breakfast Club* as media but then produces a winning performance that features that same film's signature closing song as part of the Bella mashup.

Beca's triumph as a leader stems from her ability not only to mix disparate songs to create a new whole but also from her ability to find talent in a group of diverse neophytes. The "rhetoric of lists," as Bogost calls it, resonates with the hodgepodge composition of the new Bella group. Once a group of "eight super hot girls with bikini ready bodies who can harmonize with perfect pitch," the team now consists of eight radically different female personalities and figures. For example, soloist Amy (played by Rebel Wilson) is a chubby singer from Australia, who labels herself "Fat Amy" to prevent "twig bitches" like the former Bellas from calling her that in secret. Fat Amy even toys with hairstyles that she describes as "part Jewish" and decries the habit of exercising to support her breathing capacity. Her very presence suggests a disparate part rather than a piece of the whole; her first solo features her stripping her blouse off in a raucous display of enthusiasm rather than adhering to the choreography the seniors ask the group to perform. While Amy does possess talent at matching pitch, her personality is not as easily contained as the personalities of her Bella predecessors. Additionally, it is very difficult to "make do" with what little unrefined dance and musical talent some of the girls have when they initially join the group. Beca possesses the ability to identify music and dance routines that will accent their individual talents rather than call attention to their inexperience. Once she shares her ideas, other girls come forward to share ways they can beat the competition. Asian singer Lilly (played by Hana Mae Lee), who has previously spoken only in hushed whispers, begins to speak up about their music selection and even raps part of the mashup during their final competition.

Surprising Spaces

Beca as bricoleur does more than work with unlikely objects and humans. She also learns the value of making music in unlikely settings. One of the characteristics of the bricoleur is the ability to "reappropriate the space" (de Certeau xiv). In the case of *Pitch Perfect*, the settings I will examine most specifically are Beca's dormitory co-ed bathroom and the campus's swimming pool. Having just created a new mashup by herself (we see her layering tracks of 1990s music with music of the present day), Beca enters the showers while still singing "Titanium," one of the contemporary tracks in her set list. After turning on the water and hanging her bathroom supplies on the door, Chloe, a veteran member of the Bellas, hears her, walks naked into the shower, and demands to sing in harmony with her. Even though Beca protests the lack of privacy, she eventually relents and joins in. Chloe affirms Beca's musical talent in a location where sound technology is absent: the only items present are water, towels, robes, steam, and the acoustics made possible from concrete walls. While the shower seems to be an unlikely location to harmonize, some audiophiles on discussion forums advocate for recording in bathrooms where the sound may echo and bounce in more unpredictable ways than if it were recorded in an established studio with traditional furniture and equipment. Indeed, the sound in this particular scene of the movie echoes so well that a male student hears it and opens the shower curtain to listen. This bonding moment between the two girls leads to Beca's consideration of Bella membership; it is an important scene that marks her acceptance of material music culture and, as I suggest, her pronounced role of bricoleur.

Another unlikely setting serves as a testament to the bricoleur's ability to "make do" with available resources: an empty swimming pool. This space acts as a makeshift auditorium for the singing groups to compete informally in a ritual "riff off" among the a cappella groups. This moment highlights how a space typically used for one purpose—college athletics— has been reclaimed and repurposed as a large vessel inside which to sing. The Bellas and other groups make do with this space because it allows for large groups to sing with proper outdoor acoustics (plus, as the filmmakers must have thought, it just looks really cool). This reappropriation is not without irony; while the pool appears to help those associated with sports, it is most helpful to those in the fine arts, a traditionally underfunded part of extracurricular college life.In this sense, Beca and the rest of the group undertake the kind of repurposing of space that urban explorers experience when they create street art or take photographs of abandoned buildings. The main difference is that they mark the abandoned territory with sound.

Michel de Certeau speaks to this form of material occupation with his discussion of space and place in *The Practice of Everyday Life*. He explains that although a place is a "stable" construct, space leaves room for improvisation: "A space exists when one takes into consideration vectors of direction, velocities, and time variables. Thus space is composed of intersections of mobile elements. It is in a sense actuated by the ensemble of movements deployed within it" (11). In *Pitch Perfect 2*, an eccentric billionaire ("the world's biggest a cappella fan") hosts a party where the a capella groups may compete for his entertainment via riff off. This choice of setting fits the overall mood of the first half of the sequel: a mood defined by consumerism, voyeurism, and wealth. The host has a large gong that he uses to disqualify groups, one he can barely hold up due to its immense weight. He also possesses equipment that allows the topics for the mashups to be displayed above the crowd. The performance space that the Bellas use in the sequel is, therefore, more of a place than a space since they have no agency to remake it as they see fit.

On the other hand, the pool scene showcases a large population acting as bricoleurs to circumvent boundaries that might limit other performers and artists as the singers climb down into the pool with the help of ladders they bring to the scene. The materials of the pool setting become participants similar to the singers themselves. Next to the students, whose legs swing over the poolsides, are numbers marking the depth of water that has been removed, which is significant in terms of how much space allows for the best reverberation of sound. Other objects come into view on camera: large flashlights, a singer's unicycle, a digital projection that casts a spinning wheel of musical themes on the concrete wall, and plastic cups filled with what appears to be alcohol. Since some of the singers are not legally old enough to drink, the pool becomes the site of rebellious, albeit typical, play for college students. In the midst of this network of objects, Beca asks a question of the veteran Bellas that echoes the bricoleur's purpose when she turns to a fellow singer and asks, "So we just pick any song that *works*? And just go with it?" As the groups trade Top 40 songs in a battle to outwit one another, she runs to the center and begins rapping "No Diggity," causing all the other participants some confusion at first as they see a white female reciting words from a musical genre more radical and experimental than the kind of music a cappella artists typically sing. Even though they lose the riff off on a technicality, Beca reminds her cohort when the song ends that they were awesome because "it was spontaneous" and they were "actually listening" to one another. While the success of a cappella music is the ability to carry a song without instrument, that success is augmented by the echoing choruses made more powerful by the empty pool itself. As a site of "making do" with lyrics they already know, the combination of different genres creates a temporary unification of goals when all join in with Beca's unorthodox choice of music and begin singing from all parts of the space.

The Bellas are often meeting in spaces designated for the sports teams on their campus: we view them in the gym rehearsing on more than one occasion, complete with whiteboard notes that echo a coach's diagrams for competitive sports. The empty pool acts in direct opposition to these spaces, highlighting the improvisational activities of the Bellas rather than the controlled choreography done in front of mirrors and whiteboards. When rehearsing inside the auditorium, the girls follow Aubrey's choreography and replicate previous performances. In contrast, when Beca assumes temporary leadership of the group at Aubrey's request, she leads the team back to the empty pool, where they begin to layer different tracks in their singing. The sound in such spaces is less controlled and contained, as sound engineers would know. The pool acts in direct contrast with spaces that would be considered "dry" and more soundproof. This large crowd scene acts as a moment of closure for the earlier bathroom scene in which Beca feels overwhelmed by Chloe's sudden appearance in her shower stall. While Beca originally shies away from unpredictable encounters with people and with music that does not involve her editing software, she learns to adapt to her new college community.

In this sense, the empty pool, like the showers earlier, acts as a giant echo chamber where sound waves may bounce unpredictably together, and, therefore, Beca's leadership takes on an even more important meaning. Accustomed to making sound on a laptop, where she may control and edit each moment of the tracks, Beca learns to appreciate spaces and voices in a more organic form. While acting as bricoleur, she is also ideally positioned to recognize how well human and nonhuman forces (singer and setting) work together. Appreciating material culture that, on the surface, appears less sophisticated than editing software on a computer means recognizing that, as Miller explains, "All objects, human and nonhuman alike, operate on the same flat metaphysical plane" (41). To sing well but also find a community that values her, she must work in partnership with settings and tools rather than control them through software. Frank Farmer explains the difference in digital creation and hand-made creation when talking about those who used to make zines in the late twentieth century. In this analysis of the citizen bricoleur and the ethos s/he builds through "inventive resourceful making do," he provokes the reader with an important question: "But do such arts endure in digital environments?" (76). This use of the word "but" signals a doubt that the digital world may not be capable of giving the bricoleur the same fulfillment as working in physical spaces with material tools. While I do not suggest we do away with sound mixing in favor of singing in swimming pools, what I do appreciate and what I hope to emphasize, above all else, is the way in which Beca learns to work with both analog and digital tools.

Pitch Perfect 2: Descent Into Excess

Still, the Bellas face a learning curve as their reputation grows, and their experiences in the sequel solidify the motifs of high and low tech technologies working, this time, against one another. Somewhat similar to the hoarders Jane Bennett describes in her work on new materialism and thing agency, the Bellas, when labeled champions multiple years in a row, forego the simple act of honing their pitch in order to accumulate more and more stuff in a "consumptive culture" (248–250) of fame. National championship titles result not in increased attention to harmony and originality but to a spectacle of the body and stage, with little room for original writing and singing. As the Bellas use everything from plastic rifles to flags to entertain the President, commentator John says, "Back in my day we just put on our blazers and sang. We maybe snapped our fingers if we were feeling frisky." Gail agrees, "There is so much happening onstage I don't know where to look." While such comments sound like remarks made by cynical adults of a previous generation, their concerns make sense in terms of the incongruity between a cappella's purpose and the group's ostentatious displays. The world of a cappella, by its very nature, unplugs and strips down a musical performance by eliminating tools and musical instruments.

Conversely, the more championship trophies the Bellas win, the more they accumulate objects and materials that have nothing to do with practicing pitch. The camera even reveals that they now live in what appears to be a two-story sorority house with a capital "B" engraved on the front. This setting stands in contrast to the way in which a capella groups, particularly the Bellas, appear to be scrounging for rehearsal spaces and resources in the first film. It is obvious that the world of simplicity represented by the plastic cup Beca uses has been replaced by a more materialistic approach. Music for the sake of artistry and song seems to be conflated now with spectacle and kinesthetics; Gail even comments that the Bella feet "never stop moving" during the Kennedy Center performance. Newcomer Emily, a freshman who automatically earns a spot on the Bellas roster because she is a legacy, seems confused that the rehearsals no longer focus on group singing but on athletic training and choreography. She is also disappointed because she composes her own songs and wants to share them with fellow musicians like Beca, who, as she puts it, "single-handedly created the 'Bella sound.'"

As stated in the earlier summary, their main rivals are the members of a German a capella group named Das Sound Machine (DSM), which describes itself as a "German collective, operating in concert to create sonic mastery." Barden University's administrators and the National A Capella Association forbid the Bellas from taking a victory tour due to Amy's costume ripping onstage at President Obama's birthday celebration at the Kennedy Center. This incident, one in which Amy bears all to the nation since she wears no underwear, prompts the hosts of *The View* to refer to them as a "national disgrace" and the news to label the incident "Muffgate." DSM substitutes for them, and the Bellas see them perform the first time at a car dealership. While the Bellas have given in to swag, glitter, and plastic props to enhance their stage presence, DSM members use video projection and strobe light to punctuate their own pitches before a crowd. Their first appearance in the film is appropriate, since they perform to advertise a new model of car: one that is described as reaching "automotive perfection." Here the new vehicle represents all that low tech tools do not: it has all the newest accessories and sound equipment to entice 2015 consumers. Indeed, the very idea of placing DSM alongside a company's logo rather than showcasing them outdoors or at a public event sets the stage for a game of high tech one-upmanship between the DSM members and the Bellas. Empty swimming pools now give way to stages where product placement and consumer interest are key.

Hipsters and Adults

> The thing about college a cappella is that it exists in this incredible space: college. It's the one time in life where everything is momentum. With a cappella . . . one can both step out and blend in entirely. For the same reason one joins a fraternity, or an athletic team, one joins an a a cappella group. The problem arises when you take a cappella out of the context of the college—then what is it, really? A cover band. With no instruments.
> —Mickey Rapkin, author of *Pitch Perfect: The Quest for Collegiate A Cappella Glory*

Before concluding, I want to address how adults are portrayed in the *Pitch Perfect* movies and how they act as foils to the younger characters. If going unplugged leads to innovation, and it often does, what happens when that ability to innovate ossifies into something else entirely? What happens when we grow out of young adulthood and try to maintain creative energies in the various parts of our lives?

In the first movie of the *Pitch Perfect* trilogy, a group called the Tonehangers sells CDs and sings to those in the lobby at the regional a cappella competition, held at a performing arts center at a local university. The Tonehangers are four middle-aged men who hope to make a few pennies with their "Buy One, Get One Free" CD sales, but the passersby largely ignore them. These are adults who clearly have not moved on from their college experiences of belonging to a singing group; in other words, they peaked years ago as performers but refuse to accept that their a cappella years are over. When the Tonehangers spot the current group of Treblemakers, a male group of singers from Barden University, the Treblemakers mock them for their age and their "has been" status as washed up performers. Leader of the group Bumper cries out, "Oh, look who it is! Old dudes! Get a life!"

Although every chapter in this book includes some portrayal of adults as "out of touch" and removed from the day to day challenges of growing up, the portrayal of these particular men takes a violent turn for the worse. In the university lobby, in front of everyone, they beg the current students from the day's competition to start a fight with them. The fight is meant to be comical, but the adults yell out statements like "I need to feel something! Hit me as hard as you can!" and "Fat Amy! Kick me in the balls!" Such humorous yet desperate cries affirm that these middle-aged men suffer as adults because they no longer sing and dance daily. They stress that by performing in the lobby, a liminal space, one characterized by waiting rather than doing, they are hoping to be discovered through what their leader calls "oral magic." Like Mickey Rapkin, author of the original book upon which the films are based, explains in the opening sentences above, these men are now a cover band without instruments, and the depiction of middle age without college a cappella is a dark one here despite the humor.

Sadly, in *Pitch Perfect 2*, Bumper becomes the very thing he mocks: he joins the Tonehangers, works in campus security at his alma mater, and spends most of his time attending Treblemaker functions even though, as the undergraduates remind him, he no longer "has a vote." Although his saga invokes some pity, Bumper seems to turn his life around when Amy agrees to be his girlfriend and he receives a call from the producers of the television show *The Voice*. Although Bumper's future looks promising at the film's end, and Beca and her peers graduate and then capture the World Championship title in a cappella, the third film in the trilogy then reverses this progress. The narrative then capitalizes on how empty life becomes as it follows the main characters to their first jobs, where they eventually reunite to practice their own "oral magic" for the last time. Even then, the once passionate and well respected a cappella singers must watch themselves be replaced by a new generation of college students. Because of the above examples (and because the film is quite bad, to be honest), the third film receives little attention in this chapter.

The message seems clear: life after college (and youth) often seems anticlimactic and directionless, at least in this particular universe. However, *Pitch Perfect 2* momentarily amends this perspective by adding Emily's mother, Mrs. Junk, to the narrative. Mrs. Junk looks happy and nostalgic upon visiting Barden, but she clearly has no issue separating her adult life from her former one. She shows Emily to campus but leaves her behind with enthusiasm, excited that they will belong to the same sisterhood of the Bellas. When Beca incorporates Emily's original song "Flashlight" into the World Competition, Mrs. Junk and other alumnae such as Aubrey appear onstage as backup singers. In this moment of unity, the present and past singers harmonize in a way that eliminates ageist stereotypes and offers hope to those who have just graduated. In this scene, which serves as an anomaly next to scenes of Tonehangers and adult cynicism, generational boundaries dissolve to reveal a sisterhood that appears to withstand the test of time.

Rapkin, author of the book upon which the *Pitch Perfect* trilogy bases its escapades, is accurate in describing why some materials—certain spaces and tools—are confined to a specific place and phase of life. A cappella music has always been created with certain enclosed spaces and communities in mind. Once sung in medieval churches long ago, a cappella music best suits college campus groups because college is an enclosed space where young people feel comfortable experimenting in their hobbies and friendships. Now college groups dominate the a cappella landscape, with some groups even releasing albums and touring because they have become so famous (a scene in *Pitch Perfect 2* shows the Treblemakers fighting over what to place on their album cover). Over time, people have also found creative ways to mimic instruments and sounds to accompany song lyrics rather than just to harmonize with their fellow singers.

Older characters are not the only ones under attack in these comedies. *Pitch Perfect* does offer an excellent example of what the *young* artist should *not* be. Those who collect and display old technologies may be doing so to perpetuate false images of their uniqueness rather than creating something out of nothing. We see this most clearly in Dax, the music producer boss's nephew, who works at the same recording studio with Bella in *Pitch Perfect 2*. Bella's boss chastises Dax regularly for not putting forth any real effort in the studio. His ideas are half-formed interjections, ones he has no qualms vocalizing to a captive audience during creative meetings. Dax wears glasses and skinny jeans and eats sriracha on his lunch break. He fills the workplace refrigerator with containers that he labels with his name. When asked to complete a task, Dax gives it minimal attention and/or bungles it, which leaves his uncle frustrated. This image, most often associated with the hipster, reveals that not all young adults easily move creatively from medium to medium; rather, some do the least expected and then hope for the best. This point is salient because the specter of the hipster lurks throughout the analysis of this comedic film, particularly because *Pitch Perfect* highlights middle class young people who are able to afford internships and liberal arts colleges to begin with. With money and time anyone can collect and learn about old movies and tools.

In an article from 2010, Mark Greif reminds his readers that the term hipster is notoriously slippery and misused but that we might generally think of it as an "outflanking maneuver par excellence for competitors within a common field of cool." He claims that the hipster's heyday was the 2000s when culture changed rapidly due to a spread of technology, online advertising, and new business models. Greif says hipsters may be "starving artists" or "graduate students" or "skatepunks" who attempt to rebel against traditional consumer culture but end up reifying its way of life. Janna Michael explains that a hipster "fails to convincingly establish" a "narrative of authenticity" because he "indicates a lack of personality" and "individual taste" (178). Often the hipster does experiment with art and find value in bricolage, just as Beca does. Therefore, separating the unplugged teenager from the hipster teenager frequently becomes a murky enterprise.

Although the *Pitch Perfect* films were released at the same time the hipster image was supposedly declining from public attention, the films raise interesting questions about where to draw the line between a faux artist and a real one. Indeed, Beca's talents, while innovative, do come from mixing or singing existing creations rather than coming up with her own. Although impressed by her music production instincts, Dax's boss listens to some of Beca's demos and then admonishes her for her lack of originality:

> What you gave me was more mashups.... Any kids with ears and a laptop can do that. Dax can do that. All right? So that's fine if you want a career DJing raves out in the desert, but if you want to write music producer on your tax forms someday, then you've gotta have an original voice, do you understand? You gotta show me what *you* have. Right now what I have is a demo with mashups on it.

This is why Emily Junk, the newcomer in *Pitch Perfect 2*, becomes so central to the turning point of the second film. Writing original music rather than simply mashing songs together, Emily, whose mother also belonged to the Barden Bellas in the 1980s, collaborates with Beca on a demo tape of her song "Flashlight." Through giving attention to a member of a new generation of Barden Bellas, Beca accomplishes two things: she proves she does have an original voice to share, and she has the ability to mentor someone younger than herself. In this sense, she becomes a bricoleur yet again since Emily is one of the resources she begins to draw from. One way to separate the hipster from the artist is to focus on the hipster's wide array of resources versus the artist's ability to make do with limited ones (since Emily is the only girl in the new cohort). Still, Peter Sax would argue that being called a hipster is more in the eye of the beholder, no matter what is being created. Sax characterizes the hipster as "the preferred scapegoat for any human gripe, from gentrification to the tightness of jeans" and that the "ill-defined" term acts more as a buzzword than an authentic description (Introduction). What may be at stake is the role of socioeconomic class in the young artist's life, which is something I will return to in the conclusion of this book.

Conclusion

A cappella may seem to rely on human effort, but this is far from the whole truth. Acoustics of the given space and tools that inspire certain beats and rhythm both contribute to making the sound pleasing to the ear.

As previously stated, the college setting both contains and liberates sound in unlikely places. Living an unplugged and creative life, according to the first two *Pitch Perfect* movies, is best achieved in one's undergraduate years. The joy in these films comes primarily from seeing young women in a singing group use both analog and digital tools to navigate a new phase of their lives and become close friends. While the tools they use are fascinating, the characters using them are not *initially* as compelling to watch. Most of the Barden students are middle class and privileged, mostly white, and able to attend college because their parents paid for it.

Although Beca begins the narrative as entitled and aloof, she ends by learning to collaborate with people as well as tools. What is important about Beca's characterization in *Pitch Perfect* is the emphasis on her adaptability and willingness to identify with a new group of women. Even more importantly, she identifies with her high and low tech material environments just as productively, which gives us reason to call her a bricoleur. While Beca's ability to empathize is not the topic of the film, her journey from technophilic loner to creative community leader shows how well she anticipates the needs of an audience and identifies with their values. Again, her audition illustrates this point. As a stubborn loner disinclined to change her ways of making music, the filmmakers might have chosen to showcase Beca rebelling against audition requirements, bringing in a laptop with her favorite remixed songs to share. Instead, she acknowledges the rules of singing a capella while also gently tipping the scales in her favor by employing the use of a plastic cup that marks her beats on the floor.

The film also stands out for calling attention to musical texts that are mixed in unlikely places—a bathroom, a pool—and that are created without the aid of software. What helps the viewer is the insight we gain into how someone Beca's age potentially adapts and changes her perspective without the aid of formal instruction and, even more surprisingly, without the help of screens. While Beca does not serve as a poster child for all young adults, she does raise questions that may affect our preconceived notions of what "tech-savvy" youth may accomplish and how perceptions of them might be changed in the future. *Pitch Perfect* exceeds expectations by showcasing not only Beca but all the members of the Barden Bellas as young women able to embrace change and community.

References

Bennett, Jane. "Powers of the Hoard: Artistry and Agency in a World of Vibrant Matter." *Animal, Vegetable, Mineral: Ethics and Objects*, edited by Jeffrey Cohen. Oliphaunt Books, 2012, pp. 237–69.

Blasdel, Alex. "A Reckoning for Our Species: The Philosopher Prophet of the Anthropocene." *The Guardian*, 15 June 2017, www.theguardian.com/world/2017/jun/15/timothy-morton-anthropocene-philosopher.

Bogost, Ian. *Alien Phenomenology or, What It's Like to Be a Thing*. University of Minnesota Press, 2012.

De Certeau, Michel. *The Practice of Everyday Life*. University of California Press, 1988.

Deuze, Mark. *Media Life*. Polity Press, 2012.

Farmer, Frank. *After the Public Turn: Composition, Counterpublics, and the Citizen Bricoleur*. University Press of Colorado, 2013.

Greif, Mark. "What Was the Hipster?" *New York Magazine*, 24 Oct. 2010, http://nymag.com/news/features/69129/.

"Honest Trailers: *Pitch Perfect*." *YouTube*. Directed by Screen Junkies, 15 May 2015, www.youtube.com/watch?v=Q-j8XXtwSO0.

Levi-Strauss, Claude. *The Savage Mind*. University of Chicago Press, 1966.

Michael, Janna. "It's Really Not Hip to Be a Hipster: Negotiating Trends and Authenticity in the Cultural Field." *Journal of Consumer Culture*, vol. 15, no. 2, 2015, pp. 163–82.

Miller, Adam S. *Speculative Grace: Bruno Latour and Object-Oriented Theology*. Fordham University Press, 2013.

Morton, Timothy. *Realist Magic: Objects, Ontology, Causality*. Open Humanities Press, 2013.

Pitch Perfect. Directed by Jason Moore, performances by Anna Kendrick, Anna Camp, Skylar Astin, Rebel Wilson. Universal Pictures, 2012.

Pitch Perfect 2. Directed by Elizabeth Banks, performances by Anna Kendrick, Brittany Snow, Rebel Wilson, and Hailee Steinfeld. Universal Pictures, 2015.

Pitch Perfect 3. Directed by Trish Sie, performances by Anna Kendrick, Anna Camp, Rebel Wilson, and Brittany Snow. Universal Pictures, 2017.

Rapkin, Mickey. *Pitch Perfect: The Quest for Collegiate a Cappella Glory*. Gotham Books, 2008.

Sax, Peter. *The Revenge of Analog: Real Things and Why They Matter*. Public Affairs, 2016. iBook.

Suzanne-Wong, Mandy. "Introductory Editorial: Towards Vital Materialist Aesthetics." *Eventual Aesthetics*, vol. 3, 2015, pp. 4–16.

Trowsdale, Alison, Tom Housden, and Becca Meier. "Seven Charts That Explain the Plastic Pollution Problem." *BBC News*, 10 Dec. 2017, www.bbc.com/news/science-environment-42264788.

3 Analog Dinosaurs and Abandoned Kids in *Jurassic World*

The message of the *Jurassic Park* films has never been especially subtle or nuanced. Part of this reality is that the films are blockbusters made for summer audiences, which, as Paul Lauter has described, makes for a "thinness of plot and characterization" (104). The narratives typically begin with adults assuming mastery over nature with digital and genetic technologies and conclude with these same adults' surrender as nature refuses to be programmed or controlled. While the message does not challenge us in nuanced ways that other narratives like *Get Out* (see Chapter 5) might in terms of social critique, there are aspects of this mythos that deserve some consideration, particularly when it comes to portrayals of children, analog sensibilities, and humankind's relationship to the physical world.

Ecology scholars Rachel Carson and Timothy Morton, writing more than fifty years apart, address our relationship to the physical world and how to acknowledge our limitations within it, particularly in the presence of large-scale agents, or hyperobjects, that have the power to change humankind's quality of life. One example Morton commonly refers to is climate change. He says,

> The more I struggle to understand hyperobjects, the more I discover that I am stuck to them. They are all over me. I feel like Neo in the Matrix, lifting his face in horrified wonder, his hand coated in the mirrorlike substance into which the doorknob has dissolved, as his virtual body begins to disintegrate. "Objects in mirror are closer than they appear." The mirror itself has become part of my flesh. Or rather, I have become part of the mirror's flesh. . . .
>
> (28)

Decades before Morton's studies of hyperobjects and their relationship to his own subjectivity, Carson also pointed toward one such force in nature when she explained that "a possession infinitely more valuable than individual life is our genetic heritage, our link with past and future. Shaped through long eons of evolution, our genes not only make us who we

Figure 3.1 Dinosaur Miniatures from Walmart
Source: Author photo

are, but hold in their minute beings the future—be it promise or threat" (186). Both writers hint at how certain phenomena, such as genetic code and nature, may appear understandable but actually possess an agency that defies our comprehension. Both also point toward the deflation of the individual ego in the face of sweeping change and evolution. This deflation often occurs in this particular mythos due to the consequences of scientific progress.[1] Morton appropriately calls upon an image that frequents the *Jurassic Park* films: the side-view mirror. In this side-view mirror Morton mentions that he feels much closer to the enormity of nature's forces and that it even sticks to him in ways he may not be able to undo. Likewise, the first *Jurassic Park* movie humorously zooms in on the "objects in mirror are closer than they appear" when the main characters are chased by a Tyrannosaur, a hyperobject or natural force in its own right.

Tied up in our concerns about children and technology is our concern about the future and what lies in store for humankind. In this narrative about experimental and for-profit science, the idea of going "unplugged" takes on new and special significance because the associations with analog objects and technologies become embedded in living things, not just tools. Based on Michael Crichton's book, the original 1993 film, directed by Steven Spielberg, features characters who discover a world of dinosaurs genetically created for study and display. In exploring Isla Nublar, the Costa Rican island where these dinosaurs live, paleontologists Grant (Sam Neill) and Ellie (Laura Dern) along with mathematician Ian Malcolm (Jeff Goldblum) and Hammond's children Lex and Tim, witness tycoon John Hammond's vision in its full glory. Hammond prepares for the opening of a natural park where future guests may be enchanted by benign herbivores like apatosaurs (also commonly known as brontosaurs) as well as spellbound by more dangerous creatures like the Tyrannosaur. However, Hammond must hire a legal consultant to sign off on the project since an employee died during the preparations.

The small group of characters that enters the park undergoes a test run of the exhibits, and malfunctions plague them each step of the way, putting the lives of both the young and old in mortal danger. Due to a tropical storm's arrival and the subterfuge of an employee who steals dinosaur embryos, the animals run loose from cages and fences, and fatalities rise. Hammond vows that next time he creates a park it will be flawless because they have been too dependent on automation. However, he ultimately acknowledges that his grandchildren's safety is more important than his dream, and he abandons his project to seek safety for his family and colleagues on the mainland. *The Lost World* (1997) sequel follows a somewhat similar formula: a small team visits the island Isla Sorna, and these characters must defend themselves against deadly threats from a female Tyrannosaur, this time seeking to protect her offspring. In this narrative John Hammond has retired and wishes to make amends by protecting the animals he once exploited for his own. By following his request to survey the island, the protagonists face threats from the prehistoric creatures but also from other groups of humans allied with big business and private corporations who wish to retrieve the dinosaurs for financial gain. In this sense *The Lost World* (like *Fallen Kingdom* years later) addresses issues of animal conservation and the ethical treatment of all living things when pitted against capitalism and international business conglomerates.

Released in 2015, *Jurassic World*, a blockbuster reboot of *Jurassic Park* more reflective of Generation Z sensibilities, follows two children, Zach (Nick Robinson) and Gray Mitchell (Ty Simpkins), who visit the new theme park, built by the Masrani Corporation after John Hammond's death. Their parents, on the verge of a divorce, send them away to be entertained by their aunt Claire (Bryce Dallas Howard), who manages the new park. Like Lex and Tim from the original film, Zach and Gray are the products of a soon-to-be divorced couple. Claire initially abandons her nephews to meet with investors and monitor the control room; however, by the movie's end, she reunites with them as she and Owen Grady protect the children against the newly engineered Indominus Rex. Claire signs off on the creation of the Indominus at the film's beginning but learns that the animal is too unpredictable and dangerous to control.

Although similar to *The Lost World* in basic themes and structures, *Jurassic World*'s sequel *Fallen Kingdom* takes a different turn with regard to mood, pacing, and subject matter. Claire, recently turned naturalist and animal protector of the abandoned animals at Isla Nublar, partners with Owen and former park designer and innovator Benjamin Lockwood (James Cromwell) to return to the island and rescue the remaining dinosaurs from a volcano eruption. Unfortunately, a separate extraction team, hired by a man named Eli Mills, wish to capture these same animals for auction on the mainland, and Claire and Owen must fight to save them from arms dealers and animal traffickers. Key to Mills's plan is the use of Blue, a female raptor, to act as mentor and mother to future raptors who will serve in a military capacity.

Maisie Lockwood (Isabella Sermon), the child featured in this iteration, also plays a significant role in the narrative because of her unique status. Unlike children in former films, she is not the product of a broken home but a clone created by her grandfather Benjamin Lockwood, John Hammond's former partner. Benjamin created the child in his daughter's image after she died in a car accident. Maisie, therefore, becomes a step forward in the franchise for numerous reasons: she is both literally and figuratively orphaned throughout the narrative, and she raises new questions about the ethics of cloning and the identification children have with dinosaurs bred in captivity. Maisie, who has been sequestered in a large Gothic mansion most of her life, identifies with the plight of the dinosaurs and makes repeated attempts to secure their safety.

The original *Jurassic Park*, *Jurassic World*, and *Fallen Kingdom* films remain the focus of this chapter because the narratives in those films feature more juxtaposition among old and new generations. In some cases, the alignment of dinosaur footprints next to human ones is only the beginning of how time seems suspended in this particular series of stories. The characters in *Jurassic World* pay homage to the original park, which means that the merging of prehistoric and modern worlds is now augmented by the merging of old and new designs from the late twentieth and twenty-first centuries. Therefore, *Jurassic World* allows us access to three specific eras simultaneously: the Jurassic and Cretaceous periods before recorded history, the 1990s, and the 2010s.

Children in these narratives show remarkable ability to adapt to circumstances of all three eras while adults struggle to survive. Examples from *Jurassic Park 3* and *The Lost World* are included, but the films play a smaller role in this chapter as a whole. However, they do remain relevant in one key way because they include young characters who fend for themselves under extraordinary circumstances: Kelly (Vanessa Lee Curtis), Ian Malcolm's daughter, from *The Lost World*, and Erik (Trevor Morgan), a survivor marooned on Isla Nublar in *Jurassic Park 3*.

Digital vs. Analog

In *The Revenge of Analog*, David Sax suggests that analog represents the imperfections of the entire physical realm beyond our screens, not just the specific technologies embedded within it. In his commentary on the unplugged policy at a children's summer camp, he describes the analog realm, or IRL (in real life), as the "frustrating, rough, rainy world" ("Epilogue"). Analog in these films about dinosaurs connotes variations among living and nonliving matter and involves the physical presence of something that is not *uniformly* distributed, no matter how serious the attempt to make it so. As Florian Cramer explains, two glasses of water might be analogous in their volume, but small variations will still remain. Analog makes room for glitches in design and the unpredictability of wear and tear, just like one might expect from a "rough" and "rainy" world. Although the DNA used to make dinosaurs appears to be digitally designed, since cloning of the animals happens in a lab where measurements are strictly controlled and seemingly uniform, the truth is that any creature grown in a lab is still a product of analog sensibility because each creature develops a body and mind separate from the other replicants. Moreover, these animals are patched from other DNA samples when the code breaks down, so a Frankensteinian quality exists in their blueprints, no matter how fastidious the scientists attempt to be. These dinosaurs, therefore, are unpredictable and flawed, but they are also shrewd adaptors to a new world.

This goes a long way in explaining why mathematician Ian Malcolm's theories of chaos, a complex systems theory based in the study of how small irregularities and variables change outcomes,[2] pervade the first two *Jurassic* films from the 1990s. It also explains Malcolm's disgust at the scientists who believe themselves capable of programming nature while failing to understand the consequences of their experimentation. Although not speaking strictly about science and genetics, Andrew Russell and Lee Vinsel explain that innovation has become something we value simply because it excites us and enables us to play with new toys and new ideas. Malcolm provides a similar critique in the *Jurassic Park* film: "What's so great about discovery? It's a violent penetrative act that scars." Although Malcolm is prone to hyperbole, his critique of John Hammond's new park is fair because the value placed on innovation far supersedes the value placed on maintenance and the patience for working out glitches that occur. The stewardship of the natural world falls to the side in order to find the next discovery. Like Russell and Vinsel, Sax critiques the fallacy of the new experiment or innovation, analog or digital, being necessarily better for humankind. He quotes Nicholas Carr, who says, "We assume that anyone who rejects a new tool in favor of an older is guilty of nostalgia, of making choices sentimentally rather than rationally. But the real sentimental fallacy is the assumption that the new thing is always better suited to our purposes and intentions than the old thing. That's the view of a child, naïve and pliable" ("Epilogue"). Hammond fits this description, particularly in Crichton's book, where the character plays more of an insidious role in the creation and exploitation of the dinosaurs. Even in the film, however, Hammond believes that what he is creating will benefit the greater good, even after he loses an employee to a deadly raptor attack.

The "frustrating, rough, rainy world" of nature requires maintaining equilibrium with our surroundings rather than conquering them. In the *Jurassic Park* narratives, that equilibrium is often destroyed when digital technology "improves upon" existing analog matter in this "rainy world" and, consequently, alters that matter in ways that hurt future generations. The image of Sax's unplugged summer camp is not too different from the landscape of Isla Nublar in that once the characters venture forth into the jungle, their digital technologies do them no good. Even in *Jurassic World*, where cell phones have become ubiquitous, the camera zooms in on Zach failing to grab at his phone when the Indominus turns his gyrosphere upside down and begins to crack it open. When Claire finds this same phone after the boys have escaped, she sees that the screen itself is destroyed and that the phone is no longer operable. This sight makes her panic most of all since she herself cannot imagine life without such tools. It also makes her panic because she knows how much this tool presumably means to a teenager.

Additionally, those characters invested in the early stages of digital technology, characters that could be considered the earliest digital natives, are often associated with nefarious or misanthropic tendencies. Tim, the young boy in *Jurassic Park*, chastises his sister Lex for "staying in her room all day playing on her computer." Likewise, one of the control room operators, Dennis Nedry, creates havoc in the park by first establishing a system that only he can operate to change the settings of the power grid and then trying to sell dinosaur embryos to a rival company. Those invested in early digital technology, therefore, have a reputation for individualism, isolation, and self-centered behavior. Although Lex manages to save everyone at the end by getting all security systems up, her ability to find files and follow a UNIX system are not appreciated until her brother and the adults around her feel trapped in a proverbial foxhole. As Arnold (Samuel L. Jackson), another control room specialist, says when Dennis leaves them stranded, "I hate this hacker crap." As technology advances from splicing frog DNA to fill gaps in a dinosaur's gene sequence to the actual invention of new dinosaurs in a more sophisticated lab in *Jurassic World*, the threat to humankind rises. In the hands of the Masrani Corporation, the company that succeeds John Hammond, advanced technology becomes a tool through which to weaponize animals and make even bigger profits at the expense of people's safety.

An analog sensibility prevails in these movies from their inception since the creation of new animals involves an imperfect system of gene splicing and combining with multiple species. Even more to the point, Hammond has created a park of genetically engineered dinosaurs, a "biological preserve," because he wants to create a place where people not only dream about the past but can actually "see and touch" it, which speaks directly to the quality of embodiment that analog tools convey. The 2015 reboot *Jurassic World* capitalizes on improvements in computer-generated effects to create not only a park but an immersive "World" where rides, water shows, and petting zoos augment the existing dinosaur exhibits. The camera reveals that Jurassic World features a town square similar to the Universal Studios theme park with shops, chain restaurants, and faux street signs that designate a downtown space where visitors may shop, dine, and relax. Although these improvements may seem digital due to the design of the film, the landscape is predominantly analog, with petting zoos and restaurants and water shows relying heavily on things that people can see and touch.

Still, analog settings, however luxurious, fail to satisfy those in charge of this new park. The scientists stationed at Jurassic World find ways to create a dinosaur hybrid even more terrifying than the Tyrannosaurus Rex. The philosophy among those running the park is that "bigger is better": children are no longer impressed with the average dinosaur. Adult perception of children in this film often reveals the same belief many naively have about teens and kids: that they must continue to find bigger and better forms of technological entertainment (since the dinosaurs are, in fact, engineered). In Jurassic World's Samsung Innovation Center, the PA system announces that within its walls "technology meets prehistory." Computers display holographs of dinosaurs, children may play with interactive software, and guests may take a peek at the Hammond Creation Lab, where dinosaurs are created.

The idea of hybridization is also central to the reboot *Jurassic World*. The narrative shows Claire agonizing over how to continually surpass the park experience with new exhibits that will thrill visitors, particularly when sponsors compete to finance, at twenty-six million dollars, the new fifty-foot Indominus Rex, a hybrid of raptor, Tyrannosaurus, and other reptile breeds. When Claire takes Owen to assess the holding pen containing the Indominus, she explains, "We've been pre-booking tickets for months. The park needs a new attraction every few years in order to reinvigorate the public's interest. . . . Corporate felt genetic modification would up the wow factor." Dr. Wu, the genetic engineer, later reveals that he filled some of the gaps in the DNA with cuttlefish and frog genes, which enable the creature to camouflage and avoid thermal heat detection. This lack of precision in filling in gaps leads to destruction across the island as the Indominus goes on a rampage that kills other species and humans alike. Analog and digital experiments often have the same disastrous results in these films.

If analog and digital forms of life continue to show weakness, the lesson entrepreneurs and scientists learn is that they should tirelessly but fruitlessly work toward a new model of genetically designed life. Margaret Ronda explains that the digital world is frequently associated with "greater ease, efficiency, or beauty" (79), and this characterization fits how Claire runs her departments. Claire's emphasis on numbers, profits, and what can easily be controlled suggests that while she hopes to thrill her guests, she also wants to control how that thrill occurs. In this sense, Claire desires a form of technology that in itself is hybridized: take the unique and unpredictable parts of an analog creation, such as a genetically altered dinosaur, but program it like a digital entity so that its actions toward others ensure predictable repetition and quantitative measurement. Owen even comments that Claire probably finds it "easier to pretend these animals are numbers on a spreadsheet." Likewise, contractors associated with the production of the animals at the park are looking for a way to profit off of the raptor herd mentality and develop the creatures as weapons of destruction during war. This idea also invokes an analog/digital hybridization. Hoskins (Vincent D'Onofrio), the project manager originally hired to test the raptor's intelligence, explains, "Drones can't search tunnels and caves, and they're hackable. The minute a real war breaks out all that fancy tech is gonna go dark." Hoskins is searching for something living and embodied that can be programmed—basically an analog digital hybrid that may be used as a tool for destruction.

Like digital code or binary numbers, the raptors, according to Hoskins, may be controlled with a simple hand motion or word, although Owen does his best to counter how foolish such thinking is. Owen says, "You made them and now you think you own them." Hoskins then replies, "Extinct animals have no rights," a line that appears also in *The Lost World* script when John Hammond's nephew attempts to finance a new park in San Diego. The new owner Masrani (Irrfan Khan), according to Hoskins, misuses this new genetic power to "stock a petting zoo" when he could benefit financially from selling and breeding more animals. When Owen explains that Masrani may just want to teach people "some humility," Hoskins believes such practices are futile because "progress always wins." The promotional Masrani video associated with the release of the film *Jurassic World* has Henry Wu (BD Wong) explain that "[l]ife is just a code. We're taking the code and using it for practical applications." The desire to both digitize and embody life, in an analog sense, remains central to the scientific hubris that pervades all iterations of the franchise.

Glitches

The very practice of inserting different forms of reptile DNA to make up for gaps in a genome sequence already reveals that humans are willing to make glitches in order to forge new paths in genetic experimentation. For example, in *Jurassic World*, scientists order a tracker to be placed inside the Indominus Rex, but the dinosaur promptly tears it out of her body when she escapes her paddock. Technology in the *Jurassic Park* mythos also regularly fails or provides false data. As Crichton discusses in his novel, the scientists even numbered the versions of their creatures, just as they would new versions of software. Arnold says, "As we discover the glitches in the DNA, Dr. Wu's labs have to make a new version," and Alan Grant finds himself troubled by this numbering of animals but cannot articulate exactly why ("Third Iteration," chapter 6). The reliance on digital or programmable tools actually places the characters in more danger than the use of their hands or the wielding of handheld material objects like flares, gasoline, tranquilizer guns, or land roving Jeeps. However, even the analog materials used against the dinosaurs fail to ensure the public's safety. Since both analog and digital forms of communication and defense remain inadequate, the narrative of progress suggested in *World* and *Kingdom* is that of finding a way beyond those two forms, but such a way never comes to be.

Another example of how programming and uniformity fails the scientists occurs when the animals begin to breed, even though the lab has ensured that all of the dinosaurs are female. Because glitches in DNA require Wu to insert the DNA of other creatures like frogs, Grant realizes that the dinosaurs may possess reproductive powers that mirror those of frogs who possess both sex organs. Reports of breeding shock Hammond until Malcolm explains that computers do not report tallies of animals beyond the programming that humans require. In other words, the animal population continues to grow, but, as Nedry says, the "[c]omputer allows the operator to enter an expected number of animals in order to make the counting process faster. But it's a convenience, not a flaw." Because the animal "base count" changes without warning, the machine only counts the "expected number" ("Third Iteration," chapter 13).

When materials do operate effectively, they often do so as a satire of humankind's megalomania. For example, the gyrosphere in which Zach and Gray become trapped by the Indominus breaks apart, forcing them to run for their lives. When Owen and Claire stumble upon the broken transport, the voiceover (by Jimmy Fallon no less) still works, and we hear Fallon say that "safety is our main concern." A famous example of materiality working to support this dark humor is the scene in the first film where, on board a Jeep, the characters escape the original Tyrannosaurus. As the car speeds away, operating without a hitch, the camera zooms in on the side-view mirror's view of the dinosaur, where it reads, in small font, "Objects in mirror are closer than they appear." These messages are signs that the best technology has its limits: no matter what humankind invents or operates, the forces of nature will have the last laugh. Just after Claire and the children face a near-fatal raptor attack, the following voiceover plays in the main square: "Don't forget to visit the gift shop, and remember, it's always happy hour at Margaritaville." The filmmakers even enjoy letting Jimmy Buffett make a cameo appearance as he slowly carries two frozen beverages to safety despite the danger surrounding him.

Additionally, the digital trackers that remain operable in the field are the ones on the humans, those members of the Asset Containment team that attempts to sequester the Indominus. As a reminder of how analog life cannot be controlled, the computers in the control room show flatlines on the screens as the Indominus kills them one by one. Claire, Owen, and others are helpless to look on as they witness the technological representation of death on their screens and the high-pitched alarm that accompanies it. In this case technology works fine, but its accurate representation of carnage does not comfort anyone on staff.

Indeed, most of the employees working in the control room flee the park when the animals run loose. The one remaining employee is Lowery (Jake Johnson), a man who chooses to help the extraction team take down the Indominus despite the danger to himself. It is important to see Lowery, who has volunteered to stay behind and watch the monitors, pick up his handheld dinosaur figurines just before he turns out the lights in the room at the movie's conclusion. The movie ends with this moment as well as one that follows close behind: the Tyrannosaur roaring from the helicopter-landing pad as the credits roll immediately following. In this context, the fact that we see both Lowery's toys and the Tyrannosaur as the final shots of the film suggests that analog, and all of its characteristic glitches, is alive and well.

Children of the Park (and World)

Even before adults abandon children physically on the various islands off the coast of Costa Rica, a tale of emotional abandonment unravels as the young speak about problems of divorce and isolation. In every *Jurassic Park* story, parents have separated or divorced, and this source of family stress leads the adults to outsource the job of parenting to a relative or friend. When children go missing or find themselves in physical danger, it is the result of negligence on the part of that friend or relative that creates the problem. However, the kids themselves are in those predicaments because parents leave them in loco parentis to begin with.

Kelly, Ian's daughter, says one of the most important lines in *The Lost World* when she shouts, "You never keep your word!" to her father as he leaves her with a guardian on a high hide (platform that raises humans to avoid attack) in Isla Sorna. Although Malcolm gives Kelly "his word" that he will return in one piece, the preteen is far too savvy to believe him. Adults, in essence, are not to be depended on. Children must accept this truth on a micro-level at first, as they discover that their families will break apart. Then the lack of dependability magnifies into something horrific as carnivores attack and adults often fail to protect them. Once abandoned, children seem to survive well on their own, although they should not have to do so. These young characters even find the adult theories about dinosaurs tiresome and incomplete. Although somewhat impressed with Alan Grant's career as a scientist, Erik, the young boy from *Jurassic Park 3*, admits that he does not care for Ian Malcolm's theories: "It was kind of preachy. And too much chaos. Everything is chaos. Seemed like the guy was high on himself." He also tells Alan that he has read both of Alan's books, although he "liked the first one more" because it was before visiting Isla Nublar and Grant actually "liked dinosaurs back then." Although he sounds presumptuous and arrogant for his age, Erik is actually the opposite. He manages to last eight weeks unsupervised on Isla Sorna after an accident involving his guardian. He even hoards Tyrannosaur urine to protect his hideout, a large, overturned supply truck, from other animals. When Alan Grant asks how he procured the urine, Erik simply shakes his head and says "you don't want to know." As Alan informs Erik that his parents are on the island trying to find him, the first question Erik asks is if they are together. "That's not good," he replies when Alan confirms it. "They don't do so well together." His first concern pertains to the dissolution of the family, not the eminent rescue on which he has been patiently waiting for weeks. The comment even suggests that rescue itself may hardly be pleasant if he has to endure adult fighting; sadly, perhaps living alone on the island allows him to avoid such tensions.[3]

One of the most striking observations about children and dinosaurs comes not from the screenplays of the movies but from the original Michael Crichton book upon which the first film is based. When Alan Grant ponders why children love dinosaurs, he hypothesizes that they do so because "these giant creatures personified the uncontrollable force of looming authority. They were symbolic parents. Fascinating and frightening, like parents. And kids loved them, as they loved their parents" ("Third Iteration," chapter 4).[4] If Grant is to be taken seriously, the information above about parents' absenteeism and lack of stability in the home acts as an appropriate mirror to the chaos that befalls the islands once dinosaurs roam free of electric fences and cages. In the parks and beyond, parents fail to live up to this image of authority, and nature refuses to behave. The entire series acts as a reminder of how adults and nature both fail younger generations.

Slavoj Zizek's cultural studies include references to *Jurassic Park* and the role of the father as particularly important. In comments about the original film and Steven Spielberg's vision, he observes that the very first scene featuring Alan Grant's character features him "jokingly threatening the two kids [from the Montana Badlands not Jurassic Park] with a dinosaur bone—this bone is clearly the tiny object-stain which, later, explodes into gigantic dinosaurs, so that one can risk the hypothesis that, within the film's fantasmatic universe, the dinosaurs' destructive fury merely materializes the rage of the paternal superego" (xiii). This commentary grounds itself in psychoanalytic theories that do not play a part in this argument; however, the emphasis on parenthood and its myriad forms of failure and aggression still applies. Shortly after taunting the children at his dig site, Grant emphasizes his lack of interest in having kids of his own: he tells Ellie, "They're noisy, they're messy, they're expensive," and "they smell." Although Claire in *Jurassic World* does not make similar pronouncements, she fails to note her nephews' ages, interests, or daily routines because she has not seen them in eight years. She even goes as far as to question whether they have separate bedtimes, even though both boys have matured past such issues. Both characters in the original (Grant) and the reboot (Claire) profess their dislike of anything "messy" that distracts them from their careers.⁵ In both cases, however, the characters come to accept children by proxy when trapped or attacked on the island.

The final scene of *The Lost World* film resonates with this image of parents. As preteen Kelly watches John Hammond give a press conference on CNN, Ian Malcolm and Sarah Harding are asleep on the couch. The movie ends with Kelly being the only character awake for John's entreaty: that American citizens must work with the Costa Rican government to establish "a set of rules" because the animals left on Islas Sorna and Nublar "require our absence." Kelly hears this lesson, but the adults sleep through it, which reinforces the theme of adult irresponsibility. However, more damning examples of adult irresponsibility exist. In the original *Jurassic Park*, Donald (Martin Ferrero), a lawyer sent to inspect the park, abandons two children and hides in a nearby portable bathroom just before a Tyrannosaurus Rex attacks. Both children survive but not without being pummeled inside a car. Donald's death reflects his depravity: the writers have him on the toilet when the Tyrannosaur swallows him. Zara, one of Claire's assistants in Jurassic World, meets the most gruesome and theatrical death of all as she fails to keep track of Claire's nephews during a park emergency. The young woman suffers from multiple pterodactyl attacks as she is tossed back and forth between the birds, who dive treacherously high and low and then drop her in the water. She is then eaten by the gargantuan Mososaur, who serves as a guest attraction much like SeaWorld's early Shamu the whale productions.

Part of this emphasis on children relates back to humankind's anxiety on a global scale about the environment and its "broken" and "blasted" vistas, which people would do well to accept, and even embrace, rather than avoid (Rozelle 2–4). Since Rachel Carson's publication of *Silent Spring* in 1962, a focus on how humankind influences and greatly accelerates the destruction of planetary resources through climate change has continued to influence the lives most specifically of members of Generations X, Y, and Z. Generation Z youth in particular live with the constant awareness that some form of apocalyptic event is not merely possible but probable in their future since they continually hear tales of resources depleting and plastic building up in the world's oceans. Likewise, adult and child protagonists of the *Jurassic Park* films often find themselves, either purposefully or accidentally, pitted against foolhardy antagonists who ruthlessly embrace what Carl G. Herndl and Stuart C. Brown refer to as "anthropocentric discourse, one grounded in its faith in the human ability to come to know nature's secrets (11). This anthropocentric discourse belies a tendency to perceive the world as a domain for humans with nature only subservient to their needs. Such underestimation of nature's power leads to entropy and destruction more often than not, particularly in this narrative world.

However, the protagonists are just as guilty in their anthropocentric view of the world. As she gives a tour to the prospective park donors, Claire says, "Let's be honest. No one's impressed by a dinosaur anymore. Twenty years ago, de-extinction was right up there with magic. These days kids look at a stegosaurus like an elephant from the city zoo." However, the film does not support Claire's observation. *Jurassic World* opens with an analog image of preteen Gray flipping a handheld slideshow of dinosaurs instead of viewing them online. The pictures are illustrated, not digital, and no computer is in sight. Gray also takes a disposable camera with him to the park. Also, when Zach, his older brother, promises that their parents' impending divorce will mean that they receive more gifts at holidays, Gray adamantly replies, "I don't want two of everything." The philosophy of bigger is better does not seem to be trickling down to the youngest cast member; rather, he seems to eschew anything resembling capital excess. As Claire ensures corporate sponsorship for the Indominus ("Verizon Wireless presents the Indominus Rex"), Gray only wants his family to become whole again.

The camera even cuts to Lowery, the Generation X employee at the central control panels, explaining to his coworker about his own history of divorce: "Even though I didn't meet him until I was thirteen," he says before picking up the phone and answering Claire's call, "I definitely consider Carl to be more of a dad than my real dad." While this line acts as a throwaway for a transition to a new scene of action, it still reinforces how prevalent family dysfunction remains for multiple generations, particularly in this series of films. Zach comments that his own family's separation does not matter because he "will be gone in two years anyway" and "all of my friends' parents are divorced." He encourages Gray to face reality because neither of them has any agency in the matter: "It's not up to you," he says. "There's a point you have to grow up."

Zach does not show much interest in life beyond screens, at least at the start of the narrative. He uses his smartphone for the initial few hours he tours Jurassic World, and, when not doing so, he finds teenage girls to ogle. His younger brother must pester him to pay attention to the exhibits. The audience even witnesses Zach turning away from the Tyrannosaur to take a short call from his mother. Only after the first dinosaur attack and the consequential destruction of his phone does Zach prove his ability to solve problems through an analog sensibility. First, he manages to keep his little brother calm by recollecting memories in which analog tools strengthened Gray's confidence. When the two find the old 1992 Jeep in the former park, Zach asks Gray to remember that they worked on an old model of car before with their grandfather, and their collective memories and skills from that time help them escape. Also, once the military deploys raptors to attack the Indominus, Claire puts Zach and Gray in the rear of a large truck. Gray worries that the dinosaurs will return and infiltrate the truck. Zach pacifies him by asking him to remember their fearful belief in a ghost from their former home, "the one in the garage." When Gray does recall the time, he remembers that his brother protected him by making "a battle ax out of a ruler and a paper plate." Zach's persistent recall of such times suggests that he misses a simpler era in which his parents were together and makeshift toys entertained him as much as technology.

This also explains why the two children were the cast members who end up in the abandoned buildings of the old Jurassic Park. Zach's journey consists of moving backward as well as forward through time to save his brother from harm. If, to Owen, hunting the Indominus is like "taking a walk in the woods sixty-five million years ago," Zach's timeline is much smaller and more personal in nature. While Owen tackles problems that are millions of years old, Zach's previous experiences, only ten or so years prior, continue to inform his own decisions about how to survive the trappings of a prehistoric theme park. Gray exhibits the same intuitive knowledge of dinosaurs when, despite a frightening attack, he tells Claire how to escape from the Indominus. "Twenty-four plus fifty," he says. "We need more teeth." His past knowledge of the Tyrannosaurus comes into play, and Claire radios for backup from that part of the park. However, Gray shows this kind of interest in numbers throughout the narrative (e.g., knowing the model of the 1992 Jeep and the number of teeth present in the Mososaur in earlier scenes), and some viewers on Reddit threads have even commented that he is on the autism spectrum. When Gray refers to "more teeth," he uses synecdoche to speak about the Tyrannosaur, the original analog monster from the first set of films.

Children of divorced parents come to represent humankind's difficult relationship with nature, or its lack of responsibility for creation. Yet nowhere is this more evident than in *Fallen Kingdom* with Maisie, Benjamin Lockwood's supposed granddaughter. From her first appearance during Claire's visit to the estate, the camera shows Maisie hiding or lurking behind parts of the mansion to listen to adults discuss the fate of the Isla Nublar dinosaurs. Although she remains quite confident talking with

Eli, her father's assistant, Iris, her nanny, and Benjamin, her grandfather, Maisie remains skittish around strangers and will not approach them unless they approach first. When Claire questions Eli about the child's identity, Eli confirms that she is Benjamin's granddaughter, orphaned when her mother died in a car accident. Eli confirms that she and Benjamin are "very close," which seems an odd comment until we see Maisie visit her grandfather in his sickbed and recount all of her adventures exploring the house. She excitedly tells him that she has been on "safari" with dinosaur herbivores from the Cretaceous and Jurassic periods. Since the mansion remains full of fossils and lab space for genetic experimenting, her exploring does involve a great deal of research about the animals she loves.

When Maisie questions Benjamin about her mother, he tells her that she is a "mirror image" of her. The writers never address the identity of Maisie's father, but this omission seems to speak to the need for Benjamin to act in that role. When the audience discovers that Maisie is actually genetically engineered to be a clone of Benjamin's first child, they understand how Benjamin has been trying to reverse time by undoing the trauma of losing his daughter and replacing her with someone nearly identical. Eli, who betrays Benjamin by selling the rescued animals to arms dealers and animal traffickers, refers to what Lockwood did as something "unholy" that John Hammond was right to condemn in their early years of research (*Fallen Kingdom* reveals that the split between Hammond and Lockwood occurs because both men have different opinions about how genetic engineering should be used).

The film's creators ensure that Maisie's face is repeatedly superimposed or layered on images of the dinosaur DNA or the creatures itself inside Lockwood's estate. Because she explores both the original genetics lab and the different exhibits throughout the mansion, she peers in at test tubes, and later she even sees her reflection merging with Dr. Wu's latest genetic creation, the Indoraptor, after the animal auction concludes in chaos. In this way the narrative presses the point that Maisie and the dinosaurs, even the carnivores, are motherless victims of humankind's hubris rather than accidents or aberrations that must be destroyed. Henry Wu emphasizes this point when he reminds Eli that they must keep Blue the raptor as a mother to teach the baby dinosaurs submission and respect for human commands.

Blue's presence often relays lessons about parenthood and connections among species. When Claire convinces Owen to come to Isla Nublar, she reminds Owen that Blue is still alive and that he should want to rescue her because he "raised her." Owen has kept films of Blue's childhood and reviews them before making his final decision to return to Isla Nublar. These film clips show that Blue possesses a more empathetic nature than the other animals, thereby making her an ideal mother to future raptor clones who must learn to follow human instructions. Maisie also watches

Owen train Blue on these films, and she comes to trust him because of his investment in the creature. However, it is Blue's willingness to trust Owen as the father figure, or alpha, that keeps her in the spotlight during both *Jurassic World* and *Fallen Kingdom*. Without actual parents, Blue relies on Owen as a proxy parent just as Maisie and the other children rely on guardians unrelated to them.

Manipulating Time

Part of the romantic view of dinosaurs living successfully among humans stems from the desire to experience a form of time travel, where, as Robert MacFarlane describes in his treatise on walking and exploring old terrains, "the uncanniness of the experience involves a feeling of co-presence: the prehistoric and the present matching up such that it is unclear who walks in whose tracks" (362). In each *Jurassic* film, the director's camera ensures that not only do we experience the horrors of nature's creatures run amok but that we also witness a magnificent vista where herbivores graze and stare at the humans with mild curiosity. As such animals raise their triumphant necks above the trees, the human characters look on in such awe that the moment almost compensates for the death and destruction that follows. The feeling of magic and wonder results from the seeming dissolution of time and the strange merging of different ecological eras.

In some cases the merging of different eras remains untidy, particularly if a character indulges in nostalgia. Characters who indulge in nostalgia frequently lament that the "good ole days" have passed, and that the newer technology has warped human values. Often such characters, while not exactly children in chronological years, resemble children in their desire to hold on to the past. In *Jurassic World* Lowery as a character stands out for sporting an old Jurassic Park t-shirt. Lowery claims he bought the shirt off of Ebay for $150 and adds that a mint condition version costs twice as much. When Claire chastises him for wearing the shirt to work, Lowery explains, "I understand people died. It was terrible, but that first park was legit." When Claire begins talking about how Verizon Wireless will sponsor the Indominus Rex exhibit, Lowery also interjects, "Ugh, that is so terrible. Why not just go the distance, Claire, and let these corporations name the dinosaurs? You do know these are actual animals, right?"

Even Claire and Lowery's conversations resemble a parent admonishing an irresponsible child. Lowery's work station is cluttered with mini dinosaur figurines, similar to the kind featured in the picture at the beginning of this chapter. When Claire scolds him for having a messy desk and calls it "chaotic" (a clear reminder of Ian Malcolm's philosophy of chaos theory), Lowery merely says that it is "a living system. Just enough stability to keep it from collapsing into anarchy." Although at first glance the audience may enjoy these references to the original films, a deeper examination reveals the hypocrisy of accusing others for selling out when in actuality the one indulging in nostalgia invests more money in appearances for appearance's sake. Lowery, as a member of Generation X, is actually guilty of the exact same behavior that Claire exhibits: he orders an old shirt for $150, thereby profiting off of others' misfortune from an earlier time, and his desire to keep dinosaur figurines at his desk suggests his need to set himself apart from the younger employees, who will never understand what true love of these animals means.

Although Claire's corporate liaisons appear more grandiose and thoughtless from an animal rights perspective, Lowery's own desire to set himself apart from younger employees through the wearing of the shirt and the indulgence in toys has the potential to cause even greater irritation since he claims to care about the animals whom Claire exploits but still remains oblivious to his own greed when it comes to being a collector. Claire, while cloying at times in her ambition and ruthless pursuit of financial backing, has never hidden her agenda from those who work for her. Lowery, on the other hand, fails to recognize that collecting old items off of Ebay is not that far removed from the ridiculous pursuit of finding sponsorship for living things.

Indeed, one need only to browse t-shirt collections at places like Target to find inventory that imitates these vintage shirts from the past. Now chain stores stock shirts with emblems from the 1980s and 90s simply to appeal to customers' innate sense of nostalgia. The very capitalist system that prompts Claire to make callous decisions on behalf of the genetically engineered animals in her midst is not entirely different from the kind of consumerism now involved in purchasing materials that look old despite their mass produced quantity and quality. Put another way, Lowery's investment allows him to stand out from the millennial and Generation Z characters in his midst; however, upon closer examination, it reveals a foolish belief that older is better simply because it is older. This idea is just as dangerous as the one Claire holds that newer and bigger is better simply because it is newer and bigger.

On a larger scale, the movies reveal how vulnerable humans are to misunderstanding the power of geological time and evolution as the Generation Z characters experience the conflation of ancient and contemporary ecologies never meant to mix. It seems appropriate that one of the original ideas for *Fallen Kingdom*'s title was *Ancient Futures* (Jurassic Park Wiki). Such an oxymoron would capture the inexplicable process through which past and future species collide both in design and in the wild. When *Fallen Kingdom* begins, the main characters land by plane in the abandoned main street of the former theme park. A clock is still permanently displayed on a storefront, yet the hands of the dial are missing. Such a small prop has more metaphorical weight than we might initially consider. Time and its divisions, often punctuated by cultural movements, generational divides, and/or major historical events, frame the arc of characters' lives for good or ill. Part of the problem, however, is that humans have a limited view of Crichton's description of geological time as expressed in his novel:

> Grant knew that people could not imagine geological time. Human life was lived on another scale entirely. An apple turned brown in a few minutes. Silverware turned black in a few days. A compost heap decayed in a season. A child grew up in a decade. None of these everyday experiences prepared people to be able to imagine the meaning of eighty million years....
>
> ("Second Iteration," chapter 4)

As Timothy Morton mentions in this chapter's opening quote, large forces and entities continue to remind humans that their place on Earth is precarious, always subject to the whims of nature and entropy. As Malcolm (Jeff Goldblum) says in a voiceover in the final *Jurassic World: Fallen Kingdom* trailer, "Genetic power has now been unleashed. You can't put it back in the box. These creatures were here before us. And if we're not careful, they're gonna be here after." In the case of *Jurassic World* and its sequel *Fallen Kingdom*, the presence of prehistoric life and genetic power, wielded in the hands of those who wish to profit from it, becomes a hyperobject, or large force that cannot be contained. Morton describes hyperobjects as things that "appear to straddle worlds and times, like fiber optic cables or electromagnetic fields" (29). The fact that the hyperobject most readily takes the form of large dinosaurs in a modern park allows for even more experimentation with epochal divisions of reality and how to function within those divisions Morton goes on to discuss how a hyperobject possesses a certain "viscosity" and nearness: we cannot escape it. This knowledge helps us understand the gravity of *Fallen Kingdom*'s ending, where Ian Malcolm says, without irony, "Welcome ... to Jurassic World." In the final scenes, dinosaurs escape to find their way into the lives of humans everywhere in the West (and then beyond), from Las Vegas to the California beaches. Morton offers an explanation that helps us go deeper into the implications of Malcolm's threatening (and slightly campy) proclamation.

> For some time we may have thought that the U-bend in the toilet was a convenient curvature of ontological space that took whatever we flush down into a totally different dimension called Away, leaving things clean over here. Now we know better: instead of the mythical land Away, we know that the waste goes to the Pacific Ocean or the wastewater treatment facility. Knowledge of the hyperobject Earth, and of the hyperobject biosphere, presents us with viscous surfaces from which nothing can be forcibly peeled.
>
> (31)

In part, the purpose of children in the franchise is their early awareness of this viscosity. For example, Maisie Lockwood overhears and attempts to circumvent the devious plans of those who wish to auction the animals in *Fallen Kingdom*, and she alone, as a cloned specimen, feels qualified to "press the button" that saves the creatures from a gas chamber in the basement of the mansion. Maisie echoes Lex's triumph in *Jurassic Park* when she manages to restore the security systems that will allow her safe escape. Children remain integral to the survival of their groups in all films, partly because they confront the danger without arrogance. Arrogance in this mythos frequently leads to poor decision-making in confrontations with the natural world. Adults fail because they continue to assert that there must be a workable solution to the chaos, and this belief eventually costs some of them their lives. Adults, particularly the scientists who design the animals and the parks, believe the hyperobject, which in this case is genetic power, is surmountable or easily controlled.

It is no accident that the *Jurassic Park* film series deals repeatedly in themes relating to procreation, breeding, and the parenting of youth. Such processes reflect how we measure human progress, technological invention, and the passage of time. They also allow opportunity to reflect on how adult populations of several generations continue to make the same arrogant mistakes as their ancestors. Although Maisie, Lex, Zach, Gray, and other children are lucky to survive nature's unpredictability, their older counterparts suffer casualties because they fail to acknowledge their own limitations. Partnering with the physical world requires what Owen has already mentioned: humility. Because children know that systems easily fall apart, most often in the form of families, they are more likely to retain such humility in the midst of catastrophe.

Books with pictures of brontosaurs and fossils once held their own kind of magic, even as the world progressed toward more digital platforms. Anne Lamott describes childhood and dinosaur love as a "wow" moment that persists through adulthood, especially as people accept mutability as a part of life:

> Remember first semi-sort-of being able to imagine the sheer size of dinosaurs, at five or six, trying to comprehend how a brontosaurus could be seventy-five feet long? And what those feet must have looked like? . . . And you saw paintings of them with their dinosaur families, and you saw that they did wriggly, pouncy, family stuff, the nicer ones nibbling on high leaves, like gigantic lumpy giraffes or like your grandfather taking a piece of turkey before Thanksgiving dinner. Then they were gone—kaput. When you're a little kid, that's about as trippy as science gets: These huge creatures once roamed the earth, and now are fossils: everything, from stegosaurus to your granddad, appears, roams the earth for a little while, and then vanishes.

(75)

Although Lamott's words are from a guide to prayer, not a scholarly tome, their sincerity rings true in the stories of *Jurassic Park*, where the ultimate humility is recognizing that extinction is a reality for all living things. Tied directly to this idea is the portrayal of parents who frequently fail to insulate their offspring, however innocent they may be, from that undeniable truth. Discord in nature and in families comes to represent the failures of both the analog and the digital worlds to remain under human control, yet the audience may still hope, albeit in vain, that a new generation will fix the mess left behind by their parents and find a new set of tools, neither strictly analog nor digital, to make things right again.

Notes

1. Philip Eubanks explains that the very narrative of scientific discovery and progress is a grand narrative that often needs no parsing out because it has become so common in academic culture: "Science's discovery story, is, of course, familiar to us all—we know its typified sequence of events. Scientists face an incomprehensible world, but through observation, experimentation, and rejection of ignorance and superstition, they make the world even more explainable" (35). However, science in the *Jurassic Park* films is often funded by private firms and corporations, which belies an uncertainty about how rigid or disciplined scientific methods are when profit is the major goal. For more explanation on how the term "science" is used somewhat fluidly in *Jurassic Park*, see Stern.
2. The definition of chaos theory here is the simplistic one that Malcolm shares with the other characters in the movies and the original book (see the Jurassic Park wiki). Malcolm's theory also makes it clear that some parts of chaos theory are actually predictable, that there are specific iterations that may be traced throughout the complex phenomena he studies.
3. In the final shot of the film, where Alan Grant, Erik, and Erik's parents (William H. Macy and Tea Leoni) ride a military helicopter that rescues them, the idea is that the nuclear family has been made whole again and that both Erik's parents will go home together to "nest" in Oklahoma. This complete restoration of the original family, however, is uncommon in other *Jurassic Park* films. Even when versions of families come together in the final act of the other movies, the "genetic heritage," or "link between past and future," to which Rachel Carson alludes remains broken as one parent finds a new partner (*The Lost World*) or as two people protect a parentless child (*Fallen Kingdom*). In *Jurassic World*, both parents arrive to rescue Zach and Gray, but this rescue does not belie any attempt at restoring the marriage.
4. Although the films do an admirable job illustrating the follies of humankind as it attempts to control nature, some parts of Crichton's original novel do a better job of explaining such philosophies. The eighth edition of the MLA Handbook requires that e-books be cited by listing the appropriate chapter in parentheses: e.g., (see Chapter 4). However, *Jurassic Park* as a Kindle book makes this process messy because chapters share the same names across different divisions of the narrative. Therefore, I have elected to state the major division's title alongside the number of the chapter within it. The book is divided into "Iterations" that mimic Ian Malcolm's chaos theory. Life imitates art in the sense that Crichton's way of dividing chapters and parts is a bit like controlled chaos in a digital text.

5. This fear of messy, uncontrollable scenes sounds like an aversion to analog. However, Alan is no fan of the digital world either. In the original film, he remains reticent about computers, only using them when someone else prompts him.

References

Carson, Rachel. *Silent Spring*. Fawcett World Library, 1962.
"Chaos Theory." *Jurassic Park Wiki*, http://jurassicpark.wikia.com/wiki/Chaos_theory.
Cramer, Florian. "What Is Post-Digital?" *APRJA*, www.aprja.net/what-is-post-digital/.
Crichton, Michael. *Jurassic Park*. Ballantine Books, 1990. Kindle.
Eubanks, Philip. "Poetics and Narrativity: How Texts Tell Stories." *What Writing Does and How It Does It: An Introduction to Analyzing Texts and Textual Practices*, edited by Charles Bazerman and Paul A. Prior. Lawrence Erlbaum, 2004, pp. 33–56.
"The Hammond Creation Lab: Center of Isla Nublar." *Jurassic World*, www.jurassicworld.com/intel/location/hammond-creation-lab.
Herndl, Carl G., and Stuart C. Brown. "Introduction." *Green Culture: Environmental Rhetoric in Contemporary America*, edited by Carl G. Herndl and Stuart C. Brown. University of Wisconsin Press, 1996, pp. 3–20.
"InGen Technologies: Tomorrow, Today." *Masrani*, www.masraniglobal.com/about/divisions/ingen/index.html.
Jurassic Park. Directed by Stephen Spielberg, performances by Sam Neill, Laura Dern, and Jeff Goldblum, Universal, 1993.
Jurassic Park III. Directed by Joe Johnston, performances by Sam Neill, William H. Macy, Tea Leoni, and Trevor Morgan. Universal, 2001.
Jurassic World. Directed by Colin Trevorrow, performances by Chris Pratt, Bryce Dallas Howard, Ty Simpkins, Nick Robinson, Universal, 2015.
Jurassic World: Fallen Kingdom. Directed by J. A. Bayona, performances by Chris Pratt, Bryce Dallas Howard, Isabella Sermon, and James Cromwell. Universal, 2018.
"Jurassic World: Fallen Kingdom." *Jurassic Park Wiki*, http://jurassicpark.wikia.com/wiki/Jurassic_World:_Fallen_Kingdom#cite_note-ProductionWeekly-22.
Lamott, Anne. *Help, Thanks, Wow: The Three Essential Prayers*. Riverhead, 2012.
Lauter, Paul. *From Walden Pond to Jurassic Park: Activism, Culture, and American Studies*. Duke University Press, 2001.
The Lost World: Jurassic Park. Directed by Stephen Spielberg, performances by Jeff Goldblum, Julianne Moore, Vanessa Lee Chester, and Vince Vaughn. Universal, 1997.
MacFarlane, Robert. *The Old Ways: A Journey on Foot*. Penguin Books, 2013.
Morton, Timothy. *Hyperobjects: Philosophy and Ecology After the End of the World*. University of Minnesota Press, 2013.
Ronda, Margaret. "Obsolesce." *Veer Ecology: A Companion for Environmental Thinking*. University of Minnesota Press, 2017, pp. 76–89.
Rozelle, Lee. *Zombiescapes & Phantom Zones: Ecocriticism and the Liminal From Invisible Man to the Walking Dead*. University of Alabama Press, 2016.

Russell, Andrew, and Lee Vinsel. "Hail the Maintainers." *Aeon*, 7 Apr. 2016, https://aeon.co/essays/innovation-is-overvalued-maintenance-often-matters-more.

St. George, Carlie. "We Need More Teeth." *My Geek Blasphemy*, https://mygeekblasphemy.com/2016/03/07/we-need-more-teeth/.

Stern, Megan. "*Jurassic Park* and the Moveable Feast of Science." *Science as Culture*, vol. 13, no. 3, Sept. 2004, pp. 347–72.

"What Was With the 'More Teeth' Quote?" *Reddit, Jurassic Park*, www.reddit.com/r/JurassicPark/comments/3awzlx/what_was_with_the_more_teethspoiler_quote/.

Zizek, Slavoj. "Preface to the Routledge Classics Edition: Enjoy Your Symptom—Or Your Fetish?" *Enjoy Your Symptom! Jacques Lacan in Hollywood and Out.* Routledge, 2008, pp. ix–xvi.

4 "Don't Adjust Whatever Device You're Hearing This On"

(Dis)Embodiment and Analog Technology in *13 Reasons Why*

Based on Jay Asher's book (2007), *13 Reasons Why*, a streaming drama on Netflix that premiered in 2016, immediately provoked conversation and controversy because many viewers claimed it glorified the act of harming oneself. For some, the series was an unflinching look at the ugliness of youth suicide and its ripple effects; for others, it was a teen drama that spotlighted (perhaps too affirmatively) the act of taking one's own life and seeking revenge. However, there has been little conversation about the protagonist's use of analog technology to communicate beyond the grave. In this chapter, I analyze how Hannah Baker (Katherine Langford) and her peers pay tribute to past eras without indulging in nostalgia. This choice matters because it again subverts the image of the teen digital native who never looks beyond her digital screens.

In this narrative the creation of something new does not lead to empowerment but to tragedy. Unplugging and substituting analog for digital tools ultimately ends in death, not because creating with either of these forms changes the main character's fate but because Hannah's suicide note is stored on cassette tapes rather than a computer.

Clay Jensen (Dylan Minnette), the other lead in this series, becomes the mouthpiece for Hannah's journey as he listens to all of her tapes. On each cassette tape, Hannah spotlights a student whose actions harmed her, either purposefully or accidentally. As the tapes grow in number, the incidents against her become crueler, and she finally surrenders to feelings of hopelessness as a consequence. Hannah's instructions call for each student to listen to the entirety of the tape collection and then pass them on to another student until all thirteen students are aware of their role in her death. As Clay listens, his rage at the other students for their actions continues to build, especially since he harbors more than feelings of friendship for Hannah. However, he must also confront the fact that one tape in the series is dedicated to him, and he spends most of the narrative wondering how he, too, could have hurt his friend. Clay's other close friend Tony (Christian Navarro), the first one to receive the suicide tapes and deliver them, helps him confront the truth about his role in an argument with Hannah that led to her feelings of isolation.

Figure 4.1 Compact Cassette Tape and Case
Source: Wikimedia Commons

Students Jessica (Alisha Boe) and Alex (Miles Heizer), Hannah's former best friends, also feature predominantly in the unraveling of Hannah's story. Central to the second half of the narrative is Jess's traumatic memory of a sexual assault and Alex's own suicidal ideation. The cast of teen characters includes twelve diverse students whose backgrounds are quite different: some live in the "rich" side of town, while one must escape from an addicted mother whose partners abuse him. Parents and counselors also play a supporting role in the story but have less to do with the materiality at work in the narrative.

The second season further capitalizes on the dramatic encounters among the teens associated with Hannah's cassette confessions. Instead of being narrated primarily through Clay, Season Two alternates teen perspectives according to who testifies in court. At this point in the mythos, the audience is left confused as to what Hannah's exact relationship with each cast member is; they discover that she did, in fact, have a romance with one boy whom she blamed for her death, and they find out via flashbacks that other factors, such as Hannah's parents' separation, played a role in her feelings of hopelessness.

Clay and his friends also search for ways to bring baseball player Bryce Walker (Justin Prentice) to justice for his rape of Hannah and other girls. In this iteration of the characters' lives, the analog technology most present is the use of a Polaroid camera, which Bryce and other athletes use to photograph the girls with whom they have sex in a secret location they call the Clubhouse. The narrative often shifts (sometimes haphazardly) between a focus on Hannah and a focus on bringing Bryce to justice. Although both storylines are different, Bryce's misogyny and his repeated rapes reveal another example of violence enacted on the physical form, or human body. Additionally, the season's finale includes a rape scene in which a male character is violently attacked in the school bathroom, and the ramifications of this act foreshadow what may come in Season Three.

The violence on the human body via rape or death mirrors the destruction or violence done to physical documents that could bring closure to Hannah's family and Bryce's victims. In all episodes the theme of incomplete documentation or storytelling takes center stage, but even when incomplete, the messages remain destructive. For instance, the camera loves to spotlight the enormity of vandalism and destruction of property, particularly in the second season when cast members attempt to sabotage the baseball team's championship. However, as Clay observes, "We can spray paint some shit but they clean it up the next day" ("Bryce and Chloe"). Information is obliterated just as the body is, and students consistently feel powerless to stop it. The impermanence of all forms of communication remains one of the key themes of this story.

Whether evidence of wrongdoing is confessed on tape or documented on Polaroid snapshots, the narrative focuses on gaps or erasures in knowledge, a problem that all characters must confront and move past without answering the siren call to become destructive to their own bodies and others. In this sense, analog tools function as physical reminders of holes or silences that further complicate the understanding of teenage death: the guidance counselor's datebook is missing a sheet of handwritten notes ("The Missing Page"), and the Polaroid snapshots disappear ("The Box of Polaroids"). Throughout both seasons anonymous notes are regularly placed inside characters' lockers, and slut-shaming graffiti on bathroom walls both inscribes and later revises various rumors circulating on campus. In other words, it is not just Hannah's body that is destroyed when she takes her own life but the body of information necessary to understand how each character is battling separate demons. Objects, particularly handheld objects, best represent this idea of incompleteness and loss.[1]

Walkmans and Cassettes

In Ian Bogost's series of *Object Lessons*, or mini-novels about the material world's objects (things like shopping malls, hotels, hooded sweatshirts, phone booths, dust, and remote controls), Rebecca Tuhus-Dubrow published an installment called *Personal Stereo*, which dissected the cultural implications of the Walkman as an invention in the twentieth century. This text helps argue why in *13 Reasons Why* the most significant example of analog technology is the use of cassettes and a Walkman. Tuhus-Dubrow's analysis of the Walkman does address nostalgia for the 1980s but also stresses the present day excitement for using analog in place of digital. She explains,

> We like tactile experiences. We like things that engage more than one of our senses. . . . There's something more human and fathomable

about this physicality, about sensing the connection between the observable characteristics of an object and what it does. When the tape ribbon moves, the music plays; when the ribbon is wrinkled, the music sounds garbled. This logic is the logic of our own bodies, with organs and limbs whose motions are connected to their functions, and which are susceptible to injury and gradual breakdown.

(Chapter 3)

This explanation agrees with David Sax's insistence in the *Revenge of the Analog* that people like to engage all five of their senses when they create or compose. In the above passage Tuhus-Dubrow might align herself with composition scholar Jody Shipka's view: that today's public is too often associating the word technology as a term with screens and the digital. Shipka explains, "We need to consider what is at stake—who and what it is that we empower or discount—when we use the term to mean primarily, or worse yet, *only* the newest computer technologies and not light switches, typewriters, eyeglasses, handwriting, or floor tiles as well" (21). Although it would be easy to refer to Claude Levi-Strauss and label Hannah a bricoleur, someone forced to make due with limited resources like Beca from *Pitch Perfect* (see Chapter 2), Hannah actually *chooses* analog over digital from the very start, despite the presence of both kinds of tools. She largely avoids digital methods out of a desire to compose her message in a visceral, weighted manner and purposefully selects cassette tapes in order to amplify her descent into suicidal ideation. This choice actually highlights just how important analog materials sometimes become to characters belonging to Generation Z.

Hannah initially struggles with how to use the analog technology because while cassette tapes are still available at her parents' drug store (Baker Drugs), she does not know how to record on them. Therefore, she asks Tony for help, and he explains that the process is like "recording a voice text on your iPhone, only with way more style" ("Tape 7, Side A"). Author Jay Asher has explained that he chose cassette tapes for a rather paradoxical reason:

> With technology changing so fast, it's impossible for a present-day novel to stay current if your characters use the most up-to-date material. So rather than having Hannah post her reasons online—in which case, the terminology could change overnight and the characters in the book wouldn't know it—I used an older form of recording and made the characters acknowledge it.
>
> ("Between the Lines: Thirteen Questions")

Asher makes the choice sound like one borne out of necessity, yet this decision cannot help but effect meaning in the adapted version of the narrative. Keeping the tapes as a structure and motif makes the series indebted to analog technology in a way that communicates unique perspectives on death, embodiment, and relationships. In order to understand any moment of composing or communicating, Shipka reminds us that we have to consider how a tool "impacts or alters the body and an individual's relationship with his or her body" (51).

Additionally, the use of tapes as parachronistic tools muddies and complicates the way the audience perceives time in the narrative. As explained in the Introduction to this book, a parachronism works in contrast to an anachronism; it focuses on dated tools and spaces to disrupt traditional notions of linear time. Each character in *13 Reasons* straddles the line between the past and present as s/he listens to the cassette tapes while also texting on her smartphone. This technique also reinforces the image of Generation Z moving easily between high and low tech devices and environments. Past events remain ever present in the character's struggle, so much so that the present is always infected by memory in a manner that flattens the boundary between yesterday and today. This concept works especially well in terms of Hannah's suicide because the characters who listen to her suicide note in the present are also reliving their mistakes in the past. In a sense, these mistakes disturb Clay's sense of reality so often that he demonstrates frequent mood swings, delinquent behavior (at least in the eyes of his parents and the school), and isolation from his family and friends (except Tony, who persists in helping Clay despite his fits of anger).

Tools like the cassette tape are frequently associated with Hannah's efforts to prevent students from a speedy transmission of data. Her argument in using tapes is to slow the grieving process to a crawl, especially since Clay is our narrator, and he makes his way through the tapes quite slowly. In fact, characters repeatedly ask Clay why he hasn't listened "all the way through" in one night, almost as if Hannah's tapes are akin to binging a streaming television show. Clay explains that he can only listen in stops and starts, a little at a time; otherwise, he says, "I freak out. I feel a panic attack coming on" ("Tape 2, Side A"). Building on Ron Scollon's work on mediation, Shipka testifies that reactions like Clay's are normal, for he is reacting to the habitual use of a specific tool, which changes "the physical and psychological structure of the user" embedded in a specific system of meaning making (51).

Hannah's delivery of the analog tools also reveals careful planning on her part. Clay receives the package of tapes, a shoebox wrapped in brown paper, and discovers that the box contains a set of seven cassette tapes all colored and decorated differently. On each side of the tape is a number written in blue nail polish to indicate the order in which the tapes must be heard. On top Hannah places a map of the historic business district of the town, where she will guide different listeners to different locations. Clay must find a way to listen to the tapes, so he asks his father for the "boom box" he stores in his garage. "Don't adjust . . . whatever device you're hearing this on." Clay's father comments specifically on the boom box's obsolescence as he agrees to lend it, but Hannah's tapes require this older form of technology, and according to Tony in the expositional scenes of Episode 1 ("Tape 1, Side A"), the old media "is so much better." To this comment Clay responds, "Everything was better before," perhaps alluding to his school experience before Hannah's death. This motif continues when Hannah explains why she included a city map in the shoebox with the tapes: "A map. Old school again. No Google maps, no app, no chance for the interwebs to make everything worse, like it does." While this reference from Hannah seems borne out of nostalgia, it also gestures toward the physicality of a paper map as one that engages the senses in ways that a GPS does not.

Hannah's major premise is that by putting her suicide note on seven cassettes the listeners will be forced to do two things: listen and pass them on. Because only one public copy of the tapes exists (and one is hidden as a backup, which she claims will be revealed to the authorities if the students don't finish listening), students must take the shoebox and hand deliver the package to the next person. Tapes are also harder to disguise if the listener does not complete the side. In order to make others think s/he finished the side, s/he would have to manually fast forward so that the magnetic tape looks empty on the right spool. Tuhus-Dubrow explains that part of the magic of the old analog methods of listening is that the progression of the album cannot be distorted or skipped through with ease. With the aid of an iPhone (or, formerly, an iPod), any user may surf their music with little effort, skipping over any songs or sections of podcasts not worthy of immediate attention.

Beyond the Tapes

In many instances, the perspective on digital communication remains negative in this work, yet digital communication does not hold a monopoly on pain, bullying, or isolation here. The audience recognizes the same problems with handheld tools and creations (e.g., Hannah's reaction to Ryan's zine). In other words, analog tech does not always represent a positive occurrence nor does it advocate for a certain kind of morality. In fact, Season Two capitalizes on analog delivery as a violent method of communication since characters receive tactile and unique threats to remain silent. For example, Marcus watches his father's election sign light up in flames on the sidewalk next to his house. Jessica discovers a plastic doll hanging from her porch. Again, there seems to be a purpose in this. In their work on posthumanism, Kate Birdsall and Julie Drew explain that analog technologies are often referred to as embodied technologies, ones made of atoms instead of binary code (as established by Nicholas Negroponte in the Introduction to this book. They note that the "analog self is put under erasure as the digitally-constructed other is written into code" (118). What makes this a paradox is the nature of Hannah's messages on the tapes: despite the weightiness of the tapes and the analog nature of their being, Hannah's body is still absent. She still chooses to preserve her memory with "analog language," a term Birdsall and Drew use to suggest the pre-digital forms of communication and identity formation (119). In doing so, the image of the digital native flickers and fades from view. Only when Tony makes a flash drive of Hannah's message to give to her parents does she succumb to the binary code that transmits her final words. This final step in sharing the suicide note suggests that Tony and his friends will attempt to move past the weight of carrying Hannah's death in physical form through the Walkman and the tapes. In this concluding moment, we understand that, as Bill Brown suggests in his study of objects in American literature, Hannah's message has truly "expanded far beyond the confines of the autonomous subject" and has been "dispersed throughout the material world" rather than contained as analog matter (188).

Analog affections in *13 Reasons Why* reveal themselves not only through the use of cassette tapes but through surprising instances of teen creativity and communication. These examples range from brief references to Marcus (school valedictorian to be) making an El Niño costume out of a sombrero at Halloween, one that has flickering lights and sounds of thunder ("Tape 2, Side B"), to more somber examples associated with Hannah's death. The first episode ("Tape 1, Side A") shows a close up shot of Hannah's locker decorated by different students who claim to miss her. There are handwritten notes, old photos, flowers, and a pinwheel. As the camera zooms out we see two teenagers snap a selfie with the locker and load the image to a social network with the tag "never forget." Clay observes that these same girls are sharing the photo proudly with their peers in the next class. This incident suggests a theme of hypocrisy among the students who use high tech devices. Such devices may say "never forget," but as one student complains in communications class just after the girls share the picture, he wishes they could just "move on." The student body at large often failed to show her consideration during her first year at a new school, yet suddenly her death is seen as an event that unifies them all in their grief.

In terms of analog devices, Hannah here seems most interested in the slowness of old technology, or the pauses and glitches that make each listener take stock of their part in her life and death. She also takes pleasure in *spaces* that celebrate an analog approach. In her happiest moments with Clay, the Crestmont Theater is deserted, and she and Clay are the only ones working to clean the popcorn machine and sweep tickets off the floor. Indeed, the Crestmont itself is a small venue featuring old film reels from the 1980s and 90s (as we might deduce from the posters on the walls and the unsteady stream of customers). We see the Crestmont sign repeatedly as Clay rides his bike on the town's main street. Zach, a baseball player, even uses the theater as a place to get to know Hannah so that he may ask her on a date. He and Hannah bond about the retro film showings there when Zach complains about the inanity of watching *2001: A Space Odyssey* ("The Smile at the End of the Dock"). Likewise, Hannah assists her parents in stocking and organizing Baker Drugs, their mom and pop drug store. In this work she uses her hands for manual labor rather than for texting on her smartphone; additionally, this labor gives her opportunity to locate the blue nail polish and the cassettes she will later use to compose her suicide note.

Handwritten artifacts also point Hannah's mother, Olivia Baker, toward answers about her daughter's motivation for suicide. After Hannah's suicide Olivia uses the girls' bathroom at the school, where she finds graffiti on the stall's interior. She notes the following insults as she glances around unbelievingly and snaps photos with her smartphone: "Jane is such a basic bitch," "Megan is a whore," "I love to suck cock," and "Fuck off" ("Tape 2, Side A"). Here is evidence that analog compositions, too, contain harmful and even viral messages. Mrs. Baker does allude generally to some cruel texts and Facebook comments that Hannah received ("Tape 1, Side B"), but the narrative gives us more specifics when it comes to unplugged communication like the graffiti found here. Unlike Beca in *Pitch Perfect*, whose use of the shower stall at her college helped her find friends in the public restroom (see Chapter 1), the high school bathroom reveals how distrustful and angry female students remain toward one another ("Tape 2, Side A").

Later on, as Olivia inventories Hannah's belongings, most of which are kept in shoeboxes, she then opens a box where Hannah had kept a concept map of all of the students that played a part in bullying or alienating her. While Mrs. Baker remains unaware of the circumstances surrounding Hannah's suicide, she understands that this note, while only a rough sketch, shows student names for a reason. Some names have question marks beside them, some are connected by lines, and others are circled twice in bold ink (Bryce, who rapes both Hannah and Jessica, is the main example of this). Mrs. Baker still has this analog artifact posted on her home wall in Season Two as she searches for answers to why Hannah killed herself. Only after Hannah's trial is she able to move on and leave such artifacts behind.

The circles and lines are also decorated with objects the audience sees throughout the narrative: the Crestmont marquee sign in town, a coffee cup, Clay's bicycle, and Tyler's camera. These are some of the same objects in the opening credits of *13 Reasons*, with a memorable graphic match connecting the wheels of Clay's bike with the wheels inside the tapes. Indeed, this page is placed beside other cassette tapes belonging to Hannah, ones which may have been used as early drafts of her thoughts but were probably used for music ("Tape 6, Side A"). Mrs. Baker's uncovering of Hannah's paper notes (including the one that lists the sophomore girls' various "best" attributes, where Hannah receives "best ass" ["Tape 1, Side B"]) and her observation of bathroom walls suggests that some forms of bullying never change. Passed notes and anonymous insults continue to infect the unplugged world as much as the digital one.

Sometimes handwriting on unplugged surfaces also acts as a setting for the characters who choose to meet face to face and reveal private information. We hear two characters, Marcus and Courtney (a closeted lesbian student), arguing about the dangers of texting since they fear that their conversations will be recorded for evidence. As a result, the group of teens meets face to face, as Marcus suggests, at the coffee shop, where the large blackboard behind them shows chalk writing in different colors. On this analog surface different customers write their "Chalk Thoughts" to share with the rest of the clientele ("Tape 6, Side B"), and replicas of great works of Impressionistic art decorate the walls both inside and outside the space. The coffee shop, appropriately called Monet's, becomes a central setting: it is where students have significant conversations about Hannah's suicide in the present and where Hannah, Jess, and Alex meet in the past to confess their frustrations at Liberty High. Hannah refers to these meetings with her "hot chocolate friends" ("Tape 1, Side B") as her saving grace during the first months as a newcomer in Crestmont. Although the audience sees students holding their smartphones at the tables during both the past and present narratives, they also see an emphasis on face to face conversation in the midst of a space that celebrates handwriting, chalkboards, collections of books on shelves, independent coffee, and art. Like the Crestmont Theater where Hannah and Clay work, Monet's remains characterized by analog experiences. It is fitting that the conclusion of Season Two features an entire chalkboard dedicated not only to Hannah's memory but to positive messages about kindness and tolerance ("Bye"). This shrine acts as a more authentic display of affection than the original tokens placed on Hannah's locker.

Hannah offers an overt commentary on technology's limits when she announces to the guest librarian at the school job and college fair that she does not own a Kindle; she is, rather, "a paperback, write in the margins kind of girl" ("Tape 4, Side B"). In Season Two a flashback reveals that Hannah wanted Clay to write her long letters, no postcards or computer typed messages, during his summer away from Crestmont; in fact, she specifically requests "handwritten missives filled with [his] deepest, darkest secrets" ("The Third Polaroid"). The librarian senses this love of intimate writing in Hannah and invites her to a "safe space" called Evergreen Poetry Club, which she attends for a brief time. In this space Hannah bumps into Ryan, the creator of Liberty High's zine called *Lost and Found*. In this unofficial school magazine, he features found items like old notes in the trash as part of his DIY aesthetic. As a way to gain her trust, Ryan, who writes his own poetry in a purple Moleskine notebook, presents her with a pink one—one of the specific analog tools Sax mentions in his book *The Revenge of Analog*—and tells her "her thoughts deserve a place to live." Hannah grows excited about writing and even holds the notebook to her nose, smelling the pages. This moment reminds us again how unplugged resources engage the five senses. However, Ryan's choice to publish one of Hannah's poems without her permission later leads to her humiliation ("Tape 4, Side B"). Analog, once again, does not save Hannah from torment or embarrassment.

After Hannah's death, Ryan seems contrite and plans to make a zine focused only on Hannah. This moment reveals another important example of analog tools used by Generation Z students as Ryan enlists another student, Tyler's, help with the photographs for the magazine. In this same scene, Ryan wonders why Tyler still uses this analog film to produce his pictures, and Tyler responds, "I shoot all different ways," but analog film, he explains, "really makes you focus on the image you're creating. It's not just there for you on a screen." Tyler reinforces Hannah's own plan with her tapes: she wants her listeners to listen actively rather than passively, and Tyler wants time to reflect on his projects as artifacts rather than critique them passively on his phone or computer ("Tape 2, Side B"). Tyler's desire to touch the image he shoots reinforces the need to engage the senses as he creates art, but he stresses that he is just as familiar with "all different ways" of capturing an image. He is able, therefore, to move from unplugged methods to digital ones with ease.

Although the audience might dismiss Tyler's aesthetic as nostalgia, the character is quick to correct that perception in Season Two. When Clay finds an anonymous Polaroid picture in his locker, he confronts Tyler about it, and Tyler explains that Polaroids are "amateur hipster tripe" and that they are worthless because "there's no negatives, what's the point?" When Clay presses him on the issue, he also refers to Polaroid as "retro analog bullshit," something he would not associate himself with as a true photographer, one who has won prizes at school for his talent and who cares about his art ("Two Girls Kissing"). Tyler prefers the analog method of developing film, but he does not overindulge in previous technologies simply for the sake of appearances. However, Polaroid's negative reputation precedes the twenty-first century. Another teen photographer from *Stranger Things*, which is actually set in the 1980s, will later complain in a similar fashion about Polaroid pictures and their cheap quality (see Chapter 6).

Characters' stances toward instant photography lead to questions. What is wrong with holding a photo print that possesses no negative? As discussed previously, the print still allows for touch and sensory engagement, since, as Tyler says, "If you want a print to hold on to, take a Polaroid" ("Two Girls Kissing"). The impression given is that Polaroid, in truncating the artistic process of developing images, cheapens the work in a way not completely dissimilar to digital photography. This motif of Polaroids acts as a frame for most of Season Two, since the main object characters pursue is a box of photos with high school girls in compromising positions, often related to Bryce's rape charges. When Clay wonders aloud why Bryce and his friends use Polaroids, Justin explains that it acts as "insurance" because "what happens in the Clubhouse stays in the Clubhouse" ("Smile Bitches"). On a superficial level, the lack of negative seems to safeguard against the spreadability of something photographed on a smartphone.

However, in making the Polaroid a key element of Season Two, writers and producers reinforce the disposability of the girls' bodies that visit the Clubhouse, where the baseball athletes take advantage of them and ply them with alcohol and drugs. Polaroids simply reinforce how irreverent photography can become once it acts as a trophy to document sexual conquests. This trope also reinforces what Peter Buse has said about the use of Polaroid in narrative:

> If novels and films are to be believed, after the sexually explicit it is the criminally illicit Polaroid that is most common. The use of Polaroids at crime scenes is well known, but the same qualities that make Polaroid good for dirty pictures—speed, secrecy, no compromising negative—make it ideal for committing the crime.
>
> (71)

Buse also says that since the Polaroid invokes a kind of intimacy in its usage during social gatherings, it "blur[s] the border between picture-maker, picture, and pictured" (65–67). Building on Lauren Berlant's cultural theories, Buse elaborates on the problem of this intimacy: the Polaroid creates the potential for a darker, "shadow" form of its normally "cozy and comfortable" playfulness (69). Such awareness comes with the ability to photograph via smartphone in our daily lives, but most of us have forgotten that missing negatives and lack of Internet still allows for exploitation and destruction of the photo's subjects. The Polaroid also illumines the trauma associated with memory. Since no negative exists by which to verify that the crimes in the Clubhouse occurred, the women involved are able to ignore and/or suppress any accounts they might give of what transpired there. Even Chloe, Bryce's girlfriend in Season Two's finale, is willing to look past the evidence of two Polaroids that show her unconscious while Bryce takes advantage. In Season One the audience experiences how easy it is to destroy Hannah's reputation with a viral digital photo Justin takes of her in the park. Season Two extends this horror to the tools normally considered antiquated and "cozy." This is not surprising, Buse says, because Polaroid has long "ape[d] the language and forms of the digital even while remaining firmly analog" (84). As the show's narrative continues into a second season, the line between analog and digital tools disappears here to remind its audience that the human behind the tool is at fault, not the tool itself.

Finally, analog tools and spaces become important when they also act as editing devices. Although the parachronistic nature of the Walkman seems to anchor Clay in his past mistakes, the writers and producers of the Netflix series are keen to separate the past from the present for the viewer who requires that clarity. Flashbacks are frequent throughout all episodes, and properties, costume pieces, set pieces like doors, and light all aid in the process of differentiating the past from the present. In order to help the audience navigate these abrupt and frequent shifts in time, certain objects act as markers: Clay in the present wears a Band-Aid on his forehead throughout the series (from a biking accident in "Tape 1, Side A"), while Clay's face in the past remains unblemished. In other cases, objects help scenes transition seamlessly: the ghost light on the dark theater stage shines on Hannah in the past as she hides in the empty space, and then that same light is seen as we zoom in on Jess and Justin in the present, kissing behind the curtains of the stage ("Tape 6, Side B").

Embodiment/Disembodiment

The idea of disembodiment of the young female body due to violence has been studied elsewhere in a similar narrative of rape and abuse of the female body. Ann Bliss has examined how "photographs stand in for the dead and become a metaphor for the living traumatized family" in Alice Sebold's *The Lovely Bones* (2002) and its film adaptation directed by Peter Jackson (862). Likewise, in Netflix's *13 Reasons*, the cassette tapes stand in for Hannah's absent body after her suicide. They, like photographs, act as tangible reminders of the missing corporeal body. As Clay says to Tony, "I can't hear her voice without thinking of her. Without seeing her." Tony responds, "Seems like maybe that was the idea" ("Tape 1, Side B"). While Tony does often allude to a nostalgic wish for old technology, he knows when and how to use digital means to communicate. Tony makes a digital copy of the tapes on a flash drive only when giving the story to Hannah's parents and apologizing for keeping the information from them ("Tape 7, Side A"). Tony is able to move between analog and digital delivery systems by considering his different audiences. If analog technology stands for the absence of ease and convenience, then Tony's choice makes sense, for he wishes to make the delivery as painless and easy as possible for Hannah's parents. Here tech alleviates additional emotional trauma rather than causing it. Hannah's parents need not be reminded to grieve through the use of slow technology because they have already mourned Hannah's loss more than any student on campus claims to have mourned.

Other references to the body abound in this narrative. When Ryan attempts to pry the tapes from Tony in order to ensure his silence, Tony refuses to give them up. He uses punishment of the body to describe Tony's sense of right and wrong: "Tony wouldn't budge. He's got the tapes hidden somewhere, and this medieval self-flagellating moral code"

("Tape 5, Side B"). Clay even suspects that Tony's obsession with the cassette tapes may be explained in corporeal terms, for he assumes that Tony was attracted to Hannah and unable to let her go. Later on, Tony explains to Clay that he is gay and that the tapes link him more closely to a boy than a girl since he spends most of his time comforting his best friend. It is heavily implied that he is just as fixated on Clay as Clay is on Hannah's memory.

Hannah's poetry also calls attention to the vulnerability of the body when she visits the Evergreen Poetry Club. Her first oral reading includes these lines, which Ryan later publishes without her permission:

> And I've got skin. Miles and miles of skin.
> I've got skin to cover all my thoughts like Saran Wrap
> That you can see through
> To what leftovers are inside from the night before.
> And despite what you might think
> My skin is soft and smooth and easily scarred.
>
> ("Tape 4, Side B")

The idea of Saran Wrap and leftovers reduces her human form to something that can be consumed and digested, which echoes how she feels about her encounters with men who, in previous episodes, have called her "easy." Like Ryan, Hannah learns to express her most secret thoughts in poetry form, only to have them later used against her when the student body mocks her references to "miles and miles of skin" and "lacy black underwear," a phrase used in the opening stanza. Other references in *13 Reasons* call attention to the fragility of the human body and the comforts of the nonhuman world in navigating such fragility. During Jess's party Clay and Hannah take special note of the rock collection that Jess had as a child and make some comments that suggest they find solace in the nonliving object more than the living body ("Tape 6, Side A"):

Hannah: She has a rock collection from when she was little. She used to water them and treat them as pets. . . . She can actually be pretty cool and funny. I mean, she still has her rocks.
Clay: Yes. Well, I guess an advantage of pet rocks is that they don't die.
Hannah: Mmm, yeah. They don't eat too much. And they don't crap on the floor.
Clay: (accidentally knocks the collection off the table) Uh oh. I'm killing her pets. What's that one's name? (he points to Hannah's hand)
Hannah: I think we should name him Stone.
Clay: Is that his first name or last name?
Hannah: Both.

Immediately following this banter, Clay and Hannah share their first kiss, which leads to Hannah's panic attack over being touched. Immediately after her attack, Hannah hides out of sight when other partygoers enter the room. She then sees Bryce rape Jessica during her blackout from intoxication. In these situations, the idea of corporeality, or human form, is violated repeatedly, both in Hannah's imagination when she refuses Clay's advances and then with Jess as she is unable to fend off Bryce. While having a body leads to violence, the notion of rocks or nonhuman objects suggests predictability and safety. While cassette tapes hearken back to the 1980s, the "pet rock" phenomenon recalls the 1970s. This gimmick for 70s children overlaps with Jess's own late 1990s childhood (fusing the past and present in a parachronistic manner), one not marked by screened technology but by analog toys that remind us of the past. On another level, the exchange over pet rocks remains the final moment Hannah, Clay, and Jessica are able to enjoy their innocence before Jess drinks heavily on a daily basis, Hannah selects suicide as a way out of her pain, and Clay must suffer the loss of one of his new friends Jeff in an automobile accident.

Ian Bogost has explained his love for objects as something that reminds him of youth and innocence. For Bogost, "so much of object-oriented ontology is, to me, a reclamation of a sense of wonder often lost in childhood" (Chapter 4). He further explains, "Would it really be so daft to admit that the world is simply full of interesting, curious things, all living their own alien lives, bumping and jostling about, engulfing and destroying one another, every one of them as secretive and withdrawn as the other?" (Chapter 4). The very question of what a tool or space might do beyond its initial design is one that draws from the same spirit that characterizes a group of children on a playground or in a sandbox. What looks like sand or a swing to us is something else entirely to the children using it. This enchantment characterizes Jess's love of rocks, one borne from childhood and still preserved in her bedroom. In Season Two Jess and her former boyfriend Justin even communicate via short postcards because it allows them to imagine new identities as Sid and Nancy, characters from a documentary about the punk band The Sex Pistols ("The Drunk Slut"). The idea of reclaiming innocence in childhood appears in Hannah's poetry as well: "But that doesn't matter, right? You don't care about how soft my skin is. You just want to hear about what my fingers do in the dark. . . . What if all they crave is a jungle gym to climb for a taste of fresher air?" These lines hearken back to the first tape, when Hannah visits the playground to meet Justin, only to have him snap a suggestive photo of her and show it to his friends, whose actions are further described below. What used to be a place to climb and enjoy the outdoors now represents a loss of innocence rather than a reclamation of it ("Tape 1, Side A").

Indeed, technology often highlights the disposability of human interactions and relationships, the absence of care for humans as embodied matter. We hear this kind of disposable digital concept with Hannah's first friend Kat, who moves away from town just as the students are entering sophomore year. When Hannah uses Skype (video chat) with Kat in the first episode, she asks Kat if it is all right to pursue Justin, a boy that Kat once liked. Kat merely looks confused in response, and then she realizes to whom Hannah refers. Kat explains that she had this delayed reaction because the names of her old classmates have been forgotten in the wake of meeting new ones. In her words, "those are being dragged into the trash can icon in her head." Her memory of Justin and others is now converted to "the language of computers, the binary code of 1's and 0's" (see Introduction). This kind of reaction counters Hannah's desire to maintain slowness when she painstakingly prepares seven cassettes for those who have hurt her. By moving and forgetting her friends so quickly, Kat reinforces the idea that digital media (the trash can icon in her head) works in rapid response to changing circumstances. Kat does not pause to remember her former peers; rather, she works to forget them as quickly as possible.

An even more disturbing example of disposable identity occurs when Justin photographs Hannah sliding with a skirt on in the park ("Tape 1, Side A"). Because her skirt lifts as she comes down the slide, Justin has a photo that compromises Hannah's reputation, for it suggests that the two were sexually intimate in ways they were not. The inciting moment of the series occurs when Justin unthinkingly jokes about the situation with his friends and shows them the picture. On a lark and to impress his friends, his friend Bryce forwards the photo by text to all of their peers. As Hannah arrives to communications class, she hears the incessant "dings" all around her, which signal that smartphones are receiving messages. As students open the message and see Hannah's photo, they quickly mock and judge Hannah, consistently referring to her as a "slut" for the rest of her sophomore year. Hannah views this incident as the first reason why she decides to take her life ("Tape 1, Side A"). Here the photograph stands in for Hannah's body and suggests that she, too, is disposable to the boys who spend time with her. Jess later confirms that a similar situation occurred with her and her best friend at her previous school: "I had this friend Amy. I told her everything, including my series of embarrassing sex dreams featuring various Avengers, including Scarlett Johansson. Then one day, you know, the moving trucks come, I'm like 'Bye, don't tell anyone about that Scarlett Johansson thing!' But she posts about it because that's the only communication you have anymore" ("Tape 1, Side B"). Hannah and Jess then bond about their peers' ability to twist the truth when messages go viral. Again, what Jess considers as a private dream has now been reduced to 1s and 0s. Her own humiliation is secondary to someone's need to share exciting news on a Facebook feed.

Glitches

When an object fails to work, the user becomes more attentive to its importance, since "[o]ne way taken-for-granted technologies are rendered visible is through breakdowns or disruptions" (Shipka 55). The occurrence of analog malfunction in this narrative sometimes humiliates as well as frustrates the person using the tool. Still, embarrassment and frustration are key to acknowledging how our tools, both material and digital, fail us, just as we fail others. With unplugging, the glitch often brings our shortcomings into public view through noise (e.g., Tyler's camera when he snaps photos of Hannah outside her window) and physical stress or embarrassment (e.g., the principal's key to the combination lock failing when Hannah's parents collect her things). However, exceptions occur where characters use tools to express anger or frustration. In the midst of Jess's denial of the rape she suffers at the hands of Bryce, Jess breaks an object to make her frustration known, and when Clay discovers the truth of this rape, he slams his bike into the ground and makes the chains freeze, rendering the bike temporarily useless. In both cases, Justin with Jess and Tony with Clay watch the destruction of tools with concern for their partner or friend's well-being.

One of the flashbacks in Season Two illustrates this point best: Hannah asks school photographer Tyler to take her photo by a locker that she cannot manage to open ("The First Polaroid"). Emphasis on this particular glitch continues with the principal, who cannot open Hannah's locker for her parents, who arrive at Liberty High to collect their deceased daughter's belongings from campus. He apologizes, and Hannah's father says, "You'd think there would be a master key," to which the principal responds, "There was at some point." After time passes and Hannah's shrine is removed, the new student given Hannah's locker also fails to make the combination lock work properly ("Tape 3, Side B"). It seems odd, and perhaps even parachronistic, to show today's students using the kind of lockers that characterized their parents' schools, but little has changed in terms of how lockers frustrate students ("Tape 1, Side A"). To open a faulty combination lock, the user must repetitively enter the three numbers, shifting the dial ever so slightly in each attempt. Often a stubborn combination lock, perhaps due to rust or a loose spring, will not pop free, and the owner must jiggle or pull on the object to make it work.

Clay's progression through the tapes is characterized by stops and starts that punctuate the horror of the events described. Tony remarks early on that Clay is the slowest listener of the group, as mentioned earlier. Clay repeatedly argues with Hannah's voice in the first tape, thinking that even his inclusion in the collection of cassettes must be an error. When Clay first receives the cassettes, he finds that he cannot work the boom box's eject button when it sticks ("Tape 1, Side A"). Using his father's boom box, he becomes exasperated and immobile in the face of Hannah's suicide note. In order to listen privately, Clay secretly swipes Tony's Walkman in order to start Tape 1 again. However, because the Walkman is a distinctly analog piece, it bulges from inside his pockets, making it hard to hide it from Tony as he rides his bike home. This degree of bulkiness on the part of the Walkman enables Tony to perceive Clay's attempt at theft and to track him to the first important location on Hannah's paper map.

When Clay steals the Walkman, we see Tony working with his father to repair a Mustang that needs regular maintenance because of the engine's various sounds and glitches. The car has been in his family for years, likely handed down among him and his siblings. This is the reason a tape player is installed in his car. Repeatedly we observe Tony working with his hands as he services his car and works in his father's repair shop. Additionally, when Clay curses Tony for not reacting to the rape of Jessica ("Tape 4, Side B"), the chain on Clay's bike freezes up, and he cannot leave. Tony then steps in immediately to fix the bike, reassuring Clay that he will remain by his side throughout the remaining tapes. Additionally, Tony also helps Hannah by jumpstarting her new car after the Winter Formal; his willingness to do so when, as Hannah says, "a dozen people walked past this tragedy and all averted their eyes" ("Tape 3, Side A") most likely prompts her later to choose him as her messenger and protector of the tapes. It is no surprise then that Tony shows little interest in college; he announces at the job/college fair that he "has skills," and that form of work suits him just fine.

Material objects break not only because they encounter glitches but, as I stated previously, they also break when human effort destroys them instead. Hannah's guilt over the car accident with friend Sheri leads her into a darkened theater, where the only light is a single light bulb on center stage, a ghost light left to keep the theater from going completely dark. When she sits down and stares ahead at the light, the scene transitions to Jess and Justin from the past, who use the shadows from the light to hide their secret rendezvous. In this scene Jess breaks the bulb, leaving shards of dangerous glass on the floor ("Tape 5, Side B"). While this act may hardly be called a glitch in the traditional sense of the word since a human is responsible for the wreckage, Jess's loss of control mimics what the other glitches suggest: that any attempt at a smooth encounter with humans or nonhumans will end in folly, especially after a trauma.

In his book *The Tears of Things*, Peter Schwenger explains that our relationship with objects may be best summarized by our reaction to glitches as they occur. In his chapter on "Possessed Objects," he comments, "The recalcitrant computer, the shoelace that refuses to come unknotted, the furniture that lies in wait to bruise our heel—these restore in an instant the primitive, resentful sense that objects have a will of their own" (77). He further asserts that objects reveal this sense of agency when they "become transformed into commodities, and consequently they are animated by what seems to be an independent will" (78). This argument will be central to an analysis of *Get Out* in Chapter 5. In *13 Reasons Why*, however, most objects responsible for glitches are well worn and cared for; they lack the shine or polish of newly acquired souvenirs or trophies.

While the objects discussed above are clearly lacking the finesse of new digital tools, they are reminders of how important it is to have physical contact with the material world, especially after an inexplicable loss. This contact does not have to mean that we buy or collect the materials for our own manipulative purposes; rather, it suggests that Generation Z's ability to cope with trauma is partly based on their ability to move between high and low tech environments. Still, there are examples of collections for collections' sake here: Bryce's sports trophies line the tables in his living room, Hannah's father buys her a new car to impress her cohort at the Winter Formal, and Ryan's habit of collecting other people's trash to publish it for his own pleasure are all examples of materiality run amuck for egotistical purposes. In these encounters, the student or bricoleur is not acting as a co-participant in creating something new but is reasserting his or her dominance over objects and the people around them. This attitude, left unchecked, results in assault to the human body since that body becomes just another object to be collected via Polaroid photograph.

Note

1. Although I analyze the use of objects as tools of communication in Seasons One and Two, I have purposefully excluded a study of any objects that are used as weapons to inflict bodily harm on teenagers. These include the razor blades Hannah uses in the bathtub, the guns that appear regularly in multiple character arcs, and the infamous mop scene of the Season Two finale. While the argument could be made that such objects are used to communicate, albeit in destructive form, the payoff for such a discussion is not great enough to allow for the potential harm that might stem from a thick description of such events. Nevertheless, I do argue that weapons as tools are an important part of some narratives, and this idea will be addressed later in the book within the context of racial injustice in Chapter Five on *Get Out*. For a more detailed explanation and part justification from Brian Yorkey, *13 Reasons* show creator, about his use of controversial objects, please see Dee Lockett's article.

References

Asher, Jay. "Between the Lines: Thirteen Questions for Jay Asher." *Thirteen Reasons Why*. Penguin, 2007. Kindle.
———. *Thirteen Reasons Why*. Penguin, 2007. Kindle.
Birdsall, Kate, and Julie Drew. "Wanting Ourselves: Writing (And) The Postsexual Subject." *Writing Posthuman, Posthuman Writing*, edited by Sidney I. Dobrin. Parlor Press, 2015.
Bliss, Ann. "'Share Moments, Share Life': The Domestic Photograph as a Symbol of Disruption and Trauma in *The Lovely Bones*." *Women's Studies: An Interdisciplinary Journal*, vol. 37, no. 7, 2008, pp. 861–84.

Bogost, Ian. "The Aesthetics of Physical Carpentry." *The Nonhuman Turn*, edited by Richard Grusin. University of Minnesota Press, 2015, Chapter 4. Kindle.
"The Box of Polaroids." *13 Reasons Why*, season 2, episode 12, July Moon Productions, 18 May 2018, *Netflix*, www.netflix.com/watch/80186759.
Brown, Bill. *A Sense of Things: The Object Matter of American Literature*. University of Chicago Press, 2003.
"Bryce and Chloe," *13 Reasons Why*, season 2, episode 11, July Moon Productions, 18 May 2018, *Netflix*, www.netflix.com/watch/80186758.
Buse, Peter. *The Camera Does the Rest: How Polaroid Changed Photography*. University of Chicago Press, 2016.
"Bye," *13 Reasons Why*, season 2, episode 13, July Moon Productions, 18 May 2018, *Netflix*, www.netflix.com/watch/80186760.
"The Drunk Slut," *13 Reasons Why*, season 2, episode 3, July Moon Productions, 18 May 2018, *Netflix*, www.netflix.com/watch/80186750.
"The First Polaroid," *13 Reasons Why*, season 2, episode 1, July Moon Productions, 18 May 2018, *Netflix*, www.netflix.com/watch/80186748.
Lockett, Dee. "*13 Reasons Why* Creator Defends Controversial Rape Scene: 'Talking about It Is So Much Better Than Silence.'" *Vulture*, 22 May 2018, www.vulture.com/2018/05/13-reasons-why-season-2-finale-rape-scene.html
"The Missing Page," *13 Reasons Why*, season 2, episode 9, July Moon Productions, 18 May 2018, *Netflix*, www.netflix.com/watch/80186756.
Negroponte, Nicholas. *Being Digital*. Knopf, 1995.
Sax, Peter. *The Revenge of Analog: Real Things and Why They Matter*. Public Affairs, 2016. iBook.
Schwenger, Peter. *The Tears of Things: Melancholy and Physical Objects*. University of Minnesota Press, 2006.
Shipka, Jody. *Toward a Composition Made Whole*. University of Pittsburg Press, 2011.
"The Smile at the End of the Dock," *13 Reasons Why*, season 2, episode 6, July Moon Productions, 18 May 2018, *Netflix*, www.netflix.com/watch/80186753.
Tuhus-Dubrow, Rebecca. *Personal Stereo*. Bloomsbury, 2017. Kindle.
"Tape 1, Side A," *13 Reasons Why*, season 1, episode 1, July Moon Productions, 31 Mar. 2017, *Netflix*, www.netflix.com/watch/80117471.
"Tape 1, Side B," *13 Reasons Why*, season 1, episode 2, July Moon Productions, 31 Mar. 2017, *Netflix*, www.netflix.com/watch/80117472.
"Tape 2, Side A," *13 Reasons Why*, season 1, episode 3, July Moon Productions, 31 Mar. 2017, *Netflix*, www.netflix.com/watch/80117473.
"Tape 2, Side B," *13 Reasons Why*, season 1, episode 4, July Moon Productions, 31 Mar. 2017, *Netflix*, www.netflix.com/watch/80117474.
"Tape 3, Side A," *13 Reasons Why*, season 1, episode 5, July Moon Productions, 31 Mar. 2017, *Netflix*, www.netflix.com/watch/80117475.
"Tape 3, Side B," *13 Reasons Why*, season 1, episode 6, July Moon Productions, 31 Mar. 2017, *Netflix*, www.netflix.com/watch/80117476.
"Tape 4, Side B," *13 Reasons Why*, season 1, episode 8, July Moon Productions, 31 Mar. 2017, *Netflix*, www.netflix.com/watch/80117478.
"Tape 5, Side B," *13 Reasons Why*, season 1, episode 10, July Moon Productions, 31 Mar. 2017, *Netflix*, www.netflix.com/watch/80117480.
"Tape 6, Side A," *13 Reasons Why*, season 1, episode 11, July Moon Productions, 31 Mar. 2017, *Netflix*, www.netflix.com/watch/80117481.

"Tape 6, Side B," *13 Reasons Why*, season 1, episode 12, July Moon Productions, 31 Mar. 2017, *Netflix*, www.netflix.com/watch/80117482.

"Tape 7, Side A," *13 Reasons Why*, season 1, episode 13, July Moon Productions, 31 Mar. 2017, *Netflix*, www.netflix.com/watch/80117483.

"The Third Polaroid," *13 Reasons Why*, season 2, episode 7, July Moon Productions, 18 May 2018, *Netflix*, www.netflix.com/watch/80186754.

"Two Girls Kissing," *13 Reasons Why*, season 2, episode 2, July Moon Productions, 18 May 2018, *Netflix*, www.netflix.com/watch/80186749?trackId=200257858.

Yorkey, Brian, creator. *13 Reasons Why*. July Moon Productions and Netflix, 2017–18.

5 Complicating Materiality and Generational Labels

Get Out and the Role of the Collector

Nominated for an Academy Award for Best Picture and winner of the Best Original Screenplay, *Get Out* (2017) as a narrative showcases characters who act in ways that violate the relationship between human and human as well as human and nonhuman. They do so by *collecting* objects and people rather than respecting them as partners in the creative process. The characters in previous chapters pay attention to the physical world, and this attention leads to partnership with all forms of matter, sentient and non-sentient. However, in this film the audience confronts the nasty truth that some subjects are only interested in mastering and subjugating material and human beings rather than working with or alongside them.

Get Out remains the most complicated plot to describe in simple terms. Even director Jordan Peele remarked, "I stopped writing this movie about twenty times because I thought it was impossible. I thought it wasn't going to work." Likewise, writing about Peele's work here also remains challenging since the horror of this piece sneaks up on the viewer in slow, insidious ways, some of which are hard to describe but important to understand in terms of the fears young black men such as the protagonist face in daily life. In this narrative Chris (Daniel Kaluuya) visits his girlfriend Rose Armitage's (Allison Williams) white suburban family on a weekend, only to realize that Rose's relatives (and even Rose herself) are responsible for the kidnapping and brainwashing of black Americans they capture on the street and in their home. Chris and the audience both realize that Rose's parents Dean (Bradley Witford) and Missy Armitage (Catherine Keener) keep black bodies as vessels for white people suffering from disease and old age. By keeping the black body as vessel, Mr. and Mrs. Armitage provide ways to circumvent the deaths of those they love and to use black Americans as collector's items at the same time. Likewise, they make this option available to their neighbors. Members of a secret community, the Order of the Coagula, originally led by Rose's grandfather Roman, attend a yearly party during which they auction off the current black visitor in their midst.

106 *Complicating Materiality*

Figure 5.1 Deer Head Mounted on Wall
Source: Author photo

Although Missy does her best to control Chris through hypnosis, he is able to escape because he uses materials in the Armitage home to save himself. To avoid hypnosis, he stuffs his ears with cotton. To defend himself against other family members like Rose's brother Jeremy (Caleb Landry Jones), he uses both a bocce ball and a mounted deer head as weapons. By defending himself in creative ways, Chris escapes undergoing a brain transplant with an elderly white man (Stephen Root) who wishes to use Chris's talent to become a famous photographer.

Due to the complicated ways in which humans and things are portrayed in this narrative, I take a different approach to materiality and the digital native in this chapter. First, as a counterpoint to the larger theme of this book, I demonstrate why generational labels, while helpful in understanding some cultural trends, often fail to depict those from different racial and economic backgrounds. For example, certain material objects, particularly the automobile, do not hold the same meaning as they do for the white characters in previous chapters. I then analyze how unplugged or analog tools reveal a family of collectors rather than bricoleurs. Finally, I conclude by showing how the black body then becomes just another form of collector's item for both Rose and her parents.

Rethinking Generational Labels and Analog Culture

Chris as a young character straddles the millennial and Generation Z divide, yet this description hardly explains all that he faces when he reaches the Armitage home in the countryside. Indeed, at the time of this writing and shortly after the 2018 Oscars ceremony during which Peele won his award, John Quiggen from the *New York Times* made a general observation about classifications of people according to generational cohorts: "Some may argue that the generation game, if intellectually vacuous, is basically harmless. But dividing society by generation obscures the real and enduring lines of race, class, and gender. When, for example, baby boomers are blamed for 'ruining America,' the argument lumps together Donald Trump and a 60-year-old black woman who works for minimum wage cleaning one of his hotels." This is all to say that it remains easy to lump people into one homogeneous group rather than consider how poverty and/or minority status have limited the opportunities some youth in Generation Z have confronted. *Get Out* offers an important moment in this book for many reasons, but prominent among them is that it reminds audiences to reflect on generational groupings and labels as complicated constructs, constructs that frequently neglect to take race and class into account. Chris as a bricoleur, a photographer, and a digital native is also Chris who "gets nervous when there are too many white people around," and for very good reason. Such anxiety is not a result of growing up Generation Z: instead, that feeling resonates with many black people across generations of American history.

Materiality is one way to bring such anxieties to the forefront, although the materials in this particular movie do not signify the same things they might in others, ones in which white characters use analog tools to communicate. The American automobile, for instance, acts as a major example of this change. The automobile, usually a sign of industry, masculinity, and comfort for characters in predominantly white casts (*Supernatural*, *Jurassic World*) serves here as a material reminder of the racial divisions and police brutality that made the national "Black Lives Matter" movement such a pivotal event in the 2010s. *Los Angeles Times* reporter Justin Chang comments in his review that *Get Out* is "the nerviest, most confrontational treatment of race in America to emerge from a major studio in years," partly because Peele knows "exactly how to exploit the sight of an approaching police car for maximum stomach drop." In fact, the opening sequence mirrors, almost exactly, the circumstances surrounding teenage Trayvon Martin's death in a suburban, gated community, where he had a fatal confrontation with a neighborhood watchman (Hill 108–09).

This opening scene reflects a common fear of African American men in the 2010s. Scholar and educator Howard Stevenson explains that black parents, sooner or later, have to have what he calls "the stalking talk" with their sons. In this talk parents remind young black boys, particularly those who might be wearing hoodies or other outerwear that obscures the face, to be vigilant when walking the streets at night. Stevenson records and recounts his exact words when giving this talk: "And I don't like the idea—and that's why Daddy gets mad about it sometimes and that's also why Mommy and Daddy want to teach you so that if anybody is following you that you need to know how to talk to them and to stand up for yourself, yet not under-react or over-react. Do you know what under-react means? Like it means like you pretend that nothing's happening" (68–69). Indeed, in the film, the audience first glimpses a car trailing a young black man (Lakeith Stanfield), even before the opening credits roll. The man, lost due to misdirection on his GPS, speaks on his cell phone to his girlfriend and worries about being lost. He is then followed by a white car that plays 1930s music and trails him from behind. Worried that he "sticks out like a sore thumb" around this suburban setting, he avoids eye contact with the presumably white driver, muttering under his breath, "Not me. Not today." He turns to walk back the way he originally came, but it is already too late. The driver of this vehicle tails him and later leaves the car only to manhandle and kidnap Andre (his name, revealed later), who fails to escape despite struggling. Peele heightens the tension in this scene to give the audience an idea of what a black man feels when defenseless in a predominantly white neighborhood. Ironically it is the white kidnapper who hides his face behind a mask, not the black man with a hoodie walking in the suburb.

However, the lighting design of this film obscures the details of the black man's face on purpose so that the audience must think carefully to recall him when he becomes part of the Armitage community; it is almost as if he does not fully exist until he becomes prisoner. Such erasure gives Marc Lamont Hill the title of his book about black men and incarceration, *Nobody*, because the bodies of black men cease to exist once disposed of by authorities. Chris later meets that same man, Andre Hayworth, in full daylight, under an alias at the Armitage house. He has, after the kidnapping, become Logan Smith, a physical container for the consciousness of someone's husband (presumed dead or sick). In this new incarnation of existence, Dre as Logan has a shaved face, a khaki suit, and a straw hat, which transforms him into a version of the white man his consciousness now hosts. The black Logan King, actually in Dre's body, twirls for the guests at the party who ask him to model his physique. Logan's partner, Philomena, is a white woman thirty years older than he, which suggests that Philomena arranged for Andre to take her partner's place and keep his memory alive (via the horrific Coagula experiment). It is also insinuated that Philomena uses Andre for sexual reasons, and Rod (Lil Rel Howery), Chris's best friend, continues to hypothesize that sex is one of the main reasons the Armitages and their neighbors kidnap black men in particular. Peele subverts our expectations by initially keeping the previously bearded black man's face in the dark but showing us how he is the prey, not the other way around.

The opening scene is not the only part of the story in which a car initially represents danger rather than material comfort. In the movie's conclusion, a police car pulls up in front of Chris just as he kills his young girlfriend in self-defense, for she has been firing repeatedly at him with a machine gun and ordering her relatives to kill him on sight. Once the car's lights reveal Chris next to Rose, he rises slowly with his hands up, and the assumption is that Chris will go to jail for his crimes no matter what horrors he has endured and what weapons the girl was using. After all, a young black man killing or hurting a white woman will often be judged the guilty party in such situations, no matter who fires the original shot or what she does to attack Chris both psychologically and physically. As Michelle Williams in *The New Jim Crow* has argued, "In the era of mass incarceration, what it means to be a criminal in our collective consciousness has become conflated with what it means to be black." This is because, as Williams says, one of every three African American men is likely to serve time in jail during his lifetime due to an era of mass incarceration for first time offenses (198, 9). Because the car first appears under cloak of darkness, the audience, particularly one familiar with current events, is prepared to assume the worst about the driver who steps out of the vehicle. The audience breathes more easily only when they discover that the man is Chris's best friend.

Finally, one other example of a car may seem benign, but it holds hidden meaning. When a policeman interviews Rose and Chris after Rose hits a deer on the drive to her parents' home, the man asks for Chris's license, and Rose comes to his immediate defense, explaining that he was not the driver and that the need for his identification makes no sense. In showing how supposedly aware she is of systemic prejudices in the law enforcement system, Rose hides the truth of what she is really doing when the policemen assents and leaves Chris alone. Because the cop does not take down Chris's name, he will not be found if he goes missing, so her very act of allegiance to Chris is a pretense, not a true sign of support. In this same scene, Rose shows no sympathy for the deer mortally wounded by the accident, a reaction that should signal her lack of empathy. However, Peele here plays a trick on the audience as he shows Rose as defensive of Chris because most of us are distracted and impressed by her solidarity with her boyfriend. Again, racism for Peele shows itself in subtle, insidious ways during the first act of the movie. Only later do we understand that the cop in this case would have possibly been hailed to save Chris from the family, had he been aware of Chris's full name and his home address. Since that did not occur, the police merely laugh at Rod later on when he reports a missing person, and Rod must take matters into his own hands and save his best friend on his own.

Additionally, the photographer's camera, a tool previously used by adolescent white men in the other chapters of this book, takes on a different meaning in *Get Out*. In *Stranger Things* and *13 Reasons Why*, the adolescent photographer is the outcast, someone bitter about being ostracized by his peers. However, the camera in *Get Out* acts as a tool for photographer Chris's survival in the Armitages' world of bitter *adults* who have suffered the loss of their family members. Lenika Cruz wisely interprets the motif of eyes, observation, and photographing in *Get Out*. The camera, Cruz says, is not only "a kind of protective shield between Chris and the odd behavior he encounters" but, more importantly, a reminder of "how important camera phones and video recordings have been for many African Americans experiencing police violence. . . . Cameras, *Get Out* suggests somewhat plainly, have the power to reveal." While he does possess a smartphone and uses it occasionally to take pictures or talk to his friend Rod, Chris is most often seen wandering with his camera strapped over his shoulder. The Armitages' neighbor, Jim Hudson, the one who wins the auction for Chris's body at the annual party, wants Chris's eyes more than any other part of him because Chris's camera is an "extension" of himself and his talent for photography (Cruz). Hudson admits early on that he had submitted his own photos to *National Geographic* fourteen times before bitterly realizing he "didn't have the eye" Chris possesses. His blindness, a result of genetic disease, left him, as he says, "sitting in the dark" in a physical limitation that augments his mental lack of finesse with the camera.

Hudson does not "give a flip about what race [Chris] is;" the only thing he focuses on is the body part needed to become famous. The compliments he gives Chris about his photography, calling it "brutal" and "melancholic," are not given in the spirit of admiration but out of jealousy. Like characters in other narratives discussed in this book, Hudson, as an adult, remains out of touch with contemporary issues and concerns of young people, particularly when it comes to race. As a consumer of Chris's eyes, he has no desire to evaluate or analyze the methods used by the Armitages to enslave black people; rather, he wants to purchase his goods and go.

As Cruz reminds us, even the expositional shots of the movie focus on Chris's photography before they reveal Chris himself. Chris's shots of the New York neighborhoods reveal an attention to the body as well, since one of the first black and white photos is of a round, pregnant black belly. In this instance, however, Chris does not seek to strip his subject of her body but rather to honor her life, for Chris recounts several times that he was raised by a single mother, whom he regretfully lost at an early age. Likewise, the photos in Chris's Brooklyn apartment show an attention to detail that comes partly from a need to be observant as he navigated the world without a father's protection. Zadie Smith argues that these opening shots of Chris's art suggest that he grew up within or near a housing project "where black folk hang out on sun-warmed concrete, laughing, crying, living, surviving." This world, Smith argues, is meant to be a contrast to the shots of the forest surrounding New York City, where Chris will visit Rose's family and discover how black bodies are being exploited for personal gain. Chris's photography honors his past experiences and the community in which he was raised: his view of people reveals an appreciation for the bodies he has encountered.

However, this respect for life does not render Chris naïve. His photographer's eye usually helps protect him from the world at large because he is hyperaware of his surroundings. Of his own childhood and its connection to his vision as director, Peele explains, "I grew up in New York. Single mother. Latchkey kid. I had time on my hands—time to imagine what was hiding in all the crevices of New York City" (Claude 92). Indeed, most Generation X children had time to explore their own neighborhoods in the 1980s because screened life was not a reality yet (and because most latchkey kids looked after themselves for long periods of time). However, the label's efficacy stops here. Peele suggests that his vision was honed in a way that protected him and his mother from possible harm. Rather than enjoy exploring or climbing or treasure hunting, Peele imagined the opposite in the terrain: the ways in which new, unexplored places could endanger his small family of two. Likewise, writer and scholar Te-Nehisi Coates describes how vision and the eyes in particular are important to keeping the black body safe. When meeting a new friend in Paris for dinner and worrying about his safety as he followed the man on a tour of the city, Coates would lament that his eyes stood between him and his ability to enjoy himself fully, even in a city known for its beauty and romantic vistas:

> And the entire time he was leading me, I was sure he was going to make a quick turn into an alley, where some dudes would be waiting to strip me of . . . what exactly? But my new friend simply showed me the building, shook my hand. . . . And watching him walk away, I felt that I had missed part of the experience because of my eyes, because my eyes were made in Baltimore. . . .
>
> (126)

Coates's reference to his eyes being "made in Baltimore" hints at past struggles to survive in a difficult neighborhood with limited resources. Likewise, Chris's eyes are made in New York City, far from the stretches of forest that cover the rest of the state. This fact is a problem in Chris's case because the Armitages and those similar to them are able to conduct their activities far from neighbors and crowded streets that would expose their wrongdoings. In venturing forth to the country, Chris's eyes can only accomplish so much, since the horrors he witnesses with Rose's family have no precedent in his urban life; however, Chris is observant enough to remain paranoid and on guard throughout his stay at the Armitages'.

Sadly, he trusts Rose and refuses to abandon his partner until it is almost too late. Indeed, Smith explains that "the white man in the forest" is far more sinister in this film than "the black man in the city." Chris's fears come to light when he, like Howard Stevenson's son, must figure out how to avoid over-reacting and under-reacting in this isolated setting. He errs on the side of under-reaction due to his misplaced devotion to Rose, although the camera becomes an important tool for his continued survival.

Chris later uses the camera on his smartphone to break the hypnosis that Missy Armitage has used on other black victims. In this case something digital stands between him and escape rather than something analog, although he is also skilled at using analog materials to defend himself. Chris's first attempt with the camera is inadvertent since he wishes to photograph Logan (Andre) and send the picture to Rod for investigation. Chris insists that he recognizes Logan from another place but cannot recall where. However, as soon as the phone's camera flashes, Logan/Andre panics and screams at Chris to "get out," thereby revealing the source of the film's title. In this moment Rose's mother leads Andre away to reinforce her powers of suggestion through hypnosis. Additionally, in the movie's conclusion, Chris uses the phone again to trigger Walter, Rose's grandfather in a black body, to awareness, and the technique once again works. However, as soon as Walter defends Chris from Rose by shooting her, he also shoots himself, unable to live with the way his body has been manipulated by others. By disposing of himself rather than waiting for others to dispose of him, Walter regains a small amount of agency in choosing not to live in a world where people are collected and imprisoned.

Unplugging Popular Culture in *Get Out*

Most of the narrative features the manipulation of analog objects by those who wish Chris harm. Carol Clover, a prominent scholar in the field of gender studies and horror, has explained that most evildoers in horror are what she calls "pretechnological" to begin with: "The preferred weapons of the killer are knives, hammers, axes, ice picks, hypodermic needles, red hot pokers, pitchforks, and the like" (31). In the case of the Armitage family, a letter opener, tea cup, brain saw, and lacrosse bat are just some of the objects that stand between Chris and freedom. The operating table, used to complete the transplant between Chris and Hudson, is even surrounded by candles, despite the presence of precision tools and advanced technology. Clover uses the term "pretechnological," but the word analog might also apply here. Without objects whose weight and clunkiness determine the impact of their feasibility as weapons, Chris would be unable to save himself.

Although Clover is referring to the slasher subgenre of horror, *Get Out* shares some tropes with that type of film. Jordan Peele has commented that the opening sequence where Jeremy kidnaps Dre is inspired by John Carpenter's slasher film *Halloween*, since a seemingly innocent and neighborly suburb such as Evergreen Hallow contains hidden dangers and menacing figures (Mendelson; Glaude). Dre even refers to the landscape as a "creepy, confusing ass suburb" where street names like Edgewood Way and Edgewood Lane confuse the GPS. It is worth noting that Jeremy, who does attack and trap Dre after trailing him in the car, is wearing a mask just like famous slasher villains such as Michael Meyers and Jason Voorhees. In the film's second act Jim Hudson paints Jeremy with this same brush when he later comments, with a sinister chuckle, that Jeremy's "wrangling method" of kidnapping people is more threatening than Rose's.

Indeed, *Get Out* subverts the more romantic connotations of unplugging from society. Chris's smartphone, which he frequently uses to seek his best friend's advice about the strange events and to protect himself from Walter in a concluding scene, continues to get unplugged in a sinister attempt to cut him off completely from the outside world. Each time he charges the phone on Rose's bedside table, the housekeeper Georgina (ruled by Rose's grandmother's consciousness) purposefully removes it from the electric socket. In this case the act of unplugging is no comfort; instead it leads to isolation and abuse rather than creativity. Chris finds himself unable to communicate with Rod when his life is in jeopardy. Rod, hearing only Chris's voice mail, must solve the mystery of his disappearance.

As Rod takes care of Sid the dog in Chris's apartment, the audience sees Rod drawing on a sheet of paper, making notes about Rose's family. Rod has already shown that he thinks creatively in an early scene when he tells Chris that he believes the "next 9/11" will be caused by the "geriatric" community. Reprimanded at work for "patting down an old lady," Rod, as a TSA agent, insists that a terrorist body could look like anyone, not just brown or black skinned bodies. His willingness to observe all details and people makes him an asset at his job. The reference to the old lady, while meant to be comic relief, is also important to the later discovery that Rose's grandfather is responsible for destroying the lives of innocent black men. Rod is correct that the oldest generations are responsible at least for the domestic terror they wreak on black people's lives. The opening scene of the disturbing orientation film about the Coagula experiments shows an elderly gentleman, Roman Armitage, with his hands outstretched, asking, "Is there anything more beautiful than a sunrise?" In Roman's mind, the experiments are a way to start over, a reincarnation of sorts that allows them more time to be with family. This is why the elderly members of the Order of the Coagula, afraid to confront their own mortality, are most responsible for the horrid experimentation that renders black people helpless through possession. When sitting in Chris's apartment with the dog Sid, watching television, Rod even hears a commercial that states that "millions of Americans feel the effects of aging" and begins to move with purpose and concern at that very moment.

What Rod uncovers reveals another truth about how the Armitages choose their victims. Each kidnapped man or woman has a special talent that might be exploited for their community's personal gain. When Chris uses a search engine to uncover information about Andre Hayworth, titles of news articles abound that say "Brooklyn native goes missing" and "family outraged that search is cancelled." Titles also reveal that Andre is a jazz musician and that he disappears in a place called Evergreen Hallow. A later scene cuts to Rod talking to members of the police force and explaining that the community of Evergreen Hallow has been "abducting black people, brainwashing 'em, and making 'em work as sex slaves." Because the police officers predictably laugh off Rod's ideas and refuse to take them seriously, he returns to Chris's apartment to solve the problem alone. On a piece of paper, he draws the name Armitage in a circle and makes what appears to be a concept map with different observations on it. He records the exact times of Chris's texts, branches of the Armitage family tree, and places question marks near the words "black people." This analog representation fuels his belief that Chris's life is in danger. With the laptop, phone, and tablet, Rod shows his versatility in researching the disappearances for which the Armitages are responsible. His commentary on the geriatric community has been proven true.

In this film analog life is directly related to embodiment and the threat to the black human body. It is also related to the dissolution of the body's boundaries against its will. The "stuff" in this text, however, does manage to save the protagonist at key points in the narrative but only because technology has been denied him. The entire story bases itself in the outmoded and outdated nature of things: we see a 1970s style television play a significant role in the Armitage basement, we hear frequent references to older generations and preserving them at all cost, and even an old-fashioned tea time ritual becomes significant as it is manipulated by Rose's mother. Music from the 1930s in Jeremy's car and references to Roman's failure at the 1936 Olympics remain central to the plot as well.

On another note, Peele uses race to subvert the traditional haunted house trope: most haunted residences have rotten floors and crumbling rooftops, but the horror in this film comes from the clean and groomed world of white upper class suburban life where horrors are hidden in a game room downstairs, one filled with sports equipment typical of traditional upper class families (lacrosse, dart board, bocce, foosball, ping pong). Peele explains his choice accordingly: "Many horror films go to the depth of dirty, seedy, filthy Gothic horror. I'm much more drawn to films that explore a beautiful, disarmingly attractive aesthetic. That's why I wanted to set the movie in this idyllic Northeastern-y home" (Glaude 92). Peele's comment, although not directly related to the 1982 broken windows theory of George Kelling, speaks to the now culture-wide belief that where neighborhoods fail to offer a pleasing aesthetic, crime and horror will soon follow. In his book *Nobody*, Marc Lamont Hill would take American cultural studies to task for unquestioningly believing in Kelling's research that the presence of a broken window would likely correlate to crime in a given neighborhood. This "broken windows policing," Hill argues, is one way that contemporary law enforcement officials "arrest the vulnerable" rather than seek concrete issues to societal problems (54–55). In *Get Out*, the lack of broken windows or signs of crime do not matter; instead, the seemingly "idyllic" setting, as Peele himself calls it, masks a horror much more frightening than petty theft or vandalism. The beauty of the Armitage property not only demonstrates the amount of wealth Rose's family possesses; it also acts as a brilliant smokescreen for racism and slavery of kidnapped victims.

Like other horror movies that depict serial deaths and disappearances, the danger here may begin in the outside environment, where Dean hosts his party and his auction on the lawn, but its force grows more insidious, as the horror trope would say, from *inside* the house. The mounted deer head on the game room's wall, the assortment of balls and bats, and the polished wood columns that display antiques all remind the audience that this space is defined by the philosophy of a sinister form of play, or game activity. In creating a space that reflects this kind of visual, Peele also toys with the audience's ideas of what racism looks like. He explains, "We have this association of the monsters of racism being a certain type. Being a Klan member. Being a Nazi. Being a vicious, outwardly violent, murderous police officer. They are the monsters, but in categorizing them as such, I think we often lose sight of the demon of racism" (93). The film demonstrates that such demonic energy need not stick to the most outward displays of monstrous behavior but may also "fester," as Peele says, in places where people pretend to be liberal and open-minded but "are not in touch with their inner racism" (93). The basement, which has been closed off due to "black mold," is actually the site where victims prepare for their enslavement by watching a video, being subject to hypnosis, and receiving intravenous fluids.

This game room plays a central role in the second act of the film. No one enters this space until Missy hypnotizes Chris and he is hauled downstairs to become part of the family's medical experiment. The décor of this basement, as previously stated, looks like a twentieth century game room more than a twenty-first century one due to the references to sports and hunting, yet there is camera and microphone access. Chris notices, with great trepidation, that the analog television has been repurposed to serve as one of these cameras so that the black person held in the basement may communicate with the white people who have bought the rights to his body. As Jim Hudson explains, the operation in which Chris's consciousness is traded for Jim's depends largely on their "mutual understanding" of how the transplantation will occur.

However, the central premise of the Coagula, the secret order to which the Armitages belong, is to meld different conscious minds so that one may ultimately control the other. In other words, while we often define analog in terms of its bulk or physicality, the operation that allows Jim to take control of Chris strips him of any boundaries that exist between him and another self-seeking mind. Americanist Bill Brown has explained how the surrealist artist preoccupies him or herself with trying to break down traditional barriers between words and things. However, the Armitage family in *Get Out* uses such surrealist moments for destructive purposes. Each moment of manipulation that uses words also employs an object to act as what Mrs. Armitage refers to as a "focal point" to guide someone into Phase One of the Coagula, a state of "heightened sensibility." She first uses a tea cup and silver spoon to remind Chris of his mother's death and his feelings of helplessness from the memory. The loss of Chris's mother prompts him to develop a nurturing approach to the things he loves: he even tells Rod, who acts as dog-sitter, to avoid giving Sid the dog food because he has Irritable Bowel Syndrome. Missy exploits this weakness when the spoon and cup then become tools used to provoke trauma rather than creation. While Beca's cup in *Pitch Perfect*, as analyzed in Chapter 1, expands her ability to produce analog sound out of found objects, Mrs. Armitage's use of the cup reinforces existing methods of control over both humans and capital.

In a pivotal scene after Chris discovers the truth about the Armitages, he is held prisoner and made to watch a family video where Roman, Rose's grandfather, reveals the new method by which neurosurgeons may render black bodies helpless and give white bodies extended lives. He refers to this technique as the "coagula," a term usually meant to suggest a congealed or soft mass of substance whose parts no longer hold any individual characteristics. His pronouncement, "Behold the Coagula!" in the family video is chilling; Chris now realizes his body is only part of a larger mass, or larger project, that the Armitages have devised to dissolve boundaries between people and their various parts. In the orientation film an elderly Roman Armitage explains, "You have been chosen for the physical advantages you have enjoyed your entire lifetime. With your natural gifts and our determination, we could both be part of something greater. Something perfect. The Coagula procedure is a man-made miracle." Unlike a cassette tape or zine magazine à la *13 Reasons Why*, a coagula does the opposite of analog technology: it dissolves all physical borders and glitches until there is nothing left but shapeless matter.

Collecting Souvenirs and Black Bodies

Although Peele uses materiality in new ways to describe the black experience, other cultural commentary exists through which to analyze the characters' actions. In *Get Out* the word materiality often suggests a descent into greed and accumulation of wealth, the same kind Madonna sings about in her 1980s song "Material Girl," a song referenced in the Introduction of this book. As Robert Cluley and Stephen Dunne have explained, "Commodity narcissism, in short is more than a desire to have—it is a desire to have at the expense of others" (253). In my previous research on the habit of urbex, or urban exploration, I found that zine writer and famous urban explorer Ninjalicious, appearing to make an anti-consumer argument, discusses the habits of people (often male, white middle class) who seek abandoned buildings and other off-road settings to maximize their excitement in a version of a live action video game. The zine writer mentions that urban exploration has been popular with the middle class because they have been privileged enough to have been "raised in a world built around gift shops" (20). Such privilege leads people to find true adventure elsewhere, perhaps in a series of tunnels underground or within the walls of someone's foreclosed home. Although people of color must worry about being stopped and frisked by police intent on preventing broken windows, white people may explore abandoned buildings and vacant properties without fear of punitive damage. Kelling's original article about policing practices in neighborhoods speaks to this concern:

> We might agree that certain behavior makes one person more undesirable than another but how do we ensure that age or skin color or national origin or harmless mannerisms will not also become the basis for distinguishing the undesirable from the desirable? How do we ensure, in short, that the police do not become the agents of neighborhood bigotry?

The subsequent three decades have not offered any solutions to Kelling's original question.

Additionally, a desire to escape the gift shop mentality, while creative and exciting in spirit, often results in what some people would label an exploitation of the working class and their failures to survive the Great Recession. Someone else's poverty becomes someone else's amusement park or photo op in their leisurely pursuit of entertainment. The urban explorer is not too different from the Armitage family. Dean says he wants to experience other people's cultures, but he does so by collecting souvenirs and showing them off in his home (more on this later). The Armitages and their neighbors believe that offering black people a chance to become part of their community is a privilege, even if it means stripping them of their conscious state of living.

Another angle of materiality that requires attention is the focus on nonwhite perspectives of how humans and nonhumans interact. David Grant argues that in most studies of materiality we return, time and again, to the white, European gaze. I would extend this description by adding upper middle class to the descriptors of such a gaze. After all, collectors of analog objects like typewriters, tea cups, wooden carvings, and rotary phones must have the income to spend on building such collections. To be able to indulge in analog culture, a person has to be able to afford it. For example, owning a record player in 2018 makes a statement not only about how I enjoy my music but also about how I can finance different methods of enjoying it. With this in mind, the use of analog tools has even been associated with hipsterism, a movement in which youth work to appear less susceptible to consumer trends while still affirming their desire for consumer approval (more on this in the Conclusion).

To collect is to have disposable income, and the materials the Armitages amass are proof of such financial excess. Still, it is not just fictional characterizations that are at fault. Scholars of materiality, those who would have us peek behind the curtain of how nonhuman and human agents encounter each other, often neglect the rhetorics of indigenous and black people even when such groups have *always* considered nonhumans important and agential to life. Rhetorician David Grant explains in his research how the Sioux Indian nation uses objects like a pipe, or chanupa, to bring people into the "communal or social nature" of an act of "prayer" (70). Such objects unite the community in a positive manner. However, most scholarship about materiality spends little time on such nonwhite traditions, opting instead to view ontology and material through what some consider a colonial mindset (see Todd). To recall and rethink a former example from this book's Introduction, we might consider the idea of glitch art. Put simply, glitch art is a version of art in which artists capture the technological glitches of digital and analog devices. While nonwhite, working class people might view a glitch or malfunctioning computer as an extra financial burden, those of us with money can indulge in it and repurpose it as art. The lack of stress, or stress, over a glitch separates the haves from the have nots. It creates a form of high culture that marginalized and working class people cannot enjoy in a similar way.

If such indulgence is taken to extremes, these products of culture become weapons in the hands of the elite. Objects in *Get Out* are often used as weapons against those who possess little power. Ceremonies of connecting and amalgamating resources occur in *Get Out*'s fictional settings, but their use is always about subordinating the will of the black person to the white consciousness, to something referred to in sinister terms as the Coagula. Peele, therefore, has an opportunity to not only comment on how white privilege and its associated ignorance may sabotage black agency but also to show how the materials belonging to whites are used to manipulate others rather than connect them authentically. Consider, for example, how china cups and silver teaspoons might signal an afternoon ritual, albeit an upper middle class one, of tea time during which people gather to talk and relax after a day of business. Instead, Missy Armitage uses a tea cup to render Chris and others before him submissive to her demands. At no point do we see her enjoy the tea with a community of others (except her husband); rather, this object has been weaponized in this particular narrative to trap black victims.

Additionally, Dean and his family wish to transcend material limitations in order to avoid weakness or death. Dean, standing next to the family fireplace, just before Chris is attacked, makes the statement that fire is "a reflection of our mortality. We're born, we breathe, and we die. Even the sun will die someday. But we are divine. We are the gods trapped in cocoons." Thus the Order of the Coagula is built around subverting natural processes of life and death by finding an additional cocoon or body through which to sustain their consciousness. If the Armitages and their neighbors are, as Dean says, gods, then something must be done to ensure their continued presence. Something must also be done to ensure that they have the resources to create a new world in which they remain the ultimate stewards of culture, knowledge, and medicine. This means that even the natural world must bow down to them. When Chris and Rose recount their story of hitting a deer on their way to the Armitage home, Dean says, "I say one down, a couple hundred thousand to go." The deer, he explains, are "taking over" and "destroying the ecosystem" of the region. Even Rose, when hearing the deer cry in pain after the accident, does not show any remorse. To members of the Order of Coagula, the deer are simply an expendable unit in the Great Chain of Being that culminates in human supremacy and its triumph over death. This belief makes the climax of the film a form of poetic justice since, in order to defend himself, Chris will escape the Armitage house by taking a mounted deer head and stabbing Dean with the antlers.

Early scholarship about materiality would gesture toward the problematic nature of defining things in relation to capital. Brown's "thing theory" in relation to literature contains this observation:

> [T]he word things holds within it a more audacious ambiguity. It denotes a massive generality as well as particularities, even your particularly prized possessions. . . . It functions to overcome the loss of other words or as a place holder for some future specifying operation: "I need that thing you use to get at things between your teeth."
>
> (4)

While Brown's examples come mainly from literary analysis, the description above reminds us that when things are accumulated rather than respected (as agents in their own right) the human in the scenario colonizes, captures, or controls the flow of capital in her or his midst. Things become trivial props instead of important catalysts for character transformation. The goal in collecting things becomes a contest of who finds the most treasure.

Dean Armitage, Rose's father, is the prime example of the collector, or tourist, who displays his souvenirs for all to see. When Rose and Chris enter the house, Dean immediately takes Chris on a tour to show off his collections and to brag about his past experiences. When he motions to some wooden figures he picked up in Bali, Dean says, "Pretty eclectic. I'm a traveler and I can't help it. I keep bringing souvenirs back. It's such a privilege to experience another person's culture." Chris nods and then finds Dean gesturing to photographs of his ancestors on the walls. He tells Chris that Dean's father, an athlete, failed to qualify for the 1936 Olympics due to Jesse Owens's talent, something he "almost got over." Dean then reminisces, "Hitler's up there with all this perfect Aryan race bullshit. This black dude comes along and proves him wrong in front of the entire world." Dean consistently references black culture and people as he and Chris walk around the grounds. Photos of ancestors, maps of North and South America, and mounted hunting trophies abound in the Armitage home, which calls to mind a colonial mindset. For Dean black people are part of his collection, but Chris does not know this yet. Dean's line—"My mother loved her kitchen, so we keep a piece of her in here"—later becomes significant since the black housekeeper Georgina now serves as a vessel for Dean's mother after death.

The black body as a vessel or object receives frequent attention in Peele's script. When the movie begins, the audience watches a shirtless Chris shave his face as the mirror in the apartment steams up. As this is happening, we see Rose with her nose pressed against the glass in a bakery, looking with interest at the baked goods she selects for herself and Chris. Our first views of both characters, then, are couched in the imagery of bodies and consumer goods. Marc Lamont Hill argues that boys like Trayvon Martin, Tamir Rice, and Michael Brown and other victims of "State-sanctioned violence" were "killed because they belong to a disposable class for which one of the strongest correlates is being Black" (28). Chris, having escaped poverty in adulthood after being raised by a single mother who died when he was eleven, is mostly protected by such violence until he travels with Rose to her family's home. There the idea of a disposable Black body prevails in subsequent horror, even if Rose's father claims he would have voted for Obama a "third term" and Rose refuses to let a local policeman interrogate Chris due to his color. As Ta-Nehisi Coates has explained, "In America, it is traditional to destroy the black body—it is *heritage*." He goes on to say, "Disembodiment is a kind of terrorism, and the threat of it alters the orbit of all our lives and, like terrorism, this distortion is intentional" (103, 114). Whether Rose's family is liberal or conservative is, in fact, beside the point. All of America, as Coates articulates, is complicit in ignoring and even facilitating the destruction of black bodies over hundreds of years.

Although the basement plays a large role in this film, so does the back lawn where the Armitages host their party guests. As Chris receives a tour of the property from Dean, Dean refers to the large lawn as the "piece de resistance" and the "field of play," as if surveying his kingdom as landowner over all he sees. He takes care to mention that the property is located in "total privacy" because the nearest house is "across the lake." As they walk out on the grass, Dean gestures to Walter, a black man who acts as groundskeeper, and stresses that while it may be a cliché to have black people working on a white man's property, he thinks of Walter as family since he and Georgina took care of his parents when they were ill. He mentions that "we couldn't bear to let them go," which suggests, on one literal level, that they did not want their servants to endure unemployment. On another level, the notion of not being able to let them go also implies that the collector must hoard the things that bring him pleasure. As Chris approaches both Walter and Georgina at different times, they respond in robotic fashion to his questions and comments. Their smiles appear frozen as if the expression does not belong there. This objectification reflects what Jean Baudrillard says: that the best kind of object "is ideal in that it reflects images not of what is real, but only of what is desirable. In short, it is like a dog reduced to the single aspect of fidelity." What makes the objectification of humans so desirable is that, as Baudrillard continues, we are "able to gaze on [them] without [them] gazing back on [us]" (11). Quoting Maurice Rheims, Baudrillard also refers to collecting as "a game played with utter passion" (9).

When Dean describes the upcoming party, he mentions that it was an excuse for his father to host all of his friends for sports like badminton and bocce ball. This description makes the property literally one of "play" since such activities take place on the lawn. The main game, however, is the competition for Chris's body, which all the guests entertain as they scrutinize his appearance. When Chris attends the party, several guests refer directly to Chris's form, as if he is, as his best friend Rod characterizes, "on display." Gordon, an elderly man, asks Chris to pose for him in a golfing stance. The audience discovers later that Gordon has weak hips and that he is hoping to replace them with stronger muscles from another body. The guest Lisa also admires Chris's physique in a more sexual manner, stroking his chest and arm muscles and asking Rose if the rumors about black men are true (regarding their status as good lovers). The audience later understands that she is hoping to purchase an able-bodied black person to host her paralyzed husband, who is wheelchair bound. Another male guest at the party notes that in today's world "black is in fashion" and white is no longer the popular color in society.

However, this focus on competition and collecting remains part of other scenes that take place indoors. Even the heterosexual Jeremy, Rose's brother, makes much of Chris's body the night before the party, telling him that with "his genetic makeup" and "frame" he could achieve greatness in any sport he wished. His hungry gaze grows more intense as he drinks the wine his parents provide at dinner and asks Chris if he likes mixed martial arts. Jeremy wants Chris to stand so that they may wrestle, but Chris refuses. Jeremy references acts of competition and gamesmanship at the table, describing the art of jiu jitsu, where, as he says, strength is less important than being "strategic" in one's attack and remaining "two, three, four moves ahead" of one's opponent just like in a game of chess. When Chris becomes trapped in the Armitage house, Jeremy is also holding a lacrosse bat to block his exit at the door, and he uses it against Chris until Missy manages to incapacitate him with her powers of hypnotic suggestion. Sports like badminton and lacrosse, typically associated with white, upper class players, remain a staple of those scenes that take place in or around the Armitage home. Some of this obsession with sports may stem from the grandfather Roman's anger over losing to Jesse Owens: indeed, Walter, who is the host for the grandfather's conscience, still practices running late at night, something that frightens Chris when he steps outside to smoke a cigarette the first night.

Although Chris's body receives enough explicit comment, it also receives its fair share of sly concerns from others. Rose and her parents both make disparaging remarks about Chris's smoking habits—Rose throws the cigarettes out the window as they drive to her parents' house, and Missy later offers to hypnotize Chris and make him stop this "dangerous" habit. Although Chris claims he is quitting, Dean and Missy feel that the smoking defiles the body they are interested in acquiring. When Jeremy pulls Chris downstairs after he passes out, Missy complains that Jeremy should be careful since he has "already damaged him enough." The reference calls to mind the moving of a piece of furniture without nicking the corners: the Armitages are obsessed with keeping Chris in pristine condition, even as he becomes their prisoner.

Rose herself has a history of collecting parts of bodies in a literal sense. Brother Jeremy teases her at the dinner table about her own previous childhood collection of toenails that she kept in a jewelry box. In a similar box, Rose hides photographs of her previous ties to Georgina and the man, photos that alert Chris to her possible involvement in the strangeness surrounding the Armitage party. After aiding her family in capturing Chris, she searches for the family's next black body online, and the audience watches her scroll through athlete head shots and statistics, all while snacking on Fruit Loops and drinking milk. Rose also makes an interesting list of reminders for Chris when he packs to go away with her. She asks him if he has packed his "comfy clothes," his deodorant, and his toothbrush, items that most people would pack when going away to a hospital.

During Rose's search for her next victim, the camera zooms out to reveal pictures of at least eight or more victims she has met in the past. Although these photos were not on the wall when Chris was staying in her room, they have been mounted and serialized for her to revel in once her family traps him in the game room. Baudrillard would also refer to this kind of collecting in a specific way: such collecting results in what he refers to as "limitless substitution and play" that resembles the gathering of a "harem." The "charm" of such a collection, according to Baudrillard, "lies in its being at once a series bounded by intimacy . . . and an intimacy bounded by seriality" (10). Rose states that Chris was "one of [her] favorites" as he falls under hypnosis, thereby granting him what she would consider a special place in her collection.

Control of the natural environment has often been linked to control of the bodies within that space, and Rose's parents, along with most of the supporting cast, are experts in control and exploitation of the black people they objectify. Indeed, even the deer head mounted in the game room holds special connotations to race. As A. M. Stanley reminds us, the gender of the deer is important. Another name for a male deer is buck, and this word, in the 1800s and early 1900s, served a racial epithet that "described black men who refused to acquiesce to white authority figures and were considered a menace to white America." In this sense, the mounted head in the game room reminds the imprisoned Chris that his role in the Armitage home is to become a trophy just like the animal (Stanley). However, as Stanley notes, Dean's death at the hands of Chris upends this natural order. By stabbing Dean with the antlers from the buck, the black man in this narrative uses the racialized object against the collector who tamed and mounted it.

Conclusion

The auction illustrates how the people at the Armitage party see Chris as a thing to be bought and sold. His black body, on display for all to see, must dissolve and be made part of "something greater" in order to fulfill a white community's desires. Chris escapes mainly because he defends his physical form with objects collected and displayed by those who would brainwash him. Additionally, he weaponizes his own smartphone to shock other black victims into exercising free will and defying their captors. Materiality shows how Chris's experience as an artist becomes a terrifying one because his ability to create is coveted by someone in an older generation who has faced rejection time and again. Yet he is not the only one who falls victim to this jealousy: Dre's own youth and talent as a jazz musician make him a valuable addition to a white upper class household. Members of the younger generation in this film have talent to work with both digital and analog materials, yet the Armitages would use such talent as a way to make their own community prosperous and immortal. The entire landscape of materiality in *Get Out* reinforces how manipulative people may be when they see the physical world as theirs to control and own.

Rod's own ability to see through the guise of elderly innocence (patting down the elderly plane passenger at the start of the narrative) later helps Chris to escape his circumstances. As a TSA agent, Rod knows that older adults have the ability to exploit or terrorize the young, even if he expresses such thoughts in a humorous fashion. The allusion to terrorism at Rod's job makes sense as the movie progresses: all three black men—Dre, Rod, and Chris—witness the terror that results from having the black body hijacked by the white one. Of course, they are not alone: Georgina and Walter, two black bodies taken hostage by Rose's grandparents, remain trapped in a world where they are only "passengers" of their own existence. However, the story reveals little background information on either of them, perhaps reinforcing the notion of them as plot devices or props to the larger message of terror.

Although materiality and unplugged life receive the horror genre treatment in this chapter, they still, despite their dark manifestations here, prompt us to think about how we encounter the physical world in the light of day. Rather than simply reiterate how young people navigate between digital and analog devices, the story of *Get Out* challenges the audience to consider how race and class shape human motivations just as often as generational cohorts do. Scenes from *Get Out* do highlight differences in generational philosophies, but the Armitages in particular demonstrate how family greed overrides such differences. Rose, like her grandfather before her, sees Chris as a part of her collection of bodies. Although young and worldly in her upbringing, Rose conserves the values of the white cult in which she belongs rather than challenges the status quo. Likewise, Jeremy uses violence to support his family's goals of making the Order of Coagula service available to more people than just his relatives. In several interviews Allison Williams, the actress who plays Rose, has been questioned about her character in the film. White viewers in particular, she says, are eager to find out if Rose, too, is being brainwashed just like the black victims. Her response and Jordan Peele's response have been consistent: Rose embodies the same evil that her parents and grandparents do. She is neither a victim nor an unwilling participant in what happens to Chris.

This news is not comforting if we adopt the perspective that young people are always helping us broaden our perspectives, particularly when it comes to materiality and creativity. In this particular tale, Rose reverses time to support an oppressive system of tradition and privilege. To recoup positive thoughts about Generation Z we might shift our focus to the young black men in this narrative; however, such men cannot offer a way forward without the white community admitting that we are far from post-racial or color blind in our views of the world. Only an elderly man like Jim Hudson is blind enough to suggest that the Coagula has nothing to do with color.

References

Alexander, Michelle. *The New Jim Crow: Mass Incarceration in the Age of Colorblindness*. New Press, 2012.

Baudrillard, Jean. "The System of Collecting." *The Cultures of Collecting*, edited by John Elsner and Roger Cardinal. London: Reaktion Books Ltd., 1994, pp. 7–24.

Brown, Bill. "Thing Theory." *Critical Inquiry*, vol. 28, no. 1, Autumn, 2001, pp. 1–22.

Chang, Justin. "Jordan Peele's Clever Horror-satire 'Get Out' Is an Overdue Hollywood Response to Our Racial Anxiety." 23 Feb. 2017, www.latimes.com/entertainment/movies/la-et-mn-get-out-review-20170223-story.html#nt=oft03a-1la1.

Claude Jr., Eddie S. "Interview: The Artist's Mind." *Time Magazine*, 26 Feb. 2018, pp. 90–3.

Coates, Ta-Nehisi. *Between the World and Me*. Speigel & Grau, 2015.

Cruz, Lenika. "In Get Out, the Eyes Have It." *The Atlantic*, 3 Mar. 2017, www.theatlantic.com/entertainment/archive/2017/03/in-get-out-the-eyes-have-it/518370/.

Grant, David M. "Writing Wakan: The Lakota Pipe as Rhetorical Object." *College Composition & Communication*, vol. 69, no. 1, Sept. 2017, pp. 61–86.

Hill, Marc Lamont. *Nobody: Casualties of America's War on the Vulnerable, From Ferguson to Flint and Beyond*. Simon and Schuster, 2016.

Kelling, George L., and James Q. Wilson. "Broken Windows: The Police and Neighborhood Safety." *The Atlantic; 160 Years of Atlantic Stories*, Mar. 1982, www.theatlantic.com/magazine/archive/1982/03/broken-windows/304465/.

Mendelson, Scott. "Jordan Peele Talks 'Get Out' and His Love for Horror Movies." *Forbes*, 5 Oct. 2016, www.forbes.com/sites/scottmendelson/2016/10/05/interview-jordan-peele-discusses-get-out-and-his-love-for-the-horror-genre/#78708409187e.

Peele, Jordan. "Academy Award Acceptance Speech." *YouTube*, 4 Mar. 2018, www.youtube.com/watch?v=pLjpRA1RF6c.

Sims, David. "What Made That Hypnosis Scene in Get Out So Terrifying." *The Atlantic*, 5 Dec. 2017, www.theatlantic.com/entertainment/archive/2017/12/get-out-hypnosis-scene-sunken-place/547409/.

Smith, Zadie. "Getting In and Out: Who Owns Black Pain?" *Harper's Magazine Reviews*, July 2017, https://harpers.org/archive/2017/07/getting-in-and-out/.

Stevenson, Howard C. "Dueling Narratives: Racial Socialization and Literacy as Triggers for Re-Humanizing African American Boys, Young Men, and Their Families." *Boys and Men in African American Families*, edited by Linda M. Burton et al. Springer International Publishing, 2016, pp. 55–84.

6 Solving Z for X

Extending Generational Paradigms in *Stranger Things*

Although young characters in the preceding chapters could be characterized as precocious, creative, intelligent, and resourceful, no one in these narratives quite measures up to the children in Netflix's *Stranger Things*, a 1980s era science fiction and fantasy series launched in 2016 on Netflix. Netflix renewed the show, created by the Duffer Brothers, after its first season, so two years of episodes exist now through which to analyze how young Generation X children (as they would be when the narrative occurs) echo the habits and creativity of the Generation Z young adults previously discussed. Although these young characters are born in the 1970s rather than the 1990s, the writers still promote the children's ways of thinking as unique because they move creatively from one obstacle to the next with the aid of unlikely tools. Indeed, a close up shot of one protagonist's trophies in Season One show that he and his three friends regularly win science competitions; not only do they win, but the judges have awarded them the trophy "Team Problem Solving Champions" ("Maple Street"). Such a label denotes their specific ability to communicate with one another to achieve common goals and to do so by solving mysteries and riddles others cannot.

Although the audience might not expect Generation X children, born roughly between 1965 and 1983 (Strauss and Howe), to be staring at smartphones and texting constantly, many still consider the 80s a time when children sat glued to the television, either watching Music Television (MTV), playing Atari video games, or binging movies on rented VHS tapes. David Sirocha in *Back to Our Future* reveals that the 1980s were the first decade in which most families "possessed a television, a VCR, and cable service—and nearly half had video game systems" (introduction). Indeed, most families in the 80s designed their living room furniture around the screen's placement so that hours might be spent flipping network channels if they desired. Like other characters, these children defy that stereotype in more ways than one.

The children consist of Mike (Finn Wolfhard), Lucas (Caleb McLaughlin), Dustin (Gaten Matarazzo), and Will (Noah Schnapp). Although

Figure 6.1 Vintage Portable Transceiver Radios

other young characters like the girl Max (Sadie Sink), who moves to the town of Hawkins in Season Two, and the gifted and mysterious girl named Eleven (Millie Bobby Brown) are significant, too, the team of boys mentioned above works together most often to defeat the evil forces that threaten their small Indiana town. Other supporting cast members include the parents and siblings of the four main children as well as local law enforcement in Hawkins and scientists working at Hawkins National Laboratory.

The four boys attend a public middle school where they excel in both literature and science and have caught the attention of teachers like Mr. Clarke, a mentor who encourages their various interests through the AudioVisual Club on campus. When Mr. Clarke speaks with his charges, he addresses them as peers. In conversations about middle school science, he references Carl Sagan's television program and advanced theoretical physics ("Flea and the Acrobat"). The boys are the kinds of students who have to be reminded that they may only have five books checked out from the local library at any given time. When Dustin is caught with ten books, he tells the librarian that the books are his "paddles" on his curiosity voyage and that he desperately needs his paddles ("Pollywog"). Fans of high fantasy, Mike and his friends have renamed different parts of their home town to reflect the names of regions in J. R. R. Tolkien's books about Middle Earth. Their goal in Season One is to find Will, who goes missing after a long day of Dungeons and Dragons gaming ("Vanishing").

As they search, the local police chief Jim Hopper (David Harbour) and Will's mother Joyce Byers (Winona Ryder) also canvass the area to search for answers. In doing so, they uncover the sinister experiments that the researchers at Hawkins Lab have conducted on children and how those researchers are responsible for Will's disappearance. Joyce employs creative ways to speak to Will even though he goes missing: she finds that he will communicate with her through blinking bulbs in lamps and in strings of Christmas tree lights. She also hears his voice on the landline telephone beneath the static ("Vanishing"). Likewise, Mike and Eleven (also referred to as Jane) hear Will through the static on their short-wave radio and later on the AV Club's Ham radio. These characters come to understand that Will has become trapped in a parallel universe with a monstrous creature they refer to as the Demogorgon.

Will returns by Season One's end, but his return only marks the beginning of trouble for Hawkins in Season Two, since the creatures from the other universe, which the boys term the "Upside Down," are growing in size and influence. To defeat the largest monster, a behemoth Shadow Monster (later called the Mind Flayer) with tentacles that reach throughout the Indiana countryside, the boys use traditional academic research to unravel the mystery, but they also rely on other technologies to augment their search for the truth. Mike realizes that Will's time in the Upside Down resulted in the kind of True Sight that enables him to see through an "ethereal plane" and exist in two dimensions at once. Unfortunately, Will's connection eventually leads to possession by the Shadow Monster, whose influence continues to spread.

Likewise, the rip in dimensions becomes larger until a Demogorgon army from the Upside Down escapes and begins killing. After Joyce suffers the gruesome loss of her boyfriend Bob (Sean Astin), Will's ability to connect with the Shadow Monster allows him to discover the answer to sealing the rip. Upon successfully doing so, the characters end their adventures with a Snow Ball dance at Hawkins Middle School, where most everyone is safe from the Upside Down, at least for now.

It is important to note that children of all ages in *Stranger Things*, just like in some of the previous chapters, experiment frequently with tools that have nothing to do with the analog/digital divide but rather reveal the emphasis on materiality in the narrative. Both Mike's group and Nancy, Mike's older sister (Natalia Dyer), and Jonathan, Will's older brother (Charlie Heaton), find handheld weapons to fight the monster that captured Will. Nancy and Jonathan shop for multiple weapons at the local army surplus store, where they dump bear traps, a flame thrower, lighter fluid, stakes, and a sledgehammer on the counter to purchase and then store it in the trunk of Jonathan's car ("Monster"). Nancy also prepares for battle by practicing her aim with a baseball bat ("Flea and the Acrobat"). Even Lucas finds a slingshot, something he calls his "wrist rocket," to be his most effective weapon against the monster while the adults surrounding him are firing guns ("Holly Jolly," "Upside Down"). The audience might also note that in both seasons Eleven repeatedly finds whatever tools she can to block her senses and enter the void that enables her to communicate with others from far away. In order to communicate, she uses the white noise on television and fabric to cover her eyes, thereby simulating a small version of a sensory deprivation tank. The boys even dump salt into an inflatable mini-pool to create the illusion of the tank ("The Bathtub"). These tools do not always speak to analog and digital creativity but rather to a more general bravery exhibited by those who wish to defeat the monsters from the Upside Down. However, often the two traits go hand in hand.

Therefore, the next sections examine three areas where children use tools to express themselves or compose in unlikely ways. This chapter looks carefully at the use of radio and sound, then video games and television, and finally, in greater length, Will's role as an artist. The characters' similarities to Generation Z most often fall into the categories of embracing glitches in technology rather than evading them and using a combination of contemporary and older technologies to communicate. While *Stranger Things* takes place in 1983, a year grounded mostly in analog technology, the boys in this narrative use technology that is older than the status quo for the early 1980s.

Radio and Soundscapes

While watching shows like *Dynasty* on color television in the 80s was a favorite technology and weekly ritual for nuclear families (Feuer 134–48), the writers in *Stranger Things* choose to showcase the boys frequently using radio technology, which invokes a pre-television era where narrators tell stories through a speaker. The first and most obvious example of radio usage involves walkie talkies, which Mike and his friends use to communicate with one another when separated. Mike, as president of his AV Club, who refers to his walkie as a "supercomm," often shows himself the leader in using this form of technology. When he and Lucas correspond on the radios, Mike coaches Lucas to talk in a certain way. He reminds him not to repeat his own name the way he would picking up a telephone, and he tells him to use the word "over" to signal the end of a message ("Vanishing"). The characters also develop their own language to signal danger. A particularly humorous example occurs when Dustin yells "code red" into his radio to contact Lucas. Lucas's little sister Erica picks the radio up and promptly mocks Dustin for the constant cries for help:

Dustin: Does anyone copy? This is a code red. I repeat, a code red! I really need someone to pick up here. Hopper's MIA, and I've got a code red. . . .
Erica: (picking up walkie talkie) Could you please shut up?
Dustin: Erica? Erica, is Lucas there? Where is he?
Erica: Don't know. Don't care.
Dustin: Is he with Mike?
Erica: Like I said, I don't know and don't care.
Dustin: Please tell him it's super important. Please tell him that I have a code—
Erica: Code red?
Dustin: Yep, code red. Exactly.
Erica: I got a code for you instead. It's called code shut-your-mouth.
("Dig Dug")

Only when he cannot reach his friends via radio does Dustin try the more conventional 80s approach of calling them on their home landlines. However, this form of technology is even less helpful since Mike's mother, while drinking a glass of white wine, talks to her friend Cath for over two hours on the phone, making it impossible for Dustin to break through ("Dig Dug"). Although Mrs. Wheeler may chastise the boys for playing Dungeons and Dragons for ten hours in her basement ("Vanishing"), her own use of technology shows no regard for the passage of time or the concerns of others trying to communicate through the wires.

Radio, and especially the glitches and signals accompanying its transmission, remained a central part of mass and popular culture throughout the twentieth century. Originally developed in World War II, the walkie talkie in particular allowed human voices to replace Morse code and allow two-way communication among parties ("Walkie Talkie History"). As I followed a Reddit conversation about these *Stranger Things* props and then clicked on a video link, YouTube user 7410ray shows the 1980s walkie talkie model in the show, one he purchased at a yard sale. It is a Realistic Radio TRC-214 (although Lucas has a TRC-206), which, according to the narrator of the video, is "capable of going a very far distance" and would be valuable for use even in "the event of an EMP," or electromagnetic pulse. Although the user offers no concrete evidence for these claims, this information does make some sense because the series begins with an EMP, or electromagnetic disturbance, that should have destroyed most of the tools used by characters (Joyce's telephone is "fried" as Hopper says in "Vanishing"). This particular walkie talkie model features a long antenna and, as 7410ray explains, is "very bulky" and large in appearance, a characteristic commonly applied to analog technology and especially to the 80s. As Sirocha says about the era, "Everything was big. . . . Big hair. Big defense budgets. Big tax cuts. Big shoulder pads. Big blockbuster movies" (introduction). The YouTube host also claims that such handheld radios would come in handy in a catastrophic event when other means of communication are lost. Today's "doomsday preppers," a network of people preparing for worldwide disaster situations, stock supplies like walkie talkies in case of a real electromagnetic event or nuclear fallout. The handheld radio in the case of the doomsday preppers reinforces the value of things that function in unplugged states of being.[1]

The boys' use of radio in this narrative also reverses expectations. *Stranger Things* is frequently an homage to directors and scripts of 80s cinema, which sometimes leads the audience to expect certain tropes, ones found in horror and science fiction stories told by Stephen King, Steven Spielberg, and John Carpenter, just to name a few. More specifically, the pilot script references the famous ghost movie *Poltergeist* (1982), written by Steven Spielberg and directed by Tobe Hooper. A flashback reveals that Joyce surprises Will with tickets to go see *Poltergeist* as long as he feels certain he will not suffer from nightmares, and Will promises that he no longer has this problem ("Vanishing").

For many, the film did induce nightmares of all kinds, but *Poltergeist*'s importance here in this chapter stems more from its use of technology as a motif than its capacity to scare viewers. In this film the Freeling family discovers that their house is haunted when their youngest daughter, Carol Anne, a quiet and innocent character like Will, talks to ghosts through the living room television. On several occasions, and even in the film's movie poster, the camera shows Carol Anne's body silhouetted against the screened technology, hands splayed outward as if trying to reach through the television. Carol Anne, drawn to the spirits in the television, seems glued to its contents, which again suggests the stereotype of the child who cannot look away from screens.

In the first two seasons of *Stranger Things*, the use of sound in radio and telephone transmission as opposed to television sets a different mood. Viewers must listen carefully to static through the walkie talkies and Joyce Byers's landline in order to hear Will communicate, either with discordant sets of words or through breathing. This is not to say that television and video play a nonexistent role since Joyce later finds that she can trace the Shadow Monster's shape on her screen when she watches a videotape of Will being bullied on Halloween night ("Pollywog"). Likewise, Bob (Sean Astin), Joyce's boyfriend in Season Two, often refers to video technology because he has an affinity for electronics. Eleven also uses television static similar to the kind Carol Anne experiences, only Eleven uses it for white noise rather than communication ("Dig Dug").

Still, the television hardly acts as a portal to another dimension in the same way that it does in *Poltergeist*; rather, it often appears as furniture in the background when adults are present. Even when Will does attempt to communicate after his capture by the Demogorgon, he uses the landline phone, the strings of Christmas lights, and the Heathkit Ham shack to reach out to others over the course of Season One. At no point do the adults hear his voice through the television static, but his friends and Joyce hear or see him through these older forms of technology.

Fear of radio interference, however, remains just as frightening as Carol Anne's image for some. People in the twentieth century feared that espionage or coded messages were part of radio transmissions during the Cold War era. In the 2010s articles still circulate about radio towers broadcasting "ghostly" sounds to an unknown audience (Gorvett). This has given radio technology a reputation of mystery and unpredictability. Mr. Clarke, the science teacher and sponsor of the AV Club, procures a sophisticated long-wave Heathkit Ham radio for his charges in order to show them the wonders of tuning in from greater distances across the world, even, as the boys gasp excitedly, to Australia. In order to work on what is called amateur radio, or Ham radio, users in the 1980s had to be proficient in Morse code, and Will's use of this form of transmission becomes pivotal to the action in Season Two.[2] Digital communication, as Florian Cramer explains, deals in specific amounts of information with discrete boundaries, thereby rendering something like Morse code more digital than analog. Again, the viewer sees how youth are capable of moving between digital and analog formats. The four boys even use headsets so that they may hear one another via radio while traveling by bike.

Eleven acts as a conduit for Will's voice when the boys use the Heathkit Ham shack to contact him. At this moment, the group expresses frustration when they hear snippets of Will's voice calling out to his mother for help: "It's like home, but it's so dark. It's so dark and empty. And it's cold!" As Lucas says, "The stupid radio kept going in and out," making Will's intentions unclear and his description a mystery. Rather than give up, Dustin recalls Will's words and says, "It's like riddles in the dark" ("The Body," "Flea and the Acrobat"). This reference from Tolkien's *The Hobbit* reiterates the wide reservoir of literary references the boys possess, but it also suggests something else. The idea behind riddles is that a solution exists, although finding it can be a tricky process. These characters are willing to work with the glitches that occur rather than fight them.

The Heathkit Ham radio also later becomes an object that reminds Mike of Bob Newby after he is killed by creatures from the Upside Down. Bob, a middle-aged Radio Shack manager in Hawkins, offers encouraging advice and support to both Will and his friends throughout Season Two. Upon hearing that Will has become ill, Bob brings puzzles and a Rubix cube to the house because he wants to help Will pass the time in bed. After Bob's death, Mike's glance falls on these objects and he touches the Rubix cube. He remarks, "Did you guys know that Bob was the original founder of Hawkins AV? He petitioned the school to start it and everything. Then he had a fundraiser for equipment. Mr. Clarke learned everything from him. Pretty awesome, right?" ("The Mind Flayer"). In this sense, Bob's legacy lies in that collection of equipment that Mike and his friends now use with Mr. Clarke acting as their club sponsor. Laura Tanner explains that people often cling to objects as evidence of someone's past embodiment because, as argued previously in Chapter 4, they offer "texture" and "multisensory experience[s]." When the body is lost, the object becomes a "material touchstone" that connects people to the dead (176–178).

However, soundscapes in general offer creative ways to connect human and nonhuman agents. Will explains to Mike that in the Upside Down he hears a "noise coming from everywhere," which closed captioning subtitles on Netflix characterize as "ambient rumble" ("Trick or Treat"). Will's attunement to the sounds beyond his own immediate reality deserve attention not only for their fear factor but for the unique role that attunement allows Will to play in working through, with, and against the monster's influence inside himself. While viewers may be quick to consider Will a victim in Season Two, one who loses any degree of agency he recovered when escaping the Upside Down, theorist Thomas Rickert would comment that agency never works so neatly. Indeed, Will's role as co-participant with the monster in Season Two's later episodes (to be discussed in the coming pages) reinforces the idea that humans existing in any given reality are not separate from the material world that surrounds them. Instead, "everything is intertwined and involved with everything else, twisting, changing, and coadapting: nothing is stable," and ambient sound, whether a "rumble" or a song, influences space, time, and the listener's role in both (Rickert 120).[3]

Television and Video Games

Despite the emphasis on sound, the most visible reminder of 80s technology is often the color television. *Stranger Things* includes this cultural phenomenon but often uses it as a contrast between the boys' creativity and adult complacency. As soon as the television screen loses its signal in the pilot episode, Mike's father is seen moving the antennae back and forth, hitting the machine, and dismissing it as "dang, dumb piece of junk" when it fails to work ("Vanishing"). On the other hand, no television or screen of any kind exists in the basement where Mike and his friends play Dungeons and Dragons, although plenty of radio equipment and tabletop board games do.

The basement becomes an analog haven where D and D campaigns foreshadow the larger struggles the children must face with the monsters ("Beyond Stranger Things"). Additionally, the game board itself becomes a way for Mike and Eleven to explain what Will's location means after his initial disappearance. In order to explain the Upside Down, Mike calls the top of the board Hawkins and the flip side (painted black) an alternate reality. Once the boys compare this ordinary object to the Vale of Shadows, a Dungeons and Dragons reference, they pull out binders of campaign materials and notes on locations. Their research is focused on textual and tabletop artifacts that help the boys deconstruct what it means for Will to be trapped in another dimension ("Flea and the Acrobat"). Since no maps exist to document the space where Will is, the boys must make their own model of how time and space have warped certain parts of their small town.

Additionally, Dustin's most joyous moment occurs in this basement when he links what Mr. Clarke told him about multiple dimensions in science to what is happening to the boys' compasses. Because Mr. Clarke tells them that a gate between dimensions would most likely disrupt gravity and the electromagnetic field, Dustin is the first to recognize that all of their compasses are no longer pointing "true north." This revelation leads them to form a hypothesis about the Upside Down gate's location ("Flea and the Acrobat"). Compasses, radios, research materials, and game boards in this basement all contradict the stereotype of the screen-obsessed adolescent who watches music videos all day long.

Mike and his friends also begin to recognize that they must confront the true nature of the Upside Down, where screens and lights rarely work. In the glimpses of the alternate dimension, the best descriptor of what the audience sees is a dark, apocalyptic landscape where abandoned buildings and structures pepper the horizon. Technology cannot function properly due to instability between two realities. In Season Two's premiere, Will drifts away from his friends in the arcade, as if called by an unearthly force in the Upside Down, and all of the plugged machines go dark. His only source of light is the lightning in the sky, along with a flickering, buzzing letter or two on the once bright marquee that reads "ARCADE" ("MadMax"). In this alternate dimension electricity exists only in the form of ephemeral flashes and blips.

Will's movement toward the darkness and away from the lighted spaces of the game room suggest that he is moving away from something positive and into a space of negativity, but the truth is more complicated than that. Will's departure occurs at the start of a vapid exchange among the players in the game room where his friends confront the arcade employee, Keith, who happens to know everyone's top scores and eats Cheetos while wandering aimlessly around the space. Keith's own demeanor suggests apathy and even a stoned expression as he teases Dustin, Lucas, and Mike about losing the highest score on Dig Dug to another player. When they beg him to reveal the person's identity, he only agrees if Mike will promise him a date with Nancy. This entire exchange suggests a waste of time, particularly on the part of Keith, whose refusal to share his knowledge causes Dustin to exclaim that Nancy would have nothing to do with him because he earns only $2.50 an hour ("MadMax"). The audience perceives Keith's vacant expression and lackluster personality as part of his daily life surrounded by screen technologies and junk food; on the other hand, Mike, Dustin, Lucas, and particularly Will represent the intrepid explorers able to confront the darkness beyond such machines.

Although they frequently play the video game Dig Dug, Will and Mike later resemble characters in the game who crawl beneath the earth to save their adult friend Hopper. Instead of using a game interface to simulate problem solving and adventuring, they live through the very physical act of burrowing into the earth during Season Two. Mike, Will, Bob, and Joyce forego screened technology for live action heroic behavior as they descend into the Upside Down to find their friend ("Dig Dug"). While Dig Dug remains a useful metaphor for what they do, the game remains just that—a metaphor—rather than a way of life that consumes them as it does Keith.

Although the occasional teen may be seen eating junk and staring at screens, the critique of adults remains more pointed, particularly since history often depicts Generation X parents as figures who are absent or who leave their children unsupervised for long periods of time (thereby creating the image of a latchkey on the child's neck as discussed in Chapter 1). Murray, a conspiracy theorist with whom Nancy and Jonathan speak about exposing the secrets of Hawkins Lab, summarizes most adults in this narrative with these words: "Those people. . . . They don't spend their lives trying to get a look at what's behind the curtain. They like the curtain. It provides them stability, comfort, definition" ("Dig Dug"). One of the critiques occurs when Season Two's finale opens on Mrs. Wheeler, Mike's mother (Cara Bueno), sitting in a bubble bath, engrossed in a romance novel. She has lit candles and has Barbra Streisand playing on the stereo. Meanwhile, husband Ted snores while the doorbell rings incessantly ("The Gate"). During this same time, the audience knows that her own children are in grave danger as they fight creatures from another dimension, ones intent on killing them and the rest of the town's denizens. However, they sleep and relax through any sign of suspicious activity in Hawkins rather than address the problem head on. In such cases, the television often plays in the background. Indeed, the more frequent critique of the older generation seems to center on their use of technology or screens. Although Carol Anne is the one with her hands plastered to the family television set in *Poltergeist*, the first set of hands on a living room television in *Stranger Things* are the hands of Mr. Wheeler, Mike's father, as he curses the static. Even when physically present, the audience sees parents and other adults oblivious to the needs of the young as these guardians consume television while relaxed on their La-Z-Boy recliners; Mike tells Eleven that the chair is "where my dad sleeps" ("Maple Street"). Oddly enough, Music Television only appears on one person's screen: the screen of Will's father's girlfriend Cynthia, a jaded young adult who has no sympathy for a missing boy and his distraught mother ("Maple Street"). The fact that this moment is the only one in which MTV appears is significant because, as Michael Rich explains, most teens and pre-teens were tuning in by the mid-1980s. The channel was reaching more than 27 million American homes by the middle of the decade (81–82), yet the camera never shows Mike and his friends indulging in television this way.

Television viewing is also closely associated with isolation and mental illness in this narrative. For instance, the audience sees game shows on television when Hopper and Joyce visit Eleven's mother, who suffers mental damage from her days in the MK Ultra study. This study from the 1960s caused young adults to experience adverse side effects that led to Eleven's unique powers ("The Monster"). Eleven's aunt Becky later explains, "She's just stuck, they think. Like in a dream. A long dream" ("Dig Dug"). Eleven, whose upbringing is wildly different from Mike and his friends due to her forced imprisonment in a lab, also watches television when Hopper leaves her alone in their cabin. Although she is the same age as the male protagonists, Eleven's background differs because her entire life has been spent around adults. Unlike other children in this narrative, Eleven does glue herself to the screen, but only because she has no one else with whom to communicate. Since Hopper has asked her to remain out of sight in order to avoid future capture by Hawkins Lab, Eleven spends most of her days watching soap operas and eating junk food like Eggo waffles. This feeling of isolation only ends when she moves away from the screen and begins exploring Hopper's old files of the MK Ultra case at Hawkins Lab. She finds pictures of what appears to be her mother and then decides to seek her out. Once she uses physical materials to unravel the mystery of where she comes from, she leaves the screen behind and discovers the fate of her mother and of the children who suffered with her in the lab.

In this way analog television screens become a source of mind numbing entertainment in *Stranger Things*, just as some perceive smartphone screens to be those kinds of problems in a digital age. Screens regularly point toward the negative as they represent banality in the form of Keith's constant gaming, isolation and illness in the lives of Eleven and her mother, and complete passivity in the case of parents like Mr. Wheeler. This information is damning enough, but one other example of adults and screens reveals a more sinister angle. Screens are associated with Hawkins Lab and the adult scientists who work there. When Hopper first visits the lab to investigate Will's disappearance, one employee stresses that it would be very hard for a child to go missing there since they have "over a hundred cameras" ("Holly Jolly"). Likewise, the new head of research, Dr. Owen (Paul Reiser), and his staff in Season Two monitor Will's health on a dozen television screens as Will reports the news of seeing and feeling evil outside the arcade. These same employees attempt to monitor the Upside Down with satellites, with one man even munching on snack food as he stares blankly at the transmissions from this otherworldly place ("Trick or Treat").

In sum, adults consume television passively (even when confronted with scientific or supernatural discoveries) and remain largely incapable of practicing mindful or empathetic reactions toward others. The large, unwieldy analog television becomes a piece of furniture that acts as an obstacle to normal human interaction. Mike even tells Eleven that the living room "is mostly just for watching tv" ("Maple Street"). In the final moments of Season One, Nancy, Mike's older sister, snuggles with her boyfriend Steve while Mr. Wheeler sleeps in his La-Z-Boy, a bowl of popcorn resting in his lap. This moment even more appropriately characterizes the passive parent, who remains oblivious to the events in his own children's lives. Colloquially referred to as an "idiot box" in the 80s, the television, perhaps living up to this very moniker, reinforces the lack of creativity and vision adults possess in this particular narrative. It does not, however, frame the experience of the children.

Will the Wise and Artistic Expression

Will's ability to walk away from typical technologies and into the unknown characterizes him from the start of the show. On a figurative level, Will walks away from the things other kids enjoy, thereby prompting his father and his peers to mock him for pursuing art instead of sports. Will faces pressure to conform to other notions of masculine behavior in order to appear less "queer" in the eyes of his father, but he remains steadfast in his interest in art. Jonathan explains, "He's trying to force you to like normal things. And you shouldn't like things because people tell you you're supposed to" ("Maple Street"). After his return from the Upside Down, the teasing increases as other children call him "Zombie Boy" for coming back from what appeared to be the dead. Indeed, while Lucas, Mike, and Dustin were all changed by the events of Season One's narrative, Will remains the most altered since, upon his rescue, he is now able to visualize two dimensions at once—the Upside Down and the regular world of Hawkins ("Upside Down;" "MadMax").

Despite Will's vulnerability, his friends and family remind him that there is power in being different. When Will complains that others at school call him a freak, Jonathan tells Will that being weird is the best way to navigate the world: "Do you want to be normal? Do you wanna be just like everyone else? Being a freak is the best. I'm a freak.... I would rather be best friends with Zombie Boy than with a boring nobody.... Who would you rather be friends with? Bowie or Kenny Rogers?" ("MadMax"). Jonathan and Will would both rather be Bowie likely because of his unique stage presence, writing ability, and versatility as a performer. Like many characters in this narrative, Bowie showed versatility in his career by dressing up as different characters onstage and experimenting with different types of music. As E. Ann Kaplan explains when discussing Madonna's career as a musician, part of the performative nature of music on television in the late twentieth century included stars who would change their image and character repeatedly (157). Such musicians became idols to children who were experimenting with their own identities.

Yet Will's first love is art, not music. Upon first seeing the Shadow Monster and acquiring what Mike calls "True Sight," Will explains the experience in visual terms: it is like being stuck "between two slides" on a "Viewmaster," a tool where images are advanced by a lever on a container ("Trick or Treat"). Only days later, Will finds that language cannot adequately describe what is happening when the monster attacks him. His mother suggests, "What if you didn't have to use words?" The camera abruptly cuts to Will scribbling with crayons on countless pieces of notebook papers, his gaze completely focused on the material in front of him. Will's drawing, however, one he spends hours coloring furiously at a desk, expresses information as pictures, pictures that seem unending until pieced together rather sloppily to create a map of Hawkins's underground tunnels. He draws rivers, tunnels, and connections throughout the terrain that eventually help the Hawkins citizens defeat the monster who has been killing their crops and threatening their safety. In this sense, Will taps into the "hivemind" of the creature by making the network to which he belongs a public display. Hopper and Joyce take the time to piece together the different pages until Joyce's home appears covered in art ("Will the Wise").

It is only fair to mention that Will's older brother Jonathan shares a love for visual art in the form of photography and that perhaps such a love would influence a younger sibling. Jonathan's photographs in Season One become key artifacts in locating and identifying the Demogorgon after Nancy's friend Barb disappears from Steve's backyard in "Maple Street." After the police comb the forest for clues, Jonathan searches for his brother at night, photographing parts of the ground where leaves or twigs seem altered by footprints. His choice of content seems random—the viewer cannot tell if there is a method to Jonathan's madness or if he is just too consumed by grief to capture valid evidence. Still, he acts as if he is trying to feel his way to Will rather than document it logically: the audience hears him whisper "Where are you?" in confusion as he scans the ground. Jonathan takes these photos with a Pentax, a camera whose shutter occasionally jams ("Maple Street"). Later on, in Season Two, when he discovers members of Hawkins Lab have been snooping around his house, Jonathan shows Nancy some photos lying around and says, "I don't shoot Polaroid. These aren't mine" ("The Spy"). Although Jonathan does not share his reason for eschewing Polaroid, we might conclude that such a tool reduces the ability for him to connect with his subject matter; the very work of the Polaroid is to develop shots instantaneously rather than develop them carefully in a dark room. Because he uses his camera and its lens to communicate with his missing brother, hoping the art form will provide insight that his eyes cannot, it is likely that the very slowness and methodology of photography is what draws him.

In his search for Will, he stumbles upon Steve's backyard and begins to snap photos of the teenagers drinking by the pool. He also catches one picture just before Barb disappears. In order to determine how and why Barb would be taken from this area, Jonathan uses his dark lab to "enlarge" and "brighten" the figure in the shadows behind Barb. Although such work might be more indicative of using tools for defense rather than communication, Jonathan makes telling statements about the power of the visual to communicate when words fail: "[P]eople don't really say what they're really thinking. But you capture the right moment—it says more" ("Body"). In one sense Jonathan fulfills the stereotype of the "stalker photographer" who would rather snap pictures than have conversations with others (see Chapter 4 for a similar example). For instance, Nancy and Steve discover that he even took photos of her in Steve's bedroom window, partially undressed. In another sense, Jonathan hints at the failure of words or conversation to create true meaning.[4]

Like his older brother, Will uses art in the place of language, especially since he finds himself unable to describe the way the Shadow Monster makes him feel. Unlike the Demogorgon, or monster, in Season One, which was contained by Eleven's psionic powers and Lucas's slingshot, the thing lurking outside the arcade is gargantuan. When the lab scientists question Will about the Shadow Monster he first spots outside the arcade, he responds, "There was this storm. I felt frozen. Just frozen. Like how you feel when you're scared and you can't breathe or talk or do anything. I felt . . . felt this evil, like it was looking at me" ("MadMax"). In this Season Two encounter with the Upside Down, Will says his ability to talk, and even to breathe, no longer serves him. His understanding comes from pictures and noise rather than words and sentences.

Artists of previous generations, particularly the Surrealists, practiced this kind of automatic drawing to get better in touch with the subconscious mind (*MoMA*). In the early and mid-twentieth century, these creators would engage objects and materials as co-participants in their work. Abstract painters, as Frances Turner argues, were "turning to forms of self-automation with an eye, early on, to liberating otherwise inaccessible parts of themselves, and later, to establishing explicitly democratic ensembles of people and things" (10). Although Will is small, quiet, and vulnerable, his actions here speak to the concept of an agentive bricoleur since he may only use the things in front of him. Once he runs out of notebook paper, he begins to draw on wrapping paper and any other surface he can find. This work is similar to the work of surrealists, who, as Bill Brown has argued, were among the first to celebrate the value of objects and tools as co-participants in meaning making. Additionally, Bill Brown explains that such painters were "transforming the bricolage of the dreamwork into the practice of everyday life" as they indulged in the "surrealist veneration of detritus" (11, 14). Again, here the audience sees how a child manipulates both older and newer technologies and also previous forms of expression to get results. In participating in automatic drawing, Will accesses knowledge in a new form and uses his existing tools to make it come to light.

Although Will's drawings seem abstract and banal to the casual viewer who does not understand them, he actually animates something quite solid and practical: the very lakes, rivers, farms, and detritus surrounding Hawkins. Only Bob recognizes the drawings for what they are: a map of their town. Bob in particular stresses the analog (or imprecise) nature of this map, however, when he tells Joyce he cannot know for sure where Chief Hopper is trapped beneath the earth. "The ratio isn't exactly one to one," Bob says. "If you're twisting my arm, and you are twisting my arm, I would say the X is maybe a half mile southeast of Danford?" ("Dig Dug"). Once Bob arrives there and climbs into the subterranean tunnels the Shadow Monster has been using to spread its influence, he cannot help but exclaim excitedly, "We're in Will's map! How did he know all of this?"

Will's art is not the only way in which we uncover his talent as a bricoleur. References from popular culture in the 80s continue to frame the events in *Stranger Things* and to help elucidate specific character arcs. For example, the narrative foreshadows the revelation of Will's unique abilities when he dresses as Egon Spengler from the movie *Ghostbusters* (1984) in the Halloween episode ("Trick or Treat"). This costume, although featured primarily in one episode, has implications for the rest of the season. Responsible for the theoretical side of the Ghostbusters' forays into science, Egon's hobbies include "collecting spores, mold, and fungus," while part of Will's drawings reveal the underground vines and tunnels that the Shadow Monster uses to poison the Hawkins farmland. Egon specifically deals in theoretical and historical science rather than practical applications. Likewise, Will's nickname in his Dungeons and Dragons game is not a stalwart hero but a character named "Will the Wise" whose main power is knowledge. Egon's friend and colleague Venkman teases him about previously attempting to drill a hole in his head to achieve some form of altered mental state; like Egon, Will gains a form of wisdom through strange methods, but this wisdom exists outside linguistic constructions. He says, "It's like I don't have to think. I just know things now. Things I never did before. It's hard to explain. It's like old memories in the back of my head" ("Will the Wise").

These similarities are empowering rather than deflating, although Will remains frightened of the changes to his personality in Season Two. Will's ability to "know things" means that, as he says, "It's like I feel what the Shadow Monster is feeling. See what he's seeing.... It's like he's reaching into Hawkins more and more. And the more he spreads, the more connected to him I feel." Will's voice trembles while he says the words until

Mike brings up a salient point: "Maybe that's good. You're like a spy now. A superspy. Spying on the Shadow Monster. If you know what he's seeing and feeling, maybe that's how we can stop him" ("Dig Dug"). However, most of the spying he must do does not translate to the human realm, so he continually accesses what he calls his "now-memories" and his talent for art to decode what the monster is doing to others like Hopper, who traps himself beneath the earth and becomes tangled in the monster's vines and tentacles ("Dig Dug").

Although Will dons Egon Spengler's costume at Halloween, he also associates himself with another fictional character early in the series. In flashback, the audience learns that Will uses the password "Radagast" at his outdoor fort to allow others entrance ("Vanishing"). A wizard character from Tolkien's *Lord of the Rings*, Radagast makes only a brief appearance to warn the more well-known wizard Gandalf of the approach of the enemy Sauron's army. This comparison may seem accidental if not for Will's insistence on calling himself Will the Wise and drawing himself on paper as a wizard. When Eleven tries to explain where Will has been taken in Season One, she even picks up his wizard figurine and places it upside down on the game board ("Maple Street").[5] Gandalf describes Radagast in these words: "Radagast, is of course, a worthy Wizard, a *master of shapes and changes of hue*; and he has much lore of herbs and beasts, and birds are especially his friends" (emphasis added, 250–51). This description is brief, but it and related passages reveal enough: while other wizards like Saruman and eventually Gandalf hold powers that grant them the titles of White Wizard, Radagast is referred to as the Brown. While other wizards have political power, Radagast is a chameleon whose different shapes and abilities allow him to move through the natural world without check. In this sense, Radagast may use nature as a co-participant in defeating evil, while other wizards ally themselves with humans and other races. Most importantly, his ability to communicate with other kinds of living things and ecological systems makes him valuable as the only wizard capable of rallying the natural world to defeat their enemies.

Will's talent, like Radagast's in bonding with animals, is to move beyond traditional speaking and writing habits in order to connect to multiple species. Tolkien scholar Henry Gee remarks in his study of the Orcs in *The Lord of the Rings:* "Because human beings are the only extant creatures to use language, we tend to judge the humanity of unknown entities on whether they are capable of speech even though the real world repeatedly shows that this distinction is not nearly so clear as we should like" (86). Like Radagast, Will shares connections and even common thought processes with other living things, particularly the Shadow Monster in Season Two. He spends time alone drawing in his forest fort, Castle Byers, just as Radagast dwells on the edge of Mirkwood in Middle Earth with the creatures of the woods (250). Like Egon, Radagast has a quieter influence and role than his associates, and his comforts stem from time spent with nonhuman matter: Egon with books and scientific theory, and Radagast with animals. Their shared introversion makes it hard to pay attention to their abilities in cases where they appear with their more outgoing colleagues. Like them, Will is initially overlooked as the quiet and eccentric member of his group. Still, all three possess a specific wisdom.

Still, Will is far from perfect, and Radagast as a character ultimately fails for urging Gandalf to seek help with Saruman, who has become an ally of Sauron. This failure may overshadow the interesting bits about "master of shapes and changes of hue" for fans of the Tolkien series. Likewise, Will fails in his efforts to spy on the Shadow Monster. At key points in the narrative, Will succumbs to the monster's influence by urging others to trap themselves underground in a system of tunnels where Demogorgons are hungry for blood ("The Spy"). These failures, while disturbing, do not discount the work of an unlikely hero. Jack Halberstam, a scholar who studies how failure has much to offer queer scholarship of popular culture texts, explains that failure "may in fact offer more creative, more cooperative, more surprising ways of being in the world" (2–3). This is important not just because Will falls under the monster's influence as time passes but because Will plants himself in harm's way to begin with. Determined to face his fears, he comes out of hiding and shouts "Go away!" at the giant creature coming toward him in the Upside Down. His attempt to stare down his foe ends in disaster since the Shadow Monster infiltrates all of him, passing through all parts of his body like black smoke and rendering him mute ("Pollywog"). Halberstam again emphasizes that such defeat may serve the loser of a battle more than he initially realizes:

> There is something powerful in being wrong, in losing, in failing, and that all our failures combined might just be enough, if we practice them well, to bring down the winner. . . . The concept of practicing failure perhaps prompts us to discover our inner dweeb . . . to take a detour. . . .
>
> (121)

This idea resonates with Joyce's plan to recover Will from the monster through her two-pronged attack: one mental and the other physical (she drives the monster's spirit out with extreme heat [2.9, "The Gate"]). First, Joyce begs her son to recover what Halberstam refers to as the "inner dweeb" with this memory:

> When you turned eight, I gave you that huge box of crayons. Do you remember that? It was 120 colors. And all your friends, they got you *Star Wars* toys, but all you wanted to do was draw with all your new colors. And you drew this big spaceship. But it wasn't from a

movie—it was your spaceship. A rainbow ship is what you called it. And you must have used every color in the box.

("Mind Flayer")

Joyce's comments serve as an excellent reminder of how Will uses art when others seek current technology in the form of action figures. Halberstam might agree that such actions are queer ones but not in the sense that Will's father mocks him for. In 1984, the year following the conclusion of the Star Wars trilogy, choosing crayons over Star Wars toys would make a statement about how a young person sees the world and the materials in it. It is that person, often ridiculed for being sensitive and different, who finds ways to succeed and help others that are unconventional in nature. Although it seems as if Will refuses to talk to his friends while possessed by the Shadow Monster, Chief Hopper realizes that he is "talking" just "not with words" ("Mind Flayer"). In a pivotal moment for his character, Will then spells "Close Gate" in Morse code by tapping his fingers against a chair to which he is tied, thereby warning his mother and his friends that the only solution to the attack from the Demogorgons is to seal the rip between the two realities.

The Morse code he uses is a communication system the ancient monster cannot detect. Here Will moves from analog talent in the form of art to digital talent in the discrete tapping of the fingers. Both the art and the code serve a purpose: to help fight the inexplicable powers of the Shadow Monster, who is beyond language. Actions like Will's remain necessary since all characters struggle with language when confronted with the Upside Down and must use incomplete analogies from Dungeons and Dragons to conceptualize their enemies' powers and their histories. For example, Nancy Wheeler finds it hard to describe the first Demogorgon she sees in the woods until Jonathan asks if the creature is missing a face. When she first speaks to her boyfriend Steve about what she saw, she only says, "I don't think it was a mask. I don't know. I don't know. . . . I just have a terrible feeling about this" ("The Body"). As Will alternates between digital spelling of dashes and dots in Morse code and more analog renderings of the vines in his drawings, he shows himself to be adaptable to various forms of communication and technology while others fail to articulate what exactly is happening to them and their town.

Conclusion

Traditional methods of communication that work in 80s America cannot function in the Upside Down. Instead, this alternate reality requires the work of bricoleurs who are willing to imagine plugged, unplugged, mechanical, electrical, digital, nonverbal, and analog materials in ways other characters in this book do not. The characters regularly hear static where they wish to hear words, see inexplicable art where they wished to have a map, and follow compasses where true north hardly points in the right direction. Nevertheless, Generation X navigates more than one dimension with unlikely tools. The characters never consume technology passively as the adults do, who are often featured sitting in front of the television. Additionally, Will's use of art to effect change suggests a preverbal sensibility that the earliest humans possessed, while at the same time recalling the habits of Surrealists who worked to equalize the relationships between people and things. Such creative expression shows a versatility broader in scope than one based primarily in plugged or unplugged tools.

This narrative differs from the others in setting its action in the early 1980s, but the moves it makes to demonstrate the young generation's versatility in forms of expression resemble the way that characters in 2010s narratives navigate the world through both analog and digital means. Because this show aired to an audience that included and still includes Generation Z viewers, today's young people became aware of how technology in this 80s narrative both limited and expanded the possibilities for good storytelling. The show also reminded them how varied and spontaneous communication offline could become when screens were not an option.

The objective here is not to take sides in the analog/digital "dialectic" (as Lian Amaris refers to it), but *Stranger Things* does offer repeated examples of how children maintained a form of embodied friendship that some forms of instant messaging and texting do not. The Duffer Brothers, as members of Generation X themselves, spotlight the alternatives that existed in their own youth when children enjoyed the unwieldy challenges of Morse code, crayons, walkie talkies, mixed tapes, and slingshots. While these alternatives remain full of glitches, static, and scribbles, the capacity for creative thinking multiplies when these characters embrace technological obstacles rather than resent them.

Notes

1. For more information and entertainment about preppers, check out National Geographic's television show titled *Doomsday Preppers*, which ran for five seasons. National Geographic streams multiple episodes for free online.
2. It is unclear if the four boys teach themselves Morse code or if Mr. Clarke instructs them during AV Club. In "Pollywog," Chief Hopper, in a flashback, shows Eleven how to use Morse code in order to protect her from those who believe her to be dead.
3. For example, the band Tangerine Dream uses both analog and digital synthesizers to create a soundscape based in mood rather than specific languages. Bands like them dealt in early electronic experimentation influenced by the same thing that Will's automatic drawing represents—an exploration of Surrealist thinking and artistic expression. Lead singer Edgar Froese played for Salvador Dali before beginning a long music career in creating ambient soundscapes (Perrone). The band Survive, responsible for the *Stranger Things* opening credits, based their design on previous music woven into Hollywood soundtracks by Tangerine Dream.

4. Another interesting example is how Nancy Wheeler, Mike's sister, operates sound technology in the form of taping scientists in Hawkins Lab ("Will the Wise"). Just as Jonathan uses art like Will to communicate, Nancy manipulates sound to unravel the reputation of those associated with Barb's death and Will's disappearance. Both Jonathan and Nancy do use technology in interesting ways like their siblings, but their story is often eclipsed by the love triangle associated with the two characters and Steve Harrington.
5. It is important to note that in "Pollywog," Mike, when talking to Max, refers to Will as the "cleric" of their group in Dungeons and Dragons. Although the title of cleric is not interchangeable with wizard for serious fans of the game, both types of characters are spell casters who possess great knowledge and play similar roles in guiding others (see information and message boards on the website dndbeyond.com for more information). Clerics are also known to be "intermediaries between the mortal world and the distant planes of the gods" ("Cleric"), which suits Will because he communicates with two dimensions, one more ethereal than the other.

References

Amaris, Lian. "Approaching an Analog-Digital Dialectic." *Theatre Journal*, vol. 64, no. 4, Dec. 2009, pp. 563–73.

Auner, Joseph. "Making Old Machines Speak: Images of Technology in Recent Music." *ECHO: A Music-Centered Journal*, vol. 2, no. 2, Fall 2000, www.echo.ucla.edu/Volume2-Issue2/auner/auner.pdf.

"Cleric." *D & D Beyond: Play With Advantage*, www.dndbeyond.com/characters/classes/cleric. Accessed 12 Feb. 2018.

Cramer, Florian. "What Is Post-Digital?" *H-z Journal*, vol. 19, July 2014, www.hz-journal.org/n19/cramer.html.

Feuer, Jane. *Seeing Through the Eighties*. Duke University Press, 1995.

Gee, Henry. *The Science of Middle-Earth*. Cold Spring Press, 2004.

Ghostbusters. Directed by Ivan Reitman, Performances by Dan Akroyd, Bill Murray, Harold Ramis, and Sigourney Weaver, Columbia Pictures, 1984. Amazon, www.amazon.com/dp/B008Y70TMK.

Gorvett, Zaria. "The Ghostly Radio Station That No One Claims to Run." *BBC*, 2 Aug. 2017, www.bbc.com/future/story/20170801-the-ghostly-radio-station-that-no-one-claims-to-run.

Halberstam, Jack. *The Queer Art of Failure*. Duke University Press, 2011.

Kaplan, E. Ann. *Rocking Around the Clock: Music Television, Postmodernism, and Consumer Culture*. Methuen, 1987.

Perrone, Pierre. "Edgar Froese: Leader of Electronic Band Tangerine Dream Whose Influence Has Been Felt for More than Four Decades." *The Independent*, 27 Jan. 2015, www.independent.co.uk/news/people/news/edgar-froese-leader-of-electronic-band-tangerine-dream-whose-influence-has-been-felt-for-more-than-10006676.html.

Pinch, Trevor, and Frank Trocco. *Analog Days: The Invention and Impact of the Moog Synthesizer*. Harvard University Press, 2002.

Poltergeist. Directed by Tobe Hooper, Written by Steven Spielberg, Performances by JoBeth Williams, Heather O'Rourke, and Craig T. Nelson, 1982.

Rich, Michael. "Music Videos: Media of the Youth, by the Youth, for the Youth." *The Changing Portrayal of Adolescents in the Media Since 1950*, edited by

Patrick E. Jamieson and Daniel Romer. Oxford University Press, 2008, pp. 78–102.

Rickert, Thomas. *Ambient Rhetoric: The Attunements of Rhetorical Being*. University of Pittsburg Press, 2014.

Rozelle, Lee. "Walmart of the Dead: Zombies and the Contemporary Landscape." *Lecture*. Auburn University at Montgomery, AL. 22 Feb. 2018.

Sirota, David. *Back to Our Future*. Ballantine Books, 2011. iBook.

Sterne, Jonathan. *MP3: The Meaning of a Format*. Duke University Press, 2012.

"Surrealism." *MoMA Learning*. Museum of Modern Art, New York, NY, www.moma.org/learn/moma_learning/themes/surrealism.

Tolkien, John Ronald Reuel. *The Lord of the Rings*. HarperCollins, 1994.

Turner, Frank. "Romantic Automatism; Art, Technology, and Collaborative Labor in Cold War America." *Journal of Visual Culture*, vol. 7, no. 1, 2008, pp. 5–26.

Conclusion
Blooming (and Burning) Where You Are Planted: The Optimism of Generation Z

Six-year-old Moonee from the film *The Florida Project* tells her friend Jancey that her favorite tree is one that is "tipped over" but it "still keeps growing." Likewise, the character Robby from the web-based television series *Cobra Kai* uses the image of the tree to imagine a new way of life after a period of juvenile delinquency. His mentor Daniel tells him, "You got strong roots, you know who you are, right? So now all you gotta do is visualize what you want your future to look like and then you make it happen." *Cobra Kai* and *The Florida Project* act as appropriate codas for a larger analysis of analog and unplugged technologies because the imagery surrounding childhood and teenage years returns to the natural and physical world, the unplugged canvas upon which they reshape and reimagine their futures. This conclusion also focuses on how socioeconomic class in particular shapes young characters in precarious financial situations who find confidence in believing in something (or someone) bigger than themselves. Such optimism helps redirect, at least temporarily, the negative and insidious work of characters in narratives like *Get Out*.

Previous chapters demonstrate how members of Generation Z have taken unlikely tools and spaces and transformed them into successful creations or acts of communication with others. The act of going unplugged, although once typically situated in discussions of music, acts more as a way of life than one technical choice. Although some people may use analog technologies as a way to act as collectors or to show off sophisticated audiophilic tendencies, the work of analog offers more than just a way to perform authenticity or cultural capital. It breaks the monotony of digital production. Christopher Bonanos, who traces the history of the Polaroid company, explains, "When most every bit of information you see and hear every day is digital, the great mass of it appears consistent and uniform. Digital TV has no snow; digital music (unless you're a true audiophile) sounds flawless. That eerie near-perfection leaves many people feeling a little bit numb, craving something unpredictable" (163). That said, young people are also known for using analog purchases to look and feel smarter, more authentic, and more in touch with their creative side. Tom Standage,

Figure 7.1 The Lone Cypress in California
Source: Creative Commons, www.cgpgrey.com

deputy editor of the print magazine *The Economist*, explains that even with digital versions of magazines online, his particular publication has seen sales rise not with older readers but with younger ones who see the magazine as a "social signifier." He further explains that a magazine's "finishability" provides those young readers with a sense of satisfaction, the kind a person might experience when finishing a dense prose work. Standage says, "You can't show others you're reading it with the digital edition. You can't leave your iPad lying around to show how smart you are" (Sax Chapter 5).

Standage's observation reveals just how significant social status and social class are to how Generation Z approaches the material and natural world. In previous chapters several characters would merely collect the parts of the world that improved their cultural capital. Dean Armitage in *Get Out* stores souvenirs from his vacations in order to impress guests in his home; more frighteningly, his daughter Rose collects photographs of black people she entraps in order to find her power in subjugating others. Likewise, Bryce Walker in *13 Reasons Why* collects trophies from playing sports and Polaroids from his sexual conquests. Conversely, youth from working class families have little time to indulge in collections for collection's sake. In their case a parent may be missing, or a family member may work multiple jobs simply to put food on the table. Little extra money exists through which to accumulate analog tools with which to experiment; and, in some cases, this situation reveals a form of innocence and wonder that privileged children might not possess. However, this does not mean that children from a lower income tax bracket neatly fit the bootstrap myth: remain good at heart, work hard, and all your dreams will come true. The success of *The Florida Project* and *Cobra Kai* stems not from such blind optimism but from honoring young people who choose to bloom where they are planted at a particular time in their lives. This blooming does not discount the significant socioeconomic challenges they endure or falsely indicate the possibility that the future holds easy answers to their specific dilemmas.

This is not to say that all optimism has gone out of style or that the only signifier of critical thinking need rely on a hermeneutics of suspicion. We see signs of optimism in the efforts of Generation Z to promote changes in legislation affecting gun control after a school shooting. The alumnae of Marjory Stoneman Douglas High School, who lost seventeen of their classmates to gun violence, have appeared in Washington, DC in Congress meetings as well as on stage at the 2018 Tony Awards. In this stage appearance, the group of former high school students sang one of the more optimistic numbers associated with musical theater: "Seasons of Love." Their performance suggests that optimism, while tempered with concerns for intersectional representation of race and class, may be a productive way to navigate an unpredictable world. Still, these students have matched optimism with concrete action as they tour the United States to encourage people to vote against NRA-sponsored politicians in office.

This is certainly not the first time that youth have inspired adults with their resilience. Dave Cullen's book *Columbine* ends with an encomium to the 1999 survivors of that titular event who, when a memorial was erected on the ten-year anniversary, "came back for a reunion." Their principal had noted that the students who endured the shootings "had grown up, graduated college, and started careers. Many were married and beginning to raise children" (368). To choose to raise children after enduring a senseless act of violence is in itself an act of optimism. Patrick Ireland's memorial address to his former peers at Columbine further illustrates this optimism when he states, "The shootings were an event that occurred. But it did not define me as a person. It did not set the tone for the rest of my life" (358). Although time and maturity might give someone this kind of perspective, Patrick, who was almost fatally injured and hospitalized for long periods of time, also gave a valedictory address in which he formerly had said, "When I fell out the window [of the library at Columbine], I knew somebody would catch me. That's what I need to tell you: that I knew the loving world was there all the time" (302). Such an optimistic perspective after a tragedy of that size is laudable.

Nevertheless, in all of the examples of youth showing resilience or acting as bricoleurs either in fiction or in real life, the students in the above examples had access to resources: medical care, education in affluent neighborhoods and school districts, travel to places around the world, and, in the case of the Marjory Stoneman Douglas youth, the means to travel and communicate with important people. Although all of those acts are worth noting, particularly since young people effortlessly transition between the analog and digital worlds that sometimes baffle their older counterparts, these people and many young people in the stories here had the backing of their families or the resources to prove their talent. Scarcity was never an issue that defined their pursuits. In pop culture narrative a lack of resources and stability challenge young people in ways that make us reconsider what it means to be a bricoleur, or someone who adapts an unplugged life.

The Florida Project, directed and written by Sean Baker (along with writer Chris Bergoch), features a mischievous six-year-old girl who lives in a run-down motel in Kissimmee, Florida, just a few miles away from Walt Disney World but worlds away from its opportunities and middle class adventures. Moonee's mother Halley (Bria Vinaite), an unemployed exotic dancer turned prostitute, barely gets by paying rent from week to week and has to sell the iPad to order the occasional pizza for dinner and buy Lunchables that cost "only a dollar." Despite a lack of financial security, Moonee lives in a magical world of her own design, choosing to portray the limitations of her environment as catalysts for dreaming. This is particularly true in the way she interacts with both objects and spaces. The audience sees Moonee wash and brush her toy horse's hair in the bathtub and how she finds joy in climbing through the detritus of abandoned condominiums and lighting old pillows on fire. She imagines that if she had a pet alligator she would name it Anne. In order to make her friend Jancey (Valerie Cotto) happy, she takes her "on a safari" to a neighboring field, imagining that it holds the same possibilities as the Animal Kingdom that costs over a hundred dollars to enter. All of these moments add up to reveal a child who has taken difficult circumstances and transformed them into magic.

A. O. Scott describes the success of *The Florida Project* with Moonee in mind: "No magic exists that can make the pain of reality disappear, but we don't know how to believe in anything else. This movie accomplishes something almost miraculous—two things, actually. It casts a spell and tells the truth." Indeed, most stories that honor the physical environment and its objects do the same by imbuing each nonhuman agent with some degree of magic or unknown history. Whether a belief in magic is simply blind optimism or a step toward seeing outside the individual ego for answers, Scott stresses that we as viewers "don't know how to believe in anything else." Seeing possibility and hope where there typically is none may be naïve in some circumstances, but it still requires a certain degree of imagination and reconceptualization of the immediate environment. Those who know about Disney World may be aware that jobs exist within the parks that feature mundane tasks like collecting trash or wearing bulky character costumes in sweltering heat. However, jobs within the park also include the coveted positions of Imagineers, those who "bring art and science together to turn fantasy into reality and dreams into magic." Moonee's own character journey features similar imagination, although she lives with her mother in a motel room at the Magic Castle, a purple-painted short-term residence for those down on their luck in the greater Orlando area. Moonee has learned how to entertain herself without the help of anyone: she is able to make adventure by obtaining free ice cream with tourist money, watching eccentric characters by the motel pool, and acting as bellhops to the new guests with luggage.

The second example featuring issues surrounding socioeconomic status and generational connections is *Cobra Kai*, YouTube Red's (now YouTube Premium's) surprising hit series from May of 2018. In this narrative, the young people who learn karate from former *Karate Kid* (1984) characters Daniel LaRusso (Ralph Macchio) and Johnny Lawrence (William Zabka) show an aversion to some forms of technology due to the presence of bullying and due to the limitations of some of their financial situations. One character in particular, Miguel Diaz (Xolo Maridueña), finds ways to embrace Generation X culture while also encouraging his mentor to meet him in the present. Miguel, who lives in a small apartment and is being raised by a single mother, embraces the shoddy Halloween costume his grandmother makes from discarded laundry, but then he also builds a website for his teacher's karate dojo to help attract more teen customers. Both happen with the first months of his relocation to the San Fernando Valley, where other students have begun bullying him for accidentally blowing their cover when using fake IDs.

Miguel shuttles between analog and digital worlds effectively even before he embraces his new love for karate under unemployed and down on his luck Johnny Lawrence's tutelage. Meanwhile, Johnny, the would-be mentor, starts his dojo in a sea of analog detritus. He sells an Atari game system to pay the rent on his dojo and listens to 1980s cassette tapes in his decades-old Thunderbird. Johnny still owns his Walkman and has CDs stacked in his entertainment unit. He orders Miguel to change his ring tone to Guns n' Roses and refers to recent technology as "iComputers." In order to understand Facebook, Daniel, his Generation X contemporary and nemesis, must show him to use it.

Miguel and his friend Aisha tell Johnny that bullying often happens online rather than face to face, and Johnny retorts that "back in his day" people had more respect than that. Such blatant division of how things were versus how they are now does not seem to allow any room for nuance, especially when it comes to portrayals of the young.

That said, Miguel's relationship to Johnny is based primarily on both characters showing each other how to navigate their present day lives. As a newcomer and outcast, Miguel's confidence, which develops over a series of episodes, is partly predicated on his use and embrace of analog tools that Johnny uses to teach him martial arts: a swimming pool where he must use his legs to tread water while his hands are tied, wooden slats that he must break to build momentum in his punches and kicks, and abandoned vehicles in an old car lot that he and his friends use to hide from German Shepherds that chase them. On the other hand, Miguel teaches Johnny to find a "smarter way" than just using his fists to make his case for reinstating Cobra Kai in the upcoming area tournament. By having self-control, Johnny earns the right to have his dojo back in competition ("All Valley").

Daniel also works with Johnny's teenage son Robby (Tanner Buchanan) at his car dealership and teaches him an alternative style to karate that counterbalances the one Miguel is learning. Unaware that the boy he trains is Johnny's son, Daniel, like his own character in the 1980s, encourages Robby to see the connections between mundane chores like washing windows and the choreography of blocking punches and kicks. He also encourages Robby to trim the bonsai trees he hands to guests of his dealership, which he later uses to describe how "strong roots" affect a person's ability to live a productive life. Through use of all of these tools, Robby learns how to redirect the anger he has over a broken home and absentee parents ("All Valley").

The narrative culminates in a regional competition, just as it does in the *Karate Kid* film. Miguel and Robby both make the final round, and Daniel and Johnny act as mentors. One theme that is particularly special about *Cobra Kai* is the way in which adults counter the typical narrative of ignoring, being at odds with, or resisting the ways of their young charges. Instead of fostering codependency among the children and adults, writers of *Cobra Kai* show the symbiotic nature of two different generations coming together to learn something new. This partnership between Generations X and Z is a product of the writers' skillful balance of old and new narratives to please fans of the original movies and new fans of the series. Rather than being accused of indulging in nostalgia to the point of gimmick, writers of the series received positive reviews for their masterful weaving of old and new character arcs. John Lim explains, "The characters they introduce are logical extensions of the original. They're different from the original characters, as they should be, but they aren't pitted against them. Both Daniel and Johnny take on mentor roles to new students and yet the story never forces us to sacrifice one generation for the other."

It is this last comment about not sacrificing one generation for the other that offers the most resonance here. Engaging in discussions of generational differences often leads, however inadvertently, toward the exultation of the old over the new or the new over the old. In learning how characters may move effectively between both, the emphasis should be on how intergenerational thinking improves a society whose problems are too vast for any single generation to confront alone.

Conclusion 153

Robby and Miguel confront financial instability in ways that make them stand out as members of Generation Z. They both have alternate modes of transportation: Miguel must use his bike and Robby his skateboard to get where they need to go. Neither teen has a family to help them finance a car. Robby's talent with skateboarding later translates into mastering a double kick, a challenging karate move that even Daniel has not accomplished in his past. In practicing this kick through skating, Robby has learned how an everyday object, his own board, provides transportation but also helps him master a sport he formerly knew nothing about ("Different but Same"). Although Miguel's mother and grandmother are supportive and caring, Miguel still has no father figure in his life until Johnny comes along. Both of Robby's parents remain absent—his mother spends her days flirting with men in bars, and Johnny left his son years ago, although he wishes to rectify this history by helping Robby stay in school. That said, neither Miguel nor Robby is completely destitute. Both have a roof over their heads, access to smartphones, and hobbies they enjoy.

In both *The Florida Project* and *Cobra Kai*, the main characters must learn to live without significant financial support (Moonee's case is more precarious than the two boys' lives mentioned above), and by doing so, analog tools take on new meaning. Miguel, Robby, and Moonee find ways to accept their limited realities and resources in order to, as the cliché says, "bloom where they are planted," even if the area in which they live is choked with metaphoric weeds. Although it is initially easy for us to compare these teens to characters like Beca Mitchell who uses tools and spaces in surprising ways just as Robby uses skateboarding to teach himself karate, the comparison falls short. This is because Beca uses her talent mostly to win singing competitions, not as a way to survive without financial backing, which her father happily provides as long as she remains active in college extracurricular activities. Likewise, Maeve and Marie in *Supernatural* use their own talents to stage a musical based on their favorite series of books rather than to navigate a world of financial stress. Both girls attend a private academy where they excel at both the arts and academics because of the manner in which they have been raised.

This is all to say that living an unplugged life means different things to different youth even if it points toward creative ability and problem solving. This statement may seem like common sense. However, generational labels and descriptions have limits as a methodology, and this limit is most evident when labels ignore socioeconomic class and race (as discussed in Chapter 5). Analog tools that liberate creativity may also serve as tools of oppression for others. This is evident when the appearance of different vehicles in *Get Out* signals danger to the black male characters rather than opportunities to bond over fixing machines. For Zach and Gray in *Jurassic World*, repairing the 1992 Jeep from the former park saves them from the Indominus Rex (see Chapter 3). Likewise, in *13 Reasons Why*,

154   *Conclusion*

Tony's car, likely handed down from his father just as Dean Winchester's Impala is bequeathed to him from his father (see Chapter 1), becomes like a partner to him as he repairs it with his father and chaperones his best friend around town.

The term unplugged plays a significant role in describing analog technology throughout this book, mainly because music and tools related to music production frequently appear in these stories. The narrative frame of *13 Reasons Why* is completely reliant on cassettes to tell Hannah's story in a more visceral manner than digital technology could. Beca's work with the Bellas in *Pitch Perfect* shows how she effectively navigates between analog and digital platforms to make sound. In viewing such narratives through a skeptical lens, we might be quick to dismiss these unplugged characters as the hipsters who, as Sax says, became the "scapegoats" of the 2000s and beyond (Sax introduction). Music in particular opens up this argument because a collection of LPs and cassettes speaks to two possible trends in the consumers buying them: the increase in leisure time (especially with vinyl since one must remain in the room and typically turn the record over to listen through the tracks) and the focus on collecting things as a form of promoting an image of authenticity. Moonee from *The Florida Project* and Robby and Miguel from *Cobra Kai* may dabble in all kinds of media, but they will not possess the funds to purchase and store analog items in order to impress their peers. They will also have less time and desire to focus on whether their position in any given community is viewed as authentic by others.

The *Cobra Kai* and *Florida Project* youth herald a new age of examining young people who, unlike Emma Gonzales and David Hogg from Marjory Stoneman Douglas High and fictional characters like Beca and Aubrey in *Pitch Perfect*, do not possess the money or cultural cache to travel to their nation's capital or communicate with large audiences. Rather, change for these characters happens in small increments as they take on daily tasks or explore their own backyards. Although it may appear limiting to study the bricoleur's work on this micro-level instead of paying attention to national and global platforms, it may be time to consider the smallest creative actions as catalysts for larger change and larger acts of "blooming where planted." As discussed in the chapter on *Supernatural*, small tools or props can have grand-scale consequences. In paying closer attention to those characters with fewer resources, resources that are not as traditional or sizeable as those possessed by middle class youth, people might discover entirely new ways to create and communicate that transcend any analog/digital binary that exists today. The emphasis on the tree as a representation of growth reminds the audience that in both stories nature serves not as a prop to support humans but mirrors and participates in a person's navigation of the world.

Kelly Medina-Lopez offers one term to conceptualize this future bricoleur: rasquache. Rasquache, she explains, "is a movement popular in chicanx art, cultural, and literary studies" that involves making do with limited resources, but it also reveals the "physical reality of necessity manifest through the actions and ingenuity of the underdog" and "encourages us to do these things boldly, colorfully, and unapologetically." Latinx culture plays a large role in making rasquache, but, as Medina-Lopez suggests, the term may be extended to look at other cultures. It is worth mentioning that in *Cobra Kai* the student Miguel and his family hail from Ecuador, and one of Moonee's best friends in *The Florida Project* is Scooty (Christopher Rivera), whose mother is Latina and friends with Moonee's mother. Because both narratives take place in areas where Latinx populations are greater (California for *Cobra Kai* and Florida for *The Florida Project*), this is unsurprising. However, *Cobra Kai*'s Robby, a working class white teenager from North Hills, California, also demonstrates some of the same qualities as the characters mentioned above, and Moonee herself hails from Florida, so Medina-Lopez's flexibility with the term is helpful here.

There are similarities between Claude Levi-Strauss's definition of the bricoleur, one who makes do with the resources available to him/her, and rasquache. Tomas Ybarra-Frausto explains that in rasquache "high value is placed on making do—hacer rendir las cosas. Limited resources means mending, re-fixing and reusing everything. Things are not thrown away but saved and recycled, often in different context (e.g., automobile tires used as plant containers, plastic bleach bottles becoming garden ornaments)" (6). The main difference is the emphasis on empowerment that those engaging in rasquache find through enthusiastically engaging with limitation and the status of underdog. Rasquache reaches its full meaning only when considering its origin, which, according to Maria Anderson, reflects and transforms "the sensibilities of the *barrio*." Anderson reminds us that rasquache in Spanish translates to mean "left over" or of "no value" and that its original meaning was negative. The word has changed to reflect a new aesthetic in art, and, like Medina-Lopez says, a way of life.

In other words, the plucky optimism and resourcefulness of Miguel, Robby, and Moonee is not just plucky: in some cases it is loud, messy, unrefined, or unexpected. Medina-Lopez adds that rasquache also "adopts an attitude of living in the moment: the walls of this house may desperately need repair, but at least if they are bold and bright, they will look nice when they collapse. Rasquache emerges from a sociocultural imperative to recycle, upcycle, make do, and make new meaning through whatever available bits and pieces." Moonee states it best when she takes her new friend Jancey on a tour of the hotel where she lives. She points to certain doors and says, "These are the rooms we're not supposed to go in. But let's go anyways!" Moments later the electricity in the entire hotel goes out.

As Medina-Lopez explains, rasquache does not lead to people attempting to "blend in" with their environment; rather, it invites "choices [that] are daring and colorful on purpose." Moonee's ability to subvert daily operations at a hotel is one way in which she makes the Magic Castle her home and finds agency. Although the hotel manager Bobby (Willem Dafoe) remains irked at Moonee throughout the narrative (Moonee begs tourists for tips, kills a goldfish in the pool, and spits on cars from the second floor), he also looks upon her with some affection. The trouble she invites often breaks up the monotony of a life spent doing building repairs and printing reports, although Bobby resents how Moonee's mother fails to discipline her. Bobby admires Moonee's tenacity and imagination, which save her from the anguish of knowing just how precarious life with her unemployed mother currently is.

On a different note, Miguel's original costume for Halloween, a Deadpool (superhero character) costume made by his grandmother, invokes a rasquache aesthetic when he unabashedly dons the strange mismatched bedsheets with the cut holes in the headpiece. Although he changes costumes upon pressure from Johnny, Miguel finds nothing embarrassing about wearing something his grandmother made especially for him, even if it makes Miguel, according to Johnny, look like "Poor Man" rather than a superhero ("Esqueleto"). Unlike the protagonist Daniel from the original *Karate Kid*, who feels embarrassed by his working class roots and the car his mother drives, Miguel never shies away from admitting that his family lacks money. Miguel's family and heritage remain important to him, no matter what others may think about his limited means.

The idea of rasquache helps us understand why Moonee's twisted tree, one that is dramatically "tipped over" in the fields behind her hotel, acts as an appropriate image for what Generation Z is able to accomplish. To understand fully how youth in the 2010s navigate different challenges, the image must account for a certain sideways, messy existence that rarely matches the perfectly shaped bonsais that Robby helps Daniel trim. That said, most images of bonsai in *The Karate Kid* and in *Cobra Kai* feature a tree that is crooked in nature, one that zigzags rather than grows straight in most of its manifestations. The cliché "bloom where you are planted" takes on new meaning because the growth of these characters reflects rasquache: it tips over, zigzags, and refuses to follow a set path of behaviors. Rather than be intimidated by the strangeness of such growth, we might consider it an asset. Rasquache may be best suited for an era in which large-scale problems exist in both natural and institutional spaces. Problems in the 2010s such as domestic and foreign terrorism, climate change, and corrupt government practices make room for something less docile and tame than the bricoleur. Although not all children deal with limited resources, the environmental destruction around them all signals a future where some materials will be limited in supply for *all* people. A lack of capital, therefore, becomes a form of training for an uncertain future.

Medina-Lopez stresses that we have much to learn from working class cultures that not only "make do" with limited resources but also find ways to subvert traditional expressions of art and behavior. In *Cobra Kai* and *The Florida Project*, both narratives feature characters willing to commit vandalism or arson. This action is not necessarily the rasquache that Medina-Lopez or other scholars describe or advocate. Indeed Ybarra-Frausto says that rasquache "finds delight and refinement in what many consider banal and projects an alternative aesthetic—a sort of good taste of bad taste. It is witty and ironic but not mean-spirited" (5). Nevertheless, the characters' destruction does reflect on the world of abandoned buildings and junkyards in which they are immersed.

Moonee takes her closest friends to the "Abandids," a set of empty apartment homes where drug dealing and prostitution are rumored to be common. These homes are full of leftover trash and domestic items like pillows, which Moonee uses to start a fire in one of the units. When the entire area goes up in flames, Moonee and her friends run from the scene and plead ignorance. This incident ultimately divides Moonee and Halley from Scooty and his mother, and this division catalyzes a series of events that makes it impossible for Halley to provide for her child. While Moonee's behavior causes distress, it still stands in opposition to the urban exploration that today's middle class teenagers enjoy, since urban exploration (or urbex) is often grounded in motives of colonizing the space by photographing and sharing the detritus on Instagram for aesthetic and novel purposes. Such exploration is based partly on the desire to trespass. Unlike such explorers, Moonee goes to the Abandids regularly and sees them as a logical extension of the playground that surrounds the hotels and strip malls of where she lives. Life at the Magic Castle includes the presence of such structures as seminal rather than liminal to the landscape of precarity and rootlessness experienced by all who dwell within it.

Likewise, Johnny takes his *Cobra Kai* students to a junkyard, where he encourages them to use objects as weapons and destroy old cars. In a training sequence where the song "We're Not Gonna Take It" plays raucously in accompaniment, the boys and girls of *Cobra Kai* enjoy being set loose to break and destroy things ("Molting"). At the end of the sequence, Johnny even sets large black dogs loose on his students to see how well they might defend themselves against surprise attacks. This session in the junkyard is meant to be interpreted somewhat humorously rather than seriously, yet its presence still does some cultural work in unveiling a tragic aspect of Generation Z lives. Since 2008, the amount of abandoned buildings and foreclosed homes has multiplied due to the Recession of the late aughts. The effects of this time are still being discovered and catalogued, sometimes by the middle class who repurposes these abandoned structures for their own urban exploration hobbies, but also by the working class children who live in close proximity to such sites of destruction. The once sanctimonious (and sometimes racist) promise of "broken window" policing, as discussed in Chapter 5, has failed neighborhoods completely.

Marc Lamont Hill describes the paradox of this situation in his analysis of Flint, Michigan, where these problems are magnified:

> Nearly a third of the 56,000 homes in Flint are abandoned or in an essentially unlivable state. When so many homes are unattended, arson is inevitably a popular crime; Flint has hundreds of cases each year, ranking among cities with the highest per capita incidence of arson. . . . Blame for the arsons can be attributed to gang wars or building owners looking for insurance money on a property. . . . Some cases, a few theorize, are the work of neighbors fed up with the eyesores that greet them out the window every day.
>
> (163–164)

This is where things get decidedly muddy in terms of consequences. Moonee, who torches the "Abandids," brings joy to many in the working class community at the Magic Castle because they, unlike Scooty's mother who suspects trouble, are excited to witness the structures burn down. Moonee commits arson, but she also destroys the eyesore that neighbors believe was attracting more dangerous crime to their section of town. Likewise, Johnny's students, while being destructive, are in an old junkyard littered with abandoned metal objects and cars. In some ways, the students merely break down or break apart existing trash that would have remained for years.

Even in *13 Reasons Why*, Clay and his new girlfriend get involved in "tagging" different buildings with art and writing because such work is considered creative by members of their peer group. Tagging may be seen by some as just a polite term for graffiti and vandalism, even when the ones involved possess artistic talent that transforms a space for the better. What is most obvious, however, is the motivation of Clay and his girlfriend in comparison to the motivation behind Moonee's actions. Clay's financial and domestic life are solid; they offer plentiful opportunities for him to enjoy other pursuits. Moonee's only form of entertainment, however, is the exploration of nearby sites because this activity costs nothing. Socioeconomic class plays a role in how much "exploration" of the "Abandids" is done for titillation and how much exploration is a product of where someone already lives. This is all to say that rasquache as a new form of bricolage must maintain a delicate balance between respect for the physical world and the desire to rid oneself, however possible, of unnecessary obstacles.

In one view Moonee's arson and the *Cobra Kai* lesson provide a necessary intervention in an otherwise bleak and soulless landscape. On the other hand, these children endanger themselves and others by creating more chaos and destruction in their wake. What is interesting to consider is that perhaps in this new form of bricolage we will come to accept breakdown as a central component of the creative process. Steven Jackson calls this idea "broken world thinking" (221). Broken world thinking accepts that "erosion, breakdown, and decay" may serve as useful starting points rather than end points in thinking through the work of "reinvention, reconfiguring, and reassembling" the different physical and digital materials of the world (221–222). To be clear, arson is not a technique that Jackson supports as a way to enter this new paradigm. Still, Moonee's actions and the *Cobra Kai* students' actions may be viewed a different way if Jackson's theory holds true. Instead of worrying about the destruction or burning of material, the focus would be on what will be repaired or transformed in its wake. In several classical myths the destruction of the old has to happen before making way for the new. As bizarre as it may seem, Moonee's actions lead to this very phoenix rising from the ashes motif as she leaves the Magic Castle to live with a new family. Likewise, the students of *Cobra Kai* destroy things in order to rebuild themselves. Most of Johnny's students have been victims of cyberbullying and isolation for years, and their willingness to embrace strength leads them to a new phase of agency in their lives. That said, the converse is true as well. Two of Johnny's students use excessive force in their karate competition, with one of them being disqualified for such behavior ("Mercy"). Likewise, Moonee, who has lived on the margins but fantastically so, must be ready to accept a different reality when the idea of forever losing her best friend Jancey and her mother Halley becomes reality. Destruction has consequences, both positive and negative, in these narratives.

Things get even more complicated when the way of understanding such youth changes from remembering Moonee's arson as her defining moment rather than her love for a malformed and "tipped over" tree. Both fire and nature are unplugged presences that call upon the characters to make do with whatever they may find. If, however, Moonee's arson becomes the focus of her character study, what happens to the somewhat corny notion that she "blooms where she is planted?" In the future such questions will become relevant when understanding how generations make sense of a world that is literally falling apart. If these characters see the apocalypse as a probability rather than a possibility, what valid choices remain for them to remake or reinvent a way forward? As Jackson says, "We know, now irrefutably, that the natural systems we have long lived within and relied on have been altered beyond return" (221–222).

Future studies of Generation Z are needed to address these complications. When looking at popular culture texts of the 2010s, audiences discover that children are capable of working, learning, and creating beyond screens. Analog and unplugged technologies remind young people that embodied, clunky, and otherwise outdated materials need not be sacrificed for their imperfections. Instead, imperfections are embraced as part of the messy work of learning and growing. Their generation is unique for many reasons, but a prominent characteristic is their need to wrangle with or at least confront physical materials that have been collecting in landfills, abandoned buildings, and oceans. Marc Pizarro explains that rasquache and hopefulness are intertwined because "socioeconomic limitations" provide a form of "strength" that empowers Chicano/a youth to take charge of their identities (207). More important to this book is that the empowerment happens alongside and partly because of the physical world's various materials, however banal or tacky.

Although any generation may be capable of adopting such a view, Generation Z and its pop culture narratives return time and again to images of a child or teenager refashioning existing materials to create something new as adults look on with curiosity, surprise, or, in some cases, indifference. Their creativity and resourcefulness seem to thrive rather than suffer in places like suburban junkyards (*Cobra Kai*), empty swimming pools (*Pitch Perfect*), and the ruins of old ecological parks (*Jurassic World*). Such settings anesthetize or baffle their adult counterparts. Pop culture narratives demonstrate that the story of Generation Z's legacy goes deeper than their perceived addictions to smartphones and Snapchat accounts. In these stories, young characters are doing more than staring at screens. They find new ways to bloom—and occasionally burn—in the inhospitable soil of the troubled adult world.

References

"About Imagineering." *Walt Disney World*, https://disneyimaginations.com/about-imaginations/about-imagineering/.

"All Valley." *Cobra Kai* season 1, episode 7, 2 May 2018, *YouTube Premium*, www.youtube.com/watch?v=1jTy2VMqaM4.

Anderson, Maria. "A Lesson in 'Rasquachismo' Art: Chicano Aesthetics and the 'Sensibilities of the Barrio.'" *Smithsonian Insider*, 31 Jan. 2017, https://insider.si.edu/2017/01/lesson-rasquachismo-chicano-asthetics-taste-underdog/.

Bonanos, Christopher. *Instant: The Story of Polaroid*. Princeton Architectural Press, 2012.

Cullen, Dave. *Columbine*. Twelve, 2009.

"Different but Same." *Cobra Kai* season 1, episode 9, 2 May 2018, *YouTube Premium*, www.youtube.com/watch?v=81XSlh_UKJg.

"Esquelito." *Cobra Kai* season 1, episode 3, 2 May 2018, *YouTube Premium*, www.youtube.com/watch?v=9z1nTwP2n0w.

The Florida Project. Directed by Sean Baker, performances by Brooklynn Prince, Bria Vinaite, and Willem Defoe. Cre Film, 2017.

Jackson, Steven J. "Rethinking Repair." *Media Technologies: Essays on Communication, Materiality and Society*, edited by Tarleton Gillespie, Pablo Boczkowski, and Kirsten Foot. MIT Press, 2014, pp. 221–39.

Lim, John. "How 'Cobra Kai' Is Kicking Butt at Storytelling, Marketing, and Genius." *Moving Forward*, 30 May 2018, www.bemovingforward.com/cobrakai/.

Medina-Lopez, Kelly. "Rasquache Rhetorics: A Cultural Rhetorics Sensibility." *Constellations*, vol. 1, no. 1, May 2018, http://constell8cr.com/issue-1/rasquache-rhetorics-a-cultural-rhetorics-sensibility/.

"Molting." *Cobra Kai*, season 1, episode 8, 2 May 2018, *YouTube Premium*, www.youtube.com/watch?v=9S9ydLeG-Lw&t=1374s.

Pizarro, Marc. "Racial Formation and Chicana/o Identity: Lessons From the Rasquache." *Race, Ethnicity, & Nationality in the United States: Toward the Twenty-First Century*, edited by Paul Wong. Westview Press, 1998, pp. 191–214.

Sax, David. *The Revenge of Analog: Real Things and Why They Matter*. Public Affairs, 2016. iBook.

Scott, A. O. "Review: In 'The Florida Project,' Enchantment in a Shabby Hotel." *The New York Times*, A24, 5 Oct. 2017, www.nytimes.com/2017/10/05/movies/the-florida-project-review-sean-baker-willem-dafoe.html.

Ybarra-Frausto, Tomás. "Rasquachismo: A Chicano Sensibility." *Documents of 20th- Century Latin American and Latino Art: A Digital Archive and Publications Project at the Museum of Fine Arts, Houston*, 1989, pp. 1–6, http://icaadocs.mfah.org/icaadocs/THEARCHIVE/FullRecord/tabid/88/doc/845510/language/en-US/Default.aspx.

Index

13 Reasons Why 2, 9, 18, 85–7, 89–91, 96–7, 102n1
1936 Olympics 114, 120
1967 Chevrolet Impala 23, 27

Abandids, the 157–9
abandoned buildings/places 12–14, 53, 76, 79, 117, 134, 150, 157–60
a cappella 43–4, 46, 48–50, 54, 56, 57–60
acoustics 53, 60
adults: negative portrayals 56–8, 63, 66, 72–4, 124, 135–7; resistance to change 4, 81; their views of young people 11, 149, 152, 160
analog: associated with detritus or the obsolete 9, 151; as compared to digital 7, 11, 25, 71, 83n5, 85–6, 112, 147; connected to glitches or irregularities 96, 100, 140, 159; as connected with young people 1–4, 16; in culture or sensibility 18, 31, 75–6, 93, 98, 106, 118; in 80s culture 129, 131, 133, 136–7; as embodied 8, 10, 18, 87–90, 114, 116; in language 91, 95; in nature 65, 67, 69–70, 72, 147; related to fine arts 8, 48, 90, 94, 143, 154
anthropocentric 4, 75
apocalypse 23, 27, 159
arcade 134, 136, 139
Armitage, Dean 105, 115, 117, 119–23, 148
Armitage, Jeremy 106, 113, 121–2
Armitage, Missy 105–6, 112, 115–16, 118, 122
Armitage, Roman 105, 113–14, 116, 122

Armitage, Rose 105, 109, 112, 112, 119–20, 122–4
arson 157–9
Asher, Jay 88
automatic drawing 139–40, 144n3

Baby (car) 26, 29, 39n5; *see also* 1967 Chevrolet Impala
baby boomers 107
Baker, Hannah: bodily violence 86–7, 92, 102; bullying of 93, 95, 99; connection to glitches 100; poetry by 93–4, 97; relationships 2, 92–3, 96, 98–9, 101–2; use of analog tools 18, 85, 88–93
Barden Bellas 17, 43, 45, 51, 60–1
Barden University 43–4, 56
basement 81, 114–15, 120, 130, 133–4
Battlestar Galactica 14–15
Baudrillard, Jean 121
Bennett, Jane 13, 28, 56
binary code *see* binary numbers
binary numbers 11, 70, 90–1, 99
Black Lives Matter 107
black mold 115
black smoke 35, 142
Blue (dinosaur) 66, 77–8
Bogost, Ian 50, 87, 98
boom box 89–90, 100
Breakfast Club, The 50–2
bricolage 19, 45, 47, 52, 60, 139, 158
bricoleur: Beca Mitchell as 45–6, 48, 51, 53, 55, 60–1; as compared to rasquache 149, 154–6; Hannah Baker as 88; in opposition to collector 106; role of 3, 4, 16, 34, 36–7, 54, 102, 143; Will Byers as 139–40

Index   163

broken windows theory 114
Brown, Bill 91, 116, 139
bullying 90, 92–3, 151
Byers, Will 18, 126, 128, 131–5, 137–43

Calliope 32–4, 36–7
camera 11, 75, 86, 92, 115, 138; used for survival 110, 112
Carol Anne 131
"Carry On, Wayward Son" 2, 36, 38
Carson, Rachel 63, 74, 82n3
Carver, Jeremy 23
cassette tapes: associated with glitches 100; as embodied 9, 96–7; as preferred technology 2, 18, 85–90, 154
CD (compact disc) 4, 9, 17, 34, 49–50, 57
Certeau, Michel de 53
Chandler, Mrs. 32–4
chaos theory 78, 82n2
Chevrolet Impala 23, 26–9, 36, 39n5
children: as abandoned 17, 51, 72–4, 135; as associated with rasquache 156–9; as innovative 18, 66, 76, 126, 129, 137–8; as privileged 149; representations of 12, 65, 69, 81, 98, 111
Chris (character) 18, 105–7, 109, 115–16, 120–4
Christine 28, 30
Christmas tree lights 128, 132
city map 89–90
Claire 65–6, 69–70, 74–5
cleric 145n5
climate change 25, 63, 74, 156
clock 5, 9, 14, 79
Clover, Carol 112
Coates, Te-Nehisi 111, 120
Cobra Kai 147, 149, 151–9
collector: in *Get Out* 105–6, 118, 120–1, 123; as hobby 4, 11, 79, 147
college 11, 13–14, 29–30, 53–5, 57–9, 61, 101
Colt, the 24–5
Columbine shooting 149
combination lock 100
compass 134, 144
cotton 12, 106
Cramer, Florian 10–11, 67, 132
Crestmont Theater 91–3

Crichton, Michael 65, 68, 71, 73, 80, 82n4
cursed objects 23–4, 26, 29
cyberbullying 12, 18, 159; *see also* bullying

Das Sound Machine 44, 47–8, 56
deer 109, 119
deer head (mounted) 106, 115, 123
Demogorgon 128, 132, 138–9, 142–3
Detritus 140, 151, 157
Diaz, Miguel 151–6
Dig Dug (video game) 134–5
digital: as deceptively ubiquitous 1, 13, 25, 68, 88; as different from analog 3, 7–8, 55, 55, 82n4, 96; as originally based on simple digits/processes 11, 67, 94, 132, 143; as remix 17, 45, 49–50; as satire 71–2, 99; as sterile 8–9, 147–8
digital native: definition of 31, 68; limitations of term 19, 85, 91, 107; as members of Generation Z 1–2, 11; as overwhelmed by technology 13
digital remix 45, 49–50
disembodiment 18, 96, 120
disposability 95, 99, 120
divorce 34, 65–6, 72, 75–6
DNA 67, 70–1, 77
Duffer Brothers, the 126, 144
Dungeons and Dragons 128, 130, 133–4, 140, 143, 145n5
DVDs 50

efficiency *see* digital
electricity 134, 155
Eleven (character) 127–9, 131–3, 136, 139, 141, 144n2
embodiment 18, 69, 114, 133
empty swimming pool 53–5, 57
environment: high and low tech 8, 23, 46, 55, 61, 89, 102; natural setting 115, 123, 150, 155; in terms of destruction and/or climate change 16, 47, 74, 156
eyes 27, 30, 35, 101, 110–11

"Fan Fiction" (episode) 17, 23, 25, 29–30, 32, 34–5
Fat Amy 52, 58
flash drive 49, 91, 96
"Flashlight" (song) 58

flat ontology 50
Florida Project, The 4, 19, 147, 149–50, 153, 155–7

game room 114–15, 122–3, 134
gated community 107
Generation X: as collectors 75, 79, 111, 126; parents of 135–6; as products of their culture 30–1, 34–7; as similar to Generation Z 144, 151
Generation Y *see* millennials
Generation Z: analog technology in 23, 33, 35, 88–9, 102, 129; as bricoleurs 46, 147; compared to other generations 30–2, 37, 157; definition 11–12; limitations of label 107, 124; major traits of 3, 16, 19, 75, 149, 156
genetics 64, 67
geological time 79–80
Ghostbusters (1984) 140
ghost light 96, 101
gift shop 5, 72, 117
glitch: as analog characteristic 91, 116, 129–30, 132, 144; as art 6–7, 118; as digital malfunction 7, 17; as physical or technical malfunction 8, 10, 67, 71–2, 100–2
Grady, Owen 66, 69–71, 76–8
graffiti 18, 87, 92, 158
Guardians of the Galaxy 16

Haas, Christina 5
Halloween (1978 film) 113
Halloween costume 91, 140–1, 151, 156
Hammond, John 65, 68–9, 71, 74, 77
handwriting 14, 87, 91–3
Hawkins, Indiana 127, 133, 137–8, 140
Hawkins AV Club 132, 128–9, 144n2
Hawkins Laboratory 127, 135–6, 145n4
Hayworth, Andre 108, 114
Heathkit Ham radio 132
Hill, Marc Lamont 108, 115, 120
hipster 12, 59–60, 94, 118, 154
Hudson, Jim 110, 113, 115, 124
hybridization 69–70
hyperobject 25–6, 63–4, 80–1

Imagineer 151
Indominus Rex 66, 69, 71, 75

in loco parentis 72
Isla Nublar 65–6, 68
Isla Sorna 65, 72–3, 77
isolation 48, 50, 68, 72, 136; associated with bullying or abuse 85, 89, 113, 159

Jackson, Steven 158–9
Jeep 76, 153
Jensen, Clay: encountering glitches 87, 100–1; making art 158; reacting to cassettes and Polaroid content 85–6, 89, 94–6, 100; relation to Hannah 2, 91, 97–8
Jesse 43, 50
Junk, Emily 56, 58, 60
Junk, Mrs. 58, 60
Junkyard 157–8, 160
Jurassic Park (film) 10, 63–4, 66–8, 73–5, 81–2, 82n3
Jurassic Park (location) 76, 78
Jurassic Park (novel) 71, 73, 80, 82n4
Jurassic Park 3 66–7, 73
Jurassic World 65–6
Jurassic World: Fallen Kingdom 65–6, 76–81

Kansas (band) 35–8
karate 151–3
Karate Kid, The 4, 151–2, 156
Keene, Robby 147, 152–6
Kripke, Eric 21, 23

lacrosse bat 122
landline telephone 5, 128, 130–2
latchkey kid 30–1, 37, 111, 135
La-Z-Boy recliner 135, 137
Little Bastard (car) 28–9
Livgren, Kerry 36–7
Lockwood, Benjamin 66, 77
Lockwood, Maisie 66, 76–8, 81
Lost World, The 65–7, 70, 72, 74, 82n3
LPs (records) 11, 13, 154

Madonna 5, 117, 137
Maeve 2, 31–4, 153
Magic Castle 151, 156–9
Malcolm, Ian 65, 67, 73–4, 78, 80, 82n2
Marie 2, 29–37
Marjory Stoneman Douglas High School 12, 149–50, 154
Martin, Trayvon 107, 120

Mashup 43, 45, 48–9, 51–4, 60
mask 108, 113, 143
Masrani Corporation 65, 69–70
"Material Girl" (song) 5, 117
materiality: as connected to glitches 71–2; as connected to the bricoleur 45, 49–50; as co-participant with youth 2, 23, 25, 29, 36, 44, 86, 128; in limited supply 154–60; as physical environment and structures 12, 19, 21, 28, 30, 38, 124; related to collecting 102, 106–7, 116–17, 123; in scholarship 5–7, 46, 118–19
Medina-Lopez, Kelly 154–7
memory 86, 89, 91, 95, 99, 116
mental illness 136
middle class 59, 61, 117–18, 157
millennials 12, 31
Mind Flayer *see* Shadow Monster
Miracles Out of Nowhere 36
Mitchell, Beca: in audition 45–7, 56; as a leader and bricoleur 2, 16–17, 45, 51–2, 55, 58; as privileged 43, 61, 153–4; in relationships 50; using analog technology 49, 53–4; using digital technology 45, 48, 60
Mitchell, Gray 65–6, 71, 75–6, 82n3
Mitchell, Zach 65, 68, 75–6
Moleskine notebook 11, 93
Monet's (place) 93
Moonee 4, 147, 150–1, 153–9
Morton, Timothy: nature of hyperobjects 25, 63–4, 80; respect for the environment 1, 7, 13, 47, 51
MTV 3, 16, 126, 135
Music Television *see* MTV
Mustang (car) 101

nature: as analog 68, 77, 91, 96, 114, 140, 159; as counterpoint to human arrogance 81; as related to a state of being or human character 6, 37, 56, 67, 119, 154; as threatened 12, 80; as unpredictable 4–5, 63–4, 72–3, 82, 134, 156
Negroponte, Nicolas 8, 90
noise 2, 100, 129, 131, 133, 139
nonhuman 23, 29, 38n3, 55, 97–8, 117–18
nostalgia: avoidance of 9, 85, 94; indulgence in 16, 78–9, 87, 152

object oriented ontology 6–7, 46, 51, 98
Order of the Coagula 105, 113, 116, 118–19, 124
Owens, Jesse 120, 122

parachronism 9, 10, 18, 37, 89, 100
parents: of black children 107; of Generation X 25, 30–1, 135–6; of Generation Z 30, 61, 65, 72–6, 82, 82n3, 91, 96; *see also* latchkey kid
Peele, Jordan 105, 107–9, 111, 114–15, 118, 124
pet rock 97–8
photography 94–5, 110–11, 138–9
photo negative 94–5
Pitch Perfect 15, 43–4, 53, 61
Pitch Perfect 2 43–4, 54–5, 58–60
Pitch Perfect 3 48, 57
plastic cup 17, 45–8, 56, 61
Poetry 93, 97–8
Polaroid 11, 86–7, 94–5, 138, 147
police car 107, 109
Poltergeist 131, 135
polymedia 35, 38
postcard 98
Prensky, Marc 31
privilege 30, 61, 117–18, 124

racism 109, 115
Radagast 141–2
radio 18, 48–9, 127–32
Rapkin, Mickey 57–9
Raptor 66, 70, 77
rasquache 19, 154–8, 160
record player 118
record shop 11
rhetoric 7, 15, 46, 51–2, 118
rock collection *see* pet rock
Rod (character) 108–9, 113–14, 123–4

San Jose, California 21–2, 38n1
Sax, Peter: conceptions of analog 7, 67–8, 88, 93–4, 148; definition of hipster 60, 154; unplugging 3
screen technology: as associated with Generation X 134–5; as associated with Generation Z 1, 13, 34, 75, 85, 159; as digital 3–4, 88, 94, 98; as distraction 44, 133, 136, 160; as negative 18, 37, 48, 72, 131
"Seasons of Love" (song) 149
Shadow Monster 128, 138–43

Shipka, Jody 88–9, 100
short-wave radio *see* radio
shower 53, 55, 92
Shurley, Chuck 23, 27, 33
skateboard 153
smartphone: adult use 33–4; in association with Generation Z 1, 9, 11, 13, 16, 75, 153, 153, 160; photography 95, 99; used alongside analog tools 89, 92–3, 110, 112–13
Smith, Logan *see* Hayworth, Andre
socioeconomic class 60, 147, 153, 158
soundscape 129, 133, 144n3
souvenirs 18, 116–17, 120, 148
space 91, 93, 115, 123, 156–7; as repurposed 53–5, 58–9
Spengler, Egon 140–1
Star-Lord 16
static 128, 131–2, 135
Stevenson, Howard 107–8, 112
Stonehenge 36
Stranger Things: as commentary on 80s culture 129, 133, 135–6, 144; influences 131, 140; premise 18, 126, 128
Strauss, William and Howe, Neil 11, 31, 39n6, 126
suburb 30, 107–8, 113–14
suicide note 9, 18, 85, 89–92, 101
Supernatural: fan culture 27, 31, 36, 23, 38n3; Generation X characters 29–31; Generation Z characters 17, 32–5; materiality in 21, 23–9, 35
"Swan Song" (episode) 27–8

tagging 158
tea cup 116, 118
technology *see* analog; digital
television 2–3, 9, 14, 37, 115; in 80s culture 126, 131, 133, 135–7

Thirteen Reasons Why (book) 88
Thompson, Robbie 23
thumb drive *see* flash drive
Tolkien, J.R.R. 128, 132
Tonehangers 57–8
Tony 85, 88, 90–1, 96–7, 100–1
trauma 12, 17, 37, 95–6, 101–2
tree 4, 147–8, 152, 154, 156
trophy 56, 95, 102, 120, 123
Tuhus-Dubrow, Rebecca 16, 87–8, 90
Tyrannosaur 64–5, 69, 71–2, 74, 76

uniformity 67, 71, 147
unplugged: definitions of 5, 65, 154; motivations for 106, 113; MTV show 2–3, 16; musical arrangements 36–8, 44; way of life 4, 17, 57, 61, 131, 147; in youth culture 92–3, 153, 159
Upside Down, the 128–9, 133–4, 136–7, 139, 142–3
urban exploration 117, 157

vandalism 87, 115, 157–8
video game 117, 133, 135

Walker, Bryce 86, 92, 95, 98–100
walkie talkie 129–31
Walkman 16, 87–8, 91, 96, 101
Walt Disney World 150
Wheeler, Mike 126, 128–9, 132–5, 138
whiteboard 14–15
Will the Wise *see* Byers, Will
Winchester, Dean 22, 25–31, 35, 39n5
Winchester, Sam 22, 25, 27–8, 31–4, 39n6
Winchester Mystery House 21–2, 24, 38
working class 117–18, 148, 156–8

zine 18, 55, 93–4, 117